Sweethearts

Sweethearts
THE BUILDERS, THE MOB AND THE MEN

CATHERINE WISMER

JAMES LORIMER & COMPANY LTD., PUBLISHERS
TORONTO

Copyright © 1980, 2014 by Catherine Wismer

All rights reserved. No part of this book may be reproduced or transmitted in any form or by any means, electronic or mechanical, including photocopying, or by any information storage or retrieval system, without permission in writing from the publisher.

Notice to educators

This book is available for purchase in print and ebook form. Copies can be purchased from our website at www.lorimer.ca. Copies of individual chapters or portions of the full text in print or digital form are also available for sale at reasonable prices. Contact us for details at rights@lorimer.ca.

The publisher and the author of this work expect that portions of this work will be useful for education, and expect reasonable compensation for this use. This can be readily achieved by arranging to purchase these portions from the publisher. Contrary to the view of university administrators and their legal advisors, it is unlikely that use of a chapter or 10% of this work for educational purposes with no payment to the publisher or author would be found to be fair dealing under the Canadian Copyright Act.

James Lorimer & Company Ltd., Publishers acknowledges the support of the Ontario Arts Council. We acknowledge the financial support of the Government of Canada through the Canada Book Fund for our publishing activities. We acknowledge the support of the Canada Council for the Arts which last year invested $24.3 million in writing and publishing throughout Canada. We acknowledge the Government of Ontario through the Ontario Media Development Corporation's Ontario Book Initiative.

Cover design: Tyler Cleroux

Library and Archives Canada Cataloguing in Publication

Wismer, Catherine, 1946-, author
    Sweethearts / Catherine Wismer.

Reprint of: 1980.
Includes bibliographical references and index.
Issued in print and electronic formats.
ISBN 978-1-4594-0652-0 (pbk.).—978-1-4594-0409-0 (epub)

    1. Construction industry--Corrupt practices--Ontario--Toronto--History--20th century. 2. Organized crime--Ontario--Toronto--History--20th century. 3. Criminals--Ontario--Toronto--History--20th century. 4. Construction workers--Labour unions--Ontario--Toronto--History--20th century. 5. Real estate development--Ontario--Toronto--History--20th century. I. Title. II. Title: Sweethearts: the builders, the mob and the men.

HD9715.C33T67 2014   338.4'769009713541   C2014-901451-1

James Lorimer & Company Ltd., Publishers
317 Adelaide Street West, Suite 1002
Toronto, ON, Canada
M5V 1P9
www.lorimer.ca

Printed and bound in Canada.

Contents

Foreword ... 7

PART I: INTRODUCTIONS
The Harbord Class of '33 ... 15
Bubsey, Squeaky, Little Woody and the Weasel ... 22
Beyond a Bowl of Spaghetti: Lansky and Luciano ... 32

PART II: THE REAL ESTATE BOOM, 1950–1960
The New Builders ... 45
Dippers ... 58
The Mob and Its Money ... 74

PART III: THE BRANDON GROUP CAMPAIGN
Boomtown Toronto ... 91
Zanini and Irvine ... 98
The Split ... 115

PART IV: THE GAMBLING CONNECTION
The Bahamas Adventure of C. Powell Morgan ... 129

PART V: THE UNION BUSINESS
The Bargain Builders ... 149
Gus Simone, Organizer ... 159
The Concrete Forming Campaign ... 169
The Independent Union ... 184
The Sale ... 192
The Shooting ... 199
The Mafia Is with Us ... 204

PART VI: SEMI-RETIRED
Labour Empires ... 219
End of an Era ... 225
No Regrets ... 231

Epilogue ... 239
Acknowledgments ... 242
Appendices ... 243
Select Bibliography ... 258
Index ... 260

For Agueda de Paiva, the Portuguese widow of a migrant labourer who died in a construction mishap in Toronto in 1977. Antonio de Paiva was an illegal immigrant. In his last letter home to his wife, written for him by a friend, he said, "I can't spend another winter in Canada without you. I work hard all day but the biggest sacrifice is being away from my family. This is no life at all."

Foreword

This is the untold story about the heady days of land development, the boom years of high-rise apartments of the early Fifties and Sixties and the infiltration of organized crime into all aspects of the residential construction industry. Following the Second World War, the shape of the city changed dramatically, with office towers and high-rise apartments sprouting in all parts of the city and the rapidly spreading suburbs. War veterans returned, along with an enormous influx of immigrants, mostly Italian, seeking jobs and eventually a new life in Canada. How the city was built is the subject of this story.

The housing shortage following the war attracted a whole new breed of builder who saw the opportunity to make money by assembling land and building, not ten or twelve houses a year but a hundred or two hundred. Then came the apartments, towers rising thirty, forty floors above the city, offering an alternative to single-family dwellings. Real estate was now a market for speculators who had very little knowledge of the industry. A handful of men came to dominate residential high-rise construction. They tried out their business skills by buying land and developing it. Working for the developers were the subcontractors who knew more about putting in basements and walls than business. They hoped to have enough money left from the contracts they made with developers to earn a profit after they paid for labour and material.

In the meantime, the cost of land skyrocketed through speculation; often, small builders who failed to get financing went bankrupt since few banks would lend money to such risky enterprises. Even large companies failed when they had to borrow money from private investors and the interest was very high. An example was the rapid rise and fall of Canada's biggest landlord which went into receivership in the early Sixties.

The opportunities to infiltrate a highly competitive, unregulated housing industry attracted the interest of Mafia's financial genius, Meyer Lansky. Real estate was an excellent place to put newly-laundered cash. Numbered bank accounts and lawyers acting as trustees were devices that could be used to disguise the property's true ownership. As well, real estate in Canada and the United States offered opportunities to bury cash skimmed from Lansky's gambling casinos in Las Vegas, Cuba and the Bahamas. One of Lansky's trusted couriers was John Pullman. He arrived in Toronto in the late Forties and became a financial source providing seed money for strip malls and mining ventures.

There were other methods the Crime Syndicate used to control the construction industry. Cartels were formed; bidding was rotated among the members and manipulated by the mob. The cartel didn't cost money to join. The only requirement for a subcontractor who won the predetermined tender was the percentage kickback to the mob. If you were not a "Club member" you were susceptible to finding work on any project destroyed through arson or harassment on the construction site, a strike or the negation of building supplies. Other Mafia practices included extortion; selling protection against themselves, called a "protection tax;" and ultimately, the use of violence and intimidation in order to discipline and stabilize the industry. Mafia members solved labour problems, mediated disputes, assured manpower and guaranteed *Pax* on the construction site.

After decades of Mafia infiltration into certain unions in the U.S. the Labourers International introduced an ethical code in the 1990's, specifically, barring any dealings with known organized crime figures. As it turns out, in April 2014, prompted

FOREWORD

by queries of CBC and the Toronto Star, this same Labourers union, namely, Local 183, Canada's largest construction union requested police to investigate a private company it had a collective agreement since 2012 with possible connections to organized crime. The investigation is ongoing.

The mob's move into legitimate business required a change from old-style gangster methods. Simply, the idea was to own people, professionals who act as fronts to conceal the mob's activity. Symbiotic relationships linked Mafia members and individuals operating in the legitimate sphere creating a culture that was accepted, never questioned and embedded in the industry as the Charbonneau Inquiry looking into corruption in public tenders in Quebec has found out. The affairs of the mob have become so intermingled with legitimate business that it is often impossible to tell where one stops and the other starts.

And finally, there were the workers, mostly Italian, who built the apartments of postwar Toronto. Ruthlessly exploited and unorganized, lacking safety on site and cheated of their wages, the workers were eventually signed up by unions after years of campaign. Yet, some of the newly-formed unions (when drywall replaced plaster, concrete forming replaced steel) were involved in sweetheart contracts, kickbacks, price fixing combines enforced by mob heavies, bombings, shootings and back-room deals. At key moments, union records were burned, a labour organizer was shot and a U.S. mobster arrived to intimidate an insider to keep him from talking to government investigators.

My interest in this story began when I first learned about the appalling conditions for these workers. "Tell it like it was." Those were the words of a former bricklayer turned contractor who wanted me to listen to his story. I did, and from that time became occupied and fascinated with this subject. As it happened, I was placed by chance in a position of trust by those who had never told an outsider the whole story from their point of view. I felt an obligation to piece together as much as I could through research, understand the contradictions and assemble for the first time what really took place in the apartment boom of the Fifties and Sixties.

I listened to numerous people involved at all levels of the industry, digging deeper into what was a volatile and murky business. Many evenings were spent in restaurants with extortionists, alleged Mafia associates, contractors maligned in the press and immigrant workers who spoke briefly and hesitantly about their experience.

Since this is a true story, it lacks conventional heroes and conventional villains. The main characters are individuals who move within the framework of society according to their own consciences, their own beliefs and their own perceptions of reality. At first I found it difficult to understand the men who dominate the events of this book. But eventually, I realized that if you see people in the context of the world they are a part of, it is possible to understand the true logic of their actions. This book is their story, told for the first time, beginning in the Depression years of the 1930s.

At that time (as well as the turn of the century) there was an influx of Jewish immigrants, escaping the sweep of anti-Semitism in both Europe and Russia, who were looking to start a new life in Canada. Their beginnings were fraught with barriers, excluded from resorts, private clubs, hotels, universities and Gentile firms, denied staff jobs in department stores and clerics at banks. The opportunity to overcome and succeed was education. Many became professionals, others professors, and some speculators in assembling land and developing apartment high-rise through various means of finance, at times, by private investors.

Years later, several builders turned to philanthropy to gain respect and validation by generous donations to universities, hospitals and research.

The second ethnic group was the Italians, deemed enemy aliens during the Second World War, arrested and maligned by the Canadian government for their Italian heritage. Their barrier was language as well as race and Mussolini. This is the background of the story, an ethnic history where Jews and Italians sought to break the Anglo-Saxon wall that refused entry and took every opportunity to better themselves. For a number of reasons that will become apparent, this story has no final ending.

PART I
Introductions

1
THE HARBORD CLASS OF '33

The playing field at Christie Pits was almost dark when the last hitter from Harbord Collegiate sliced a fast pitch, curving the ball high before it was snapped out of the air by an outfielder. There was a hoarse cry as the umpire called the 6–5 win, and the game between St. Peter's and Harbord was over. The crowd started to break up and wander up the slopes toward home.

Suddenly someone unfurled a canvas with a black swastika on a small mound on the north side of the park. The moment it was noticed, hundreds of youths started after the flag-bearer, the banner now tight in his fist as he raced down some side street and into a ravine.

Fights broke out on every corner. Bits of wood studded with nails, lead pipes, bottles were yanked out of pockets; cars were halted on Bloor Street as the crowd swarmed the area. Early casualties limped off into the darkness while other boys raced off on bicycles as far away as Spadina Avenue, alerting street gangs of Jews and Italians who raced up moments later in the back ends of several trucks, armed with wooden planks. Five people were taken to hospital.

The city Softball Championship between St. Peter's, which had mostly Gentiles in its line-up, and the Harbord team of Jews was the excuse for open battle. The rabbis, city officials and spokesmen for the baseball players flatly denied any responsibility for the riot. The games, they protested, had been used as an occasion for a fight by onlookers and partisans, street gangs of Irish toughs and their rivals, a local band of Jewish strong-arm boys who had been spotted earlier, drifting through the spectators with sticks up their shirts.

Nobody mentioned anti-Semitism. Nor had there been much public expression of this sentiment, at least not until this year, 1933. In January, a Toronto insurance company cancelled most of the policies held by Jews. Only when the government intervened were they reinstated. Next, a "Gentiles Only" sign appeared one night on the dance-hall door at Lambton Park. In the worst incident, two weeks before the riot at Christie Pits, a newly organized Swastika Club marched on the public boardwalk in front of the exclusive Balmy Beach Sporting Club, campaigning to rid the area of boisterous and indecent bathers who had crowded the beaches, trying to escape the summer heat. Some were apparently dressing and undressing in cars without using side curtains. As beach club members hastily removed swastikas posted on their building, some fifty Jewish youths arrived by truck, armed with broom handles and lacrosse sticks. They were taunted by the crowd on the boardwalk — which had swelled by the late evening, marching now in lines of five or six abreast — with this doggerel sung to the tune of "Home on the Range":

> *Oh give me a home where the Gentiles may roam,*
> *Where the Jews are not rampant all day;*

*Where seldom is heard a loud Yiddish word,
And the Gentiles are free all the day.*

One newspaper later reported that four gunmen had arrived uninvited from the U.S. but had left the scene, disgruntled, at the request of Jewish youths determined to handle their own affairs. The shouts of *Heil Hitler* rang into the night at the end of the long, hot holiday weekend.

However, it was that white canvas with Hitler's cross flung against the side of a hill and the nine hours of rioting that followed that sent hundreds of Jews into the streets of Toronto the day after the game. Many of the city's Jewish residents had only just left a Germany where Hitler was on the rise. Arriving in Canada in the midst of a depression, they found unemployment, overcrowding and discrimination. They were denied staff jobs in department stores and clerical positions in banks. They were excluded from many private clubs, hotels and resorts and denied leases to apartments in better residential areas. Employment was not available for professionals in Gentile firms. And now the taunts of *Heil Hitler* from carloads of youths destroyed the faith of some in Canadian justice and the British tradition.

During the night, the windows of several shop-owners were shattered by stones and bottles. Garbage pitched from passing cars rotted on the doorsteps of Jewish homes in the area where most of the new immigrants had settled.

There was talk the next day of reprisals. The League for the Defence of Jewish Rights met in the afternoon. Weeks before, they had blamed the heat for the incident at the east end beaches. Now they found no excuse. They revived the Canadian Jewish Congress, a committee to protect the rights of Jews across the country; a former editor of the *Jewish Times*, Archie Bennett, agreed to run the Toronto office, which would open officially a year later.

Earlier efforts to establish a recognized association for the scattered communities of Jews had been less than successful. In 1919, the Congress met for the first time, and a paper on national rights prepared by Bennett was read. Funds were raised for victims of the Great War. But enthusiasm for the association waned in spite of the influx of Jewish immigrants during the 1920s. There were many divisions among the newcomers, who were arriving from a wide range of European countries including Poland, Ukraine and Russia. By 1933, Toronto's Jewish neighbourhood had moved west, from the narrow streets of the Ward, lined with one-storey frame cottages and privy pits, toward Dundas, College and Harbord. It was here, in the days after the riot, stunned by the burst of anti-Semitism, that Jews began to renew their efforts to organize as a community. Many now turned to the Canadian Jewish Congress.

The Congress was committed to protecting the social and economic rights of Jews, providing relief for Jews forced to leave Germany and petitioning Canadian governments to refuse incorporation to Nazi groups. Chairing the Toronto activities was Archie Bennett, a long-time advocate of communal organization and a major force behind the re-establishment of the Congress. He had served as a publicist for the Federation of Jewish Philanthropies, a fundraising organization headed by Montrealer Samuel Bronfman, once a liquor broker for Scottish distilleries. Within a year of Bronfman's election to the presidency of the Congress, a position he held for 23 years, Bennett was appointed coordinator of an emergency refugee operation. Money raised from associations affiliated with the Congress was used to provide relief to immigrant newcomers and later to support the state of Israel. The Congress itself would become the official voice of Canadian Jewry, where previously there had been none.

If there was any part of the city where being a Jew made a child fearful by instinct, it was here in the back lanes of the old fish market and beyond, going as far north as Dundas, College and the neighbourhood school, Harbord Collegiate. These backyard alleyways bordered by wood and wire fencing offered a single schoolboy no escape from an attack by a street gang of Irish toughs or the swastika boys of the Pits gang. It had not been uncommon for Jewish pedlars to be dragged from their carts there and pelted with stones. Fear of the same treatment was instilled in the young students who raced these narrow stretches to reach the doorsteps of Harbord. In this area, Jewish parents warned their children to remain inconspicuous, if only to lessen the chance of a beating in the streets.

Many Harbord students came from immigrant homes made even poorer by the Depression. Few if any had the price of a piece of chalk in their pockets. Crowded in row housing near the stench of fish markets and factory smoke, their families believed there was only one way out of the Jewish quarter, and that was through education. Harbord Collegiate became the vehicle, if not the only hope, for these children.

Among the better-known Harbord graduates of the late 1920s and '30s: Louis Rasminsky, later governor of the Bank of Canada; Sam Shopsowitz, owner of a hot-dog empire; Victor Feldbrill, conductor of the Toronto Symphony Orchestra; Charles Best, co-discoverer of insulin; Lou Applebaum, director of the Ontario Arts Council; CBS newsman Morley Safer; Melissa Hayden, prima ballerina with the New York City Ballet; Gordon Stulberg, president of Twentieth Century Fox. There was certainly something vital about the school in the 1930s. It was the first to have its own symphony orchestra, and years later no less than one-quarter of the members of the Toronto Symphony were Harbord graduates. There were full-scale productions of Gilbert and Sullivan operettas, Shakespearean drama and farcical comedy, with gags written and staged by something called the Oola Boola Club.

And there were sports. One of the toughest end tackles for the school rugby team was Eddie "Fighting" Goodman. Eddie lived on Palmerston Avenue, a broad tree-lined street close to the school. At home, he talked of Zionism, politics and law. His ancestors were Jews from Austrian Galicia who had fled to Canada during the nineteenth-century pogroms that swept parts of Europe. His grandfather had peddled pots and pans from a pushcart through small Ontario towns; his father was a lawyer. Eddie Goodman wanted to be a judge.

Playing first string flying wing for the same rugby team was Philip Givertz, a latecomer who quit his school in Parkdale to get a Harbord education after his father, a Polish immigrant who sewed men's trousers for $3 a week, yelled at him in Yiddish, "You can be anything you like — a bum, a gangster, anything at all — but first, by God, you finish school!"

Then there was Max Goldhar, so poor he stuffed cardboard in his shoes to plug the leaks whenever it rained. Two of Goldhar's classmates were the moving force behind the Oola Boola Club. Sitting in the same row of desks, separated only by Eddie Goodman, were the two stars, Louis "the Lug" Weingarten and Frank Shuster; Goodman was the conduit for wisecracks scripted on bits of paper, jokes like this:

First kangaroo: Annabelle, where's the baby?
Second kangaroo: My goodness, I've had my pockets picked!

Some years later, Louis Weingarten changed his name to Johnny Wayne, and he and Frank Shuster became professionals in the entertainment world. But in 1937, with the war around the corner, Louis Weingarten had other ideas: "In a few years, I shall enter the greatest fight of my life, but I will enter it with the same brave words with which millions of others have entered it — I DO!"

Philip Givertz volunteered for the air force but was turned down because of poor eyesight. Instead, he changed his name to Givens, studied political science at the University of Toronto, then went to Osgoode Hall law school. Max Goldhar couldn't afford the tuition fees to study medicine, so he took a course in accounting before he became a land developer. Eddie Goodman enrolled at Osgoode for a law degree, but quit to join the army. In 1941, he went overseas.

That year Leonard Blatt graduated from Harbord. To put himself through school, Blatt and his partner, Philip Roth, had set up a diamond polishing business that had earned them $100,000 by graduation. Blatt and Roth became rich years later as apartment developers, as did their colleague Herb Stricker, another 1941 Harbord graduate.

Phil Givens, whose own political star rose when he became mayor of the city, gave this explanation for the success of his classmates: "The kids at Harbord had to prove something to themselves and their parents. In addition, they had to compensate for a degree of anti-Semitism that was around at that time. Many of them aimed very high, and they scored."

2
BUBSEY, SQUEAKY, LITTLE WOODY AND THE WEASEL

Nearly a mile north of Harbord Collegiate there was a railroad junction where the Canadian Pacific and Canadian National tracks crossed. There was no particular name for this neighbourhood, nor were the people who lived there of any particular origin. It was to this district, a drab little quarter where the trains passed daily, that the Ungerman family moved in 1931. They carted their boxes of clothes and china from the predominantly Jewish Kensington neighbourhood to Dupont Avenue, relocating their poultry business in a small store where, in the rear, the chickens were hand-plucked and hung by their necks.

Several streets east across the CN tracks was Millicent Avenue, where Giobatte Zanini lived. He was an immigrant construction worker, a bricklayer by trade. Some years earlier he had left his family in his native village in northern Italy to join work gangs in several parts of Europe before coming to Canada in the 1920s. It was often the father of a family who came first, alone, with the experience of a man who has worked as a sheepherder or farmer on some rocky hillside; later when the wives came they had to face the unaccustomed patterns of city living in a foreign country where people spoke only a foreign language.

The Zanini family was reunited in 1929 after Giobatte made the decision to remain in Canada. Of the ten children born to his wife, seven had survived; and among these seven, who came to Canada that year, was a stocky, red-haired boy named Bruno, a sensitive, energetic child who took easily to the life he saw in the streets, racing the alleyways at all hours of the day and night.

He was one of the foreign-born (as Anglo-Saxon social workers were inclined to say), restless little newcomers whose exuberant behaviour and spirited nature constituted a social problem for the Toronto community. Some blamed this random play on overcrowded living conditions forced upon immigrants. Others claimed it was peculiar to southern and eastern Europeans. The problem was to fit these children into Canadian schools where punctuality, industry and schoolbook intelligence were rigidly enforced. For this reason, the school-age children of immigrants were not always regarded with warmth and understanding. One speaker at a private club in Toronto, concerned about the future citizenry of Canada, said this: "The children of our new immigrants, in the natural course of events, may be expected to become good Canadians, but it will require education if they are to appreciate the advantages of Imperial unity so patent to most of us who come from British stock."

As the wave of Jewish immigrants following the First World War increased, so too did Italian migration. But the reasons were different. Unlike the Jews, the Italians were less concerned with finding a new home. They came attracted largely by the opportunities to earn money and then return home. It was only after they had spent some time here that more and more Italians thought of bringing out their families to settle in Toronto. By 1933, the Italian population had increased to 14,000.

A few Italian homes were scattered in the area around Millicent and Dupont, some on the fringes of streets at the north end of the Jewish quarter at Harbord. As more Italians moved into the neighbourhood, the owners of corner stores there began to replace their stock of biscuit tins with bags of pasta.

The nearest Catholic school was St. Rita's. On several occasions, Bruno Zanini distinguished himself as a fighter at mid-morning breaks until finally the nuns expelled him. Happily, he attended a public school for the remainder of his elementary education; however, on most days of the week he could be found squatting on a curb, tossing a pair of dice. Gambling had its own rewards, so in time he was looking for money to support this pastime; he found it stealing safes from factory warehouses. Boxing, too, had its advantages. Bruno took instruction from an old man at a neighbourhood youth centre. Nearly every immigrant boy learned to box at one time or another, as a form of protection as well as status. Joey Bagnato boxed. So did Irv Ungerman — it was a project he undertook after someone hit him with a geography book. "I fixed that kid pretty good," he recalled years later. "I got him in the cloakroom one day when he knocked my coat off the hook. I guess I must have whacked him into a few of those big coat-hooks because even the top of his head was bleeding and I couldn't have hit him up that high. He never bothered me again." Ungerman later became a boxing promoter.

Both Ungerman and Zanini learned quickly about prejudice. It was Ungerman who went to the steam baths, usually off limits to Jews, with Zanini one day. The doorman paused, then stepped aside for "Ungy," as he was affectionately called, while barring entry to Zanini. How Ungerman got in was a mystery, but Zanini, not for the first time, had been mistaken for a Jew. On another occasion late one night, coming out of a side alley near Christie Pits, he was spotted by a swastika gang of Irish toughs and chased home. Whether it was his curly hair or the Roman nose, long by anyone's standards, there was a measure of racial discrimination Bruno Zanini grew to expect. He eventually forgot most of his Italian. In time, his Italian expressions were limited to the scores of operas like *La Boheme* and *La Traviata,* heard in weekend radio concerts by nearly everyone in the household. They inspired Zanini to take voice instruction from a local teacher. Zanini's English was a street language, created by immigrant kids who were determined to hide their differences.

Out of this common anxiety to belong and to have some self-protection emerged street gangs, haphazard collections of half-grown men, 15 or 16 or 17, their pants cut off at the knees, their feet laced in ankle boots, squaring off behind some deserted shed for a late-afternoon boxing spree. Some groups were more ambitious than others, staking out their territory like cats, patrolling street corners, where they planned raids, harmless outings at first that soon were replaced by more sophisticated adventures. There was no reason to think that Zanini was the mastermind of such sport, although he regularly gave advice to his group. There was Bubsey, Squeaky, Little Woody and the Weasel — swearing oaths, pledging allegiance not as British subjects to their country but rather to each other. There was little justice or protection for immigrant kids, so together they concocted their own system, their own rules, and together they scrambled in and out of warehouse windows, pinched cement vaults and split the contents.

They were not always successful. In 1933, on November 12, Zanini was arrested and charged with theft. He was 12 years old.

Three years later, his family moved to the north side of the tracks, to 62 Wiltshire Avenue, a narrow brick duplex in the middle of a block, across from the Reed Metal Products brass foundry and the Brunton Lumber Company. Although his residence changed, Zanini's territory remained the same. When Johnston's gas station was built at the corner of Symington and

Davenport, it was instantly claimed by members of his gang, some of whom returned to that spot year after year, as if to recapture some sacred past.

The closest rivals to the Symington gang were a band of mostly Italian boys who operated around Silverthorn. Other streetwise youths found themselves in similar groups throughout the city. In the east end, near Gerrard and Dundas, six stocky Italians — the Volpe brothers — shared a background similar to Zanini's. These gangs shared one common passion: gambling. Stone quarries were used for craps games; back lanes for euchre. There was nothing unusual or uncommon about these groups, as one social worker had explained nearly a decade earlier: "The gang spirit is very strong in the city. Outstanding characters in boy life have no difficulty in keeping a strong body of retainers, ready to back them up in anything they say or do — and, as a rule, faithful in any trouble or dispute in which the gang may be involved."

During the next four years, Zanini was charged with break and enter, theft and vagrancy eight times, until in 1938 he was sent to Guelph reformatory, a training school for delinquent boys. At Guelph, enclosed by a wire fence, inmates learned to make bricks.

After his release Zanini got a job as a bricklayer, but his inability to shun Johnston's gas station and his old associates hastened a second arrest some months later. A crime reporter for one of the city's English newspapers filed this item:

YOUTH FEARS REFORMATORY VOICE EFFECT

Cultivation of Vocal Organs is Whole Ambition, Officer Quotes Safe Thief — Is Remanded

. . . The charge to which the accused pleaded guilty

was that of breaking into the store of Kevin Kirby, at 1560 Danforth Avenue, and stealing a safe containing $172.13.

"He made a statement admitting that he and two other young men had entered the store and stolen the safe which they had taken out on the highway and forced open," testified Detective Sergeant Norman Tinsley. "He stated each had taken $57.

"He also said in his statement that he had a fine tenor voice, the cultivation of which was his whole ambition and that he had definitely resolved to lead a different life. He stated he would willingly accept five years probation rather than three months in the reformatory where smoke would interfere with his voice."

"This young man has definitely made up his mind to lead a proper life," said J. W. Teskey, defence counsel. "He is very much in earnest."

Zanini was sentenced to two years less one day. Only his mother ever came to visit him. "I can still see her, you know," he said later. "She was standing there, shaking her head and saying in Italian, 'Our family is not like this, nobody has ever been in trouble before.'"

But there were still more confusing times ahead. On June 10, 1940, Benito Mussolini declared war on Britain and its allies. That night a brick was thrown through the window of Joe Bevaconti's shop on Queen Street. Stones shattered the storefront of Tony Ungrassi's fruit store on Gerrard. About the same time, the window at Peter's Shoe Store splintered and broke from a flying brick, scattering glass over the pavement. Someone tossed a flowerpot into Charles Cira's fruit store on Parliament Street. On St. Clair Avenue, an elderly man carrying a rock approached a fruit store and yelled, "Down with the jackals. Drive them out. They want to get in for the kill but we'll show them." He then sent the rock crashing through the store window.

The following day, all unnaturalized Italians in Canada were required to register. Those considered suspicious were taken from their families and interned by the Royal Canadian Mounted Police. All Italian unnaturalized aliens receiving public relief were stricken from the welfare rolls. Twenty-four hours after the minister of justice authorized internment, Toronto police arrested a hundred Italians, including two professors and a city policeman with the force for twenty-seven years. They were taken to police stations and later removed to headquarters, where they were photographed and fingerprinted. Some were sent to Stanley Barracks; others were held at the Exhibition grounds. Nine were detained in Don Jail for further inquiry. The Italians arrested offered no resistance to police.

Other influential Italians were included in the police roundup of suspected "enemies." One of the city's most popular restaurants was closed after the arrest of the owner. An Italian with a criminal record who had successfully evaded the police for years was also picked up, fingerprinted and photographed. "Well, here I am," he told a reporter, "I guess I need a rest — I guess I will be away for a long time." A father and son were taken from their home by police. An Italian doctor was arrested at his office while he was treating patients; an old priest was led away from his house. Giobatte Zanini and his wife were taken away by a police cruiser to be questioned, then released. There had been no warning.

Those under arrest were imprisoned in the Automotive Building at Exhibition Park in four long pens, 40 men in each, with two rows of beds, two bunks high. Held in one pen was an organist who had been picked up during his choir practice. Two Italians who had served with the Canadians in the First World War were also interned. Most of those held here were later removed to an internment camp in Niagara-on-the-Lake, where a special compound had been built.

And a large bronze statue of Romulus and Remus was removed from City Hall, where it had been on exhibit for six years. It had been a gift from the Italian government to mark the 100th anniversary of Toronto. The statue was smashed and sent to a munitions factory to be converted into shells.

To most of Toronto's Italian residents, the arrests and imprisonment were a totally unexpected development. People who had been law-abiding were suddenly suspect solely because they were Italian. Some protested. Others sent statements of loyalty to Canadian newspapers. Many lived alone with their fear, split from families, divided, scorned by a war that raged several thousand miles away.

In 1942, despite the boom in the many fast-growing war industries, there was little work available to Italians, especially those who refused to change their names. It was at this time that Bruno Zanini was released from prison. He was penniless. Hampered by a criminal record and his Italian background, he found it difficult to secure work, so he turned to other sources of income. The war had spared no luxury: rations on gas, coffee, liquor, even rubber tires were imposed, creating a lucrative black market, appropriate for Zanini, who readily applied his skills along with some members of the old Symington gang. Everyone was cheating the system and the wartime rationing, Zanini rationalized. Then too, none of his "scores" were wilful or malicious; he only dealt with illegal operators. For example, one night in late December, he and Little Woody slipped into a bootlegger's basement for several cases of liquor. Woody's contact, a man of some status, was willing to pay them $15 a bottle. But someone had tipped off the police, and they gave chase. Zanini ended up wading across the Humber River; he had to crawl out and climb the nearest eavestrough to the roof of a house to hide from his pursuers.

Two years later, in an incident that led to his arrest, Zanini joined a plan to steal the winnings of a gambler who used crooked dice. He arrived late, shortly after his singing lesson with Maestro Rossellini, and the place looked empty. When he stepped inside, he was startled to hear someone coming up the stairs. The ensuing fight woke up the neighbours, who called the police. Zanini resisted arrest, then fell to the ground as though he had blacked out, but ran away when he got a chance. Two days later, he was charged with breaking and entering, assault and escaping custody. The judge sent Zanini to the Kingston Penitentiary for two years.

Everybody in Kingston looked thin in those years, probably because of the war and food rationing. Zanini joined the prisoners' choir but quit because they practised only once a week; instead he vocalized at night, singing to cellmates after the lights were shut off. During the day, he studied books about medicine, psychology, fossils and ancient history. In time, he got his high school diploma. As he explained, "If you don't discipline your mind in there, you grow weak, you get old and your teeth fall out."

If there was any excuse for his behaviour and his past, it had been his environment, he concluded. He did not feel like a criminal. Still, he did have one weakness: gambling. Someone approached him while he was indulging his habit at a card game a year after his release, wanting to sell a bracelet. The price was $500. "Is it hot?" he asked. (Had it been stolen?) There were repeated denials. To establish a fair price, Zanini asked a jeweller to appraise the bracelet. The jeweller promptly informed the police, because the bracelet had in fact been taken in a major robbery. Zanini was charged in 1947 with receiving stolen property. Despite his protestations of innocence, he did another twenty months in Kingston.

Finally, in May 1949, four years after the war ended, Zanini was returned to society. He still didn't think of himself as a criminal. And he still wanted to be an opera singer. By the end of the year, with his earnings from bricklaying, he had left for Genoa, an Italian seaport, where he planned to join an opera company.

3

BEYOND A BOWL OF SPAGHETTI: LANSKY AND LUCIANO

In the spring of 1933, Salvatore Luciano — better known as Lucky Luciano — held a meeting in his suite at the Waldorf Towers in New York City with his business partners to discuss plans for the end of Prohibition. It had taken Luciano some time to get to the Waldorf. His New York life had begun in 1906 at the Bend, where Mulberry Street crooks like an elbow, in the core of New York slums on the Lower East Side.

This district was a maze of narrow streets, filth, rotting fruit, tenement rooms crowded with boarders; families slept on floors, the children in boxes. It was the home of pedlars and rag-pickers, largely Italian. Forty families would be packed into five two-storey homes; the crowds in the streets were dotted with bandannas and on Sundays, men squatted around a wooden crate for a game of cards. Salvatore Luciano had arrived here with his father, a day labourer who quit the sulfur mines in Sicily to start again in the New World ghetto that was flourishing below Fourteenth Street. Of the five children, only Salvatore refused to change or shorten his name. At 14, five years after his arrival in New York, Salvatore left school to learn his English in the streets.

Turning off Mulberry Street at Bayard was Jewtown, where bearded men haggled for goods and women walked with babies at their breasts. Here even the bread was different, baked in doughy wreaths. Luciano made inroads into this territory by selling protection to young Jewish boys in the district. For a penny or two a day, he made sure his clients escaped the regular attacks from older Irish and Italian gangs. In time, he collected his own band of Sicilian boys, eager to make money by selling protection. Once, they cornered a young Russian Jew called Maier Suchowljansky: "If you wanna keep alive, Jew boy, you gotta pay us five cents a week protection money." The boy, who called himself Lansky, stared back at Luciano, then spat out, "Fuck you!"

Months later, the two boys met again. By then Lansky had organized his own gang of Jewish toughs to deal with life on the streets. After a handshake, Lansky agreed to join forces with Luciano. It was the first Italian-Jewish defence pact on the Lower East Side. Their first joint effort was breaking into a riverfront warehouse. After a score of successful thefts, profits began to mount and they opened a bank account. One early Lansky associate, Daniel Francis Ahearn, broke the code of silence some years later, shedding light on the activities of the Lower East Side gang. He said Lansky had told him one day he was "connected with crap games" and "making some money, with unions and so forth." In those early days both management and unions used street gangs to settle their disputes. Some were hired to protect factories from workers threatening to burn down the buildings while unions used their own gunmen in self-defence, for protection against management troublemakers.

But for Luciano, who acted as the front man, and his colleague Lansky, the biggest opportunity for profit came in 1920 when the U.S. government banned the manufacture, sale and transportation of liquor and beer. At once, the Lower East Side set up a supply line of liquor, offering some of the finest Scottish brands for wealthy customers who began to frequent speakeasies. Crates of liquor were purchased from a Canadian, Samuel Bronfman, who had close ties to one of Lansky's lieutenants, Abner "Longie" Zwillman. Both the Lansky and Bronfman families had been part of the same exodus from Europe, fleeing the pogroms that had ripped through the eastern countries. According to Luciano, Samuel Bronfman was "bootlegging enough whiskey across the Canadian border to double the size of Lake Erie." However, Bronfman's export activities were considered legal in Canada. Emerging as one of the most wealthy families in North America, the Bronfmans owed their success to the start they got during this period. Sam Bronfman later explained how their business worked: "We loaded a carload of goods, got our cash and shipped it. We shipped a lot of goods. I never went on the other side of the border to count the empty Seagram's bottles."

Getting the liquor out of Canada was easier than getting it into the U.S. Often boats were chartered in Canada to take shipments to an obscure foreign port; once they were in international waters they would rendezvous with speedboats from the U.S. side, which would run the supply to the American shore. To facilitate border-crossing in the Prairies, the Bronfmans set up satellite warehouses and a transport company, properly accredited to move between the two countries. Drivers of Hudsons, Studebakers, Packards and Chryslers drove from the U.S. to the Canadian depots for their loads of booze. Some of these cars, completely stripped of upholstery and with reinforced springs, could carry forty cases of whiskey worth $2,000 south to a thirsty population.

Some of this imported liquor was sold directly to customers. The rest was watered, cut with grain alcohol. This generated a need for bottles looking like the originals to rebottle the booze. So

Lansky and Luciano went into the bottle business. They needed labels identical to the original Johnnie Walker, Haig & Haig, Dewar's, so they went into the printing business. The bottles had to be stored in warehouses so they went into the real estate business. The crates had to be shipped, so they became owners of huge trucking companies. In the peak years of Prohibition, Lansky and Luciano were operating a $12-million empire in New York based on the sale of illegal liquor alone. Al Capone, another child of the Lower East Side, left the city to set up his own operation along these lines in Chicago.

Their new-found fortune gave Luciano and Lansky mounds of cash that could be used to finance other ventures. So they became moneylenders. Quick, ready cash was needed in a number of high-risk businesses, such as the garment industry. Since banks were unwilling to advance short-term loans to garment manufacturers, new sources of financing were found. A number of businessmen turned to associates of the Lower East Side gang for loans, making loansharking a highly profitable enterprise, as Luciano once remarked: "They was gettin' anywhere from double to 1,000 percent interest for short-term loans, and of course, if the loans wasn't repaid, no excuses was accepted."

If a company was unable to repay a loan, but the business looked good, it would soon have the Lower East Side gang as a partner. Lansky's thinking was this: "We won't worry about the non-payment of interest for a while. Our money will be repaid all right. We should offer to forget about the loan altogether and even give them back their interest if they've paid any. Instead we should suggest that we become silent partners in their business. You must explain," he advised his colleagues, "that we will not interfere in the way they run their business. But we'll draw up legal documents giving us a share of the business with the profits divided up fairly. With our financing, nothing can keep us from growing."

Working the other end of the industry at the same time, loan sharks also funnelled large amounts of cash into unions to finance their organizing drives. When a union failed to repay its loan, its local organization came under the control of such enterprising men as Luciano and Lansky. The takeover of union locals also yielded profits for the syndicate. The union became a tool: the syndicate could extort money from businesses by interfering in labour matters or threatening strikes. Later unions were used to swell the coffers of the syndicate with a regular income skimmed from the union membership's monthly dues. A specified percentage of money was also taken from the workers' welfare and pension funds. This was done easily since there was no regulation, inspection or audit of any kind by government officials.

Through certain union locals, the syndicate gained enormous power in a number of industries that were poorly regulated and highly competitive. One example was the construction field. Imaginative schemes were used to squeeze money at all levels of this industry. Contractors who refused to meet payments became victims of sabotage, arson and vandalism. The damage was often extensive enough to force these men out of business forever. Syndicate-controlled unions were used by cutthroat competitors to force out rival companies through lengthy illegal walkouts or violence. When racketeers offered management a chance to gain a monopoly in business, they demanded a percentage of the company's profits in return. In the end, the people most exploited were the honest and legitimate contractors and workers.

The syndicate's scheme to work both ends of an industry led to a new level of cooperation between management and unions. Fearful that unions would drive them out of business with demands for higher wages, owners soon learned that, for a fee, labour racketeers were at times willing to hold wage scales at a reasonable level in their union contracts.

The skilful manoeuvring of companies and unions in the garment and construction businesses was repeated in several other industries dependent on the transport industry. The mob's trucking operation expanded rapidly after three of the four biggest fresh-food businesses in the U.S. were persuaded to cooperate, giving up a percentage of sales — as much as half a cent a loaf for bakeries, for instance. Dairies, too, became part of the mob's business. Milk, like bread and vegetables, spoils quickly. Drivers for these companies were to be organized by Teamster boss James R. Hoffa, whose circle of acquaintances included a number of top-ranking syndicate bosses. In the meat industry, mobsters again collected from both ends of the industry: from the packers, to ensure prompt delivery, and the restaurants, who paid protection for the same prompt, regular delivery service.

The diversification into new businesses was made possible largely because of the money made on bootlegging. However, this unlimited supply of cash from the illicit liquor trade was cut short when Prohibition ended, nine months after the Waldorf convention in the spring of 1933. There both Luciano and Lansky, who made one of his rare appearances, stressed to their colleagues the importance of moving their operations into legitimate business ventures.

At that spring meeting, Luciano was the first to speak to the roomful of high-powered businessmen representing syndicates throughout the country. There was discussion about legitimate business operations and the need to diversify further. Lansky announced his intention to move into gambling. The idea, he explained, was to open a casino offshore where gambling would be viewed as a legitimate and profitable tourist attraction. The spot he had chosen was Havana, where Lansky already had ties with Fulgencio Batista, a Cuban strongman and friend from the earlier days of Prohibition.

However, as he explained to the syndicate chiefs, this new venture required $500,000 as an investment from each partner. At the mention of this figure, the room exploded. Chuck Polizzi from Cleveland screamed so loud the veins in his neck looked like rope. Half a million dollars during the Depression was outrageous. Still, Lansky persisted, finally persuading Polizzi that it was better to spend the money on a casino than send it to the income tax boys in Washington. So in September Lansky flew to Havana and asked Batista to join him in his hotel room. At the appropriate moment, a suitcase bulging with packets of bills totalling $3 million was shown to the Cuban politician. An additional offer of $3 million was extended to him for every year Lansky had a monopoly on the casino planned for the Hotel Nacional. Batista agreed, and Lansky opened a Swiss bank account for his friend in Zurich.

A number of other sites were chosen for gambling casinos, in Florida, California and Nevada. But for Lansky the gem was Cuba, this delightful island just off the tip of southern Florida. His idea was to establish an entire gambling resort, not just a casino. Once the casino was set up, Lansky arranged for money to be skimmed from the profits of the casino and sent by courier to a numbered bank account in Switzerland. Later, its origins and ownership obscured, the money was returned to the U.S. to be invested in the stock market or to finance some legitimate business that syndicate members would control. These gambling profits seeking a tax-free home in Swiss bank vaults were carried in suitcases or locked pouches by only a few trusted men. One was Sylvain Ferdmann, a Swiss with degrees in banking and economics. Another was John Pullman, an associate of Lansky's since 1920 and a former member of the Kid Cann gang of Minneapolis–St. Paul, who played a major role in the Minneapolis combination, bootlegging Canadian whiskey. The city had been a major market for Sam Bronfman's Saskatchewan "boozoriums" during Prohibition days. One of Bronfman's most profitable arrangements with American bootleggers had been with a Minneapolis liquor broker, Fred Lundquist.

Gambling was only one aspect of the big push for diversification. Plans had long ago been made to move into the legitimate business of importing whiskey as well as for transforming speakeasies into restaurants and nightclubs. Arrangements were made with foreign distillers for the sole importing and distribution franchises. Lesser notables such as Lewis Rosenstiel and Sam Bronfman emerged on their own as heads of domestic distilleries, Schenley and Seagram's respectively.

But the move into legitimate business was not always that simple or popular. Often Lansky's ideas were met with resistance from other associates. It was Luciano who remarked on this: "The toughest fight of all was gettin' into real estate. In a way, it was crazy that so many guys objected to it. There was no rackets, no shakedowns. It was all out in the open, clean. You had a nice buildin' which maybe didn't pay off like a slot machine, but the money come in regular. Some of the guys only knew things like rackets and the big score. When Lansky and I talked about buyin' into real estate, they looked at us like we was nuts. 'What're we gonna do with a buildin'?' We lost out on a lotta terrific deals which if we owned today would be worth a thousand million dollars. That was always my big objection to the brainpower in the Unione [the Italian mob]. Some of them guys could never see beyond a bowl of spaghetti."

But it was the rackets like prostitution that fired the imagination of crime-busters in the 1930s. U.S. attorney Thomas Dewey, flanked by a team of detectives from the vice squad, rounded up hundreds of lieutenants employed by Luciano in that racket in February 1936. Luciano was never linked directly to the prostitution ring but he was arrested anyway, tried and convicted on the evidence of Florence Brown, known professionally as Cokey Flo.

Meanwhile Lansky continued to promote casino ventures. The Second World War ended his efforts in Havana for a time; nobody wanted to go to an island where the waters were patrolled by submarines. Next Lansky tried Florida. Using some local businessmen to front his operation, he bought control of the Colonial Inn in Broward county, just north of Miami. The county sheriff supplied armed deputies to guard the illegal casino and to protect the armoured cars carrying the money to and from various banks. In return, the sheriff was permitted to operate a numbers racket from his office and control slot machines under the name Broward Amusement Company.

Rival establishments sprang up all around the Colonial Inn, mostly run by small independent promoters. But when a nightclub operator leased a large building to open a casino, his lawyer was visited by a stranger who dropped $250,000 on his desk and announced that the club was under new management. When this failed to impress Lansky's new competitor, two men made a second visit, to the office of the nightclub operator's business associate in the casino deal, explaining how they were his new partners. The two men were ordered out. The rival casino operator was later found dead in his car with two .38-calibre slugs in his head.

Lansky's move into Las Vegas began in 1945, when he and ten partners purchased the El Cortez Club. The club was sold a year later and the money invested in the Nevada Projects Corporation, which would build the Flamingo casino and hotel in the desert. Building supplies following the war were scarce; so was skilled labour. Top wages were paid to bring in carpenters, electricians and plumbers. The casino opened in 1946, but lost heavily and was closed until the hotel was completed. The second time it opened, the profits again were unimpressive. Gambling operator Bugsy Siegel was shot — with Lansky's consent, it was assumed — only twenty minutes before Morris Sidwirtz, Gus Greenbaum and Morris Rosen walked into the Flamingo and announced they were the club's new managers. And Las Vegas began to boom.

Not everyone was entirely enthusiastic about the casinos; a few civic organizations in Florida were particularly concerned about crime on the east coast of their state. In 1948, ninety such organizations met and discussed ways to secure injunctions against the major gambling clubs. An injunction closed the Colonial Inn at the end of the year. Lansky countered by campaigning through various paid media sources for the legalization of gambling. But his efforts were cut short when a senator from Tennessee, Estes Kefauver, announced an inquiry by the Special Senate Committee to Investigate Organized Crime in Interstate Commerce. As committee chairman, Kefauver was soon to embark on one of the most thorough probes of crime and politics ever undertaken by U.S. authorities.

It was just a few months before the Kefauver hearings began that an associate of Meyer Lansky, John Pullman, left Miami to join his relatives in Toronto. Pullman was to play a major role in the more sophisticated operations of the syndicate after the war, first from his new base in Canada and later operating from Switzerland.

Pullman was born in 1901 in Romania, but came as a young child with his family to Canada. He attended school here until the age of 10, then had a brief career as a bellhop working at an island resort at Penetanguishene. In 1917 Pullman left for the U.S., where he worked in the bakery business and in an automobile parts retail chain. He got involved with the Kid Cann gang in Minneapolis, the area where Sam Bronfman had his best customers, and ran afoul of the law in 1931 when he was convicted of bootlegging. Later he ran a nightclub in Miami with a Toronto stockbroker named Louis A. Chesler. was a promoter of mining stocks, and on occasion worked with Lansky on Canadian mining deals.

How Pullman became connected to Lansky isn't clear, but he never made a secret of his affection for the "Little Man." As he once told a newspaper reporter, "Yes, I know Meyer Lansky. He's a wonderful man . . ."

Soon after his arrival in Toronto in 1949, Pullman registered a business and became active as an investor in both stocks and real estate. Meanwhile he continued to travel widely, from Toronto to Switzerland to the Bahamas and to the U.S., as a trusted courier for Lansky. Pullman's specialty was money. And money was something that Meyer Lansky and his associates had lots of.

PART II
The Real Estate Boom, 1950-1960

4
THE NEW BUILDERS

By 1950 Canada's postwar housing boom was on. During and after the war, there had been a serious shortage of housing, particularly in the large cities. To meet the demand, the government hastily built a number of wartime units, small, temporary frame houses that alleviated the crisis. But the population continued to swell. There were returning war veterans, displaced Europeans and other immigrants concerned now with settling into a civilian way of life, raising a family and owning a home of their own. This demand was so strong that the relatively small number of house builders were unable to ease the shortage. The government continued its interim housing program until 1949, when the homebuilding industry seemed to be back on its feet.

Nearly every business had been hurt and disrupted by the Depression and then the war. In construction, a whole generation of builders had been wiped out during the Thirties and Forties, as sons gave up their fathers' skills and sought work elsewhere. Contributing to the declining activity was the scarcity of construction materials. As business tapered off, the ranks were further depleted. So when the demand suddenly became strong again, there were few skilled builders available.

The possibilities of making big money in housing had never fully been explored before this boom. A builder used to complete only ten or twelve houses a year. Now thousands of new homes were needed. The demand attracted a whole new breed of builder to the industry. Few were experienced or skilled, but almost everyone saw a chance to make some money. The more successful and ambitious opportunists quickly expanded their operations, building a hundred or two hundred homes a year. Later in the Fifties the boom spread to apartment construction. Starting out with three-storey buildings, it did not take long for the most successful builders to move into tall high-rise apartment buildings of a type that had never been seen in Canada. Along with all this activity, particularly in the new suburbs, came the shopping centres, at first small strips of stores alongside supermarkets, later enormous plazas incorporating two or three department stores.

All this new growth was on undeveloped farmland, and it didn't take long for speculators and investors to discover that there was also big money in land. Hundreds of acres were converted into streets, house lots, parks and shopping centres. Traditionally, the small house builder bought land already serviced with water and sewers, since he would be unable to pay for these services himself. With the demand for land increasing, the small builder was suddenly confronted with rising real estate costs as more and more speculators moved in, making a quick dollar by buying raw land, hiking the price and selling it. In fact, real estate overnight became the darling of speculators who knew a good deal, seasoned traders who began buying and selling land as they had previously bought and sold penny mining stock. Often values were pumped up artificially by the traders as they bought and sold among themselves. Through these syndicates and partnerships, large tracts of land were tied up all around the city.

Some of these land speculators were also builders, buying land and developing it, bringing their business talents to the home-building industry. As their profits rose, promoters abandoned their careers as stockbrokers, diamond merchants, furriers and pharmacists to converge on the housing business. These new builders, unlike the small, traditional house builders, knew little about construction. The responsibility for work crews and equipment they passed on to subcontracting companies.

The use of this cutthroat system, where inexperienced developers subcontracted work to the firm with the lowest bid, nearly always guaranteed a rock-bottom price. To step up competition among the subcontractors who did the foundation, carpentry, brickwork and plastering, some developers promised nonexistent work, creating a surplus of companies. The bidding served a cosmetic purpose only; the subcontractor usually took the price the builder gave him, if only to get the project. Some developers resorted to a private kickback scheme, replenishing the subcontracting firm with money under the table when the winning bid, even after an open tender among competitors, was outrageously low. This system was a long way from the traditional method of bidding on work by tenders in sealed envelopes, opened one at a time by the general contractor builder, who would then choose the lowest price without further haggling.

A number of small subcontractors who refused to accept payment in the form of kickbacks fell into bankruptcy, unable to compete at such low prices without cheating their workers. Those who saw their future in the house building industry had to face continually dropping prices for the work they performed. Some moved into the commercial building sector; others stayed in housing, forced at times to cut hours off their workers' weekly paycheques to stay in operation. Devising numerous methods to meet the residential builders' prices, these subcontractors wrote worthless cheques, changing company names to avoid payment, fled the country or hired workers on probation, then fired them weeks later without pay. On occasion labourers were required to pay a percentage of their salaries back to their bosses in the form of dues for the Queen of England — or so they were told. The money was then used by the subcontractor to flesh out his meagre profit.

The majority of the new subcontracting firms were operated by immigrant labourers who eagerly sought work from the developers. Rarely did these companies hire skilled or union tradesmen, since the wages they demanded were considerably higher than they could afford; instead they employed hundreds of immigrants, mostly Italian, whose lack of skills and language didn't bar them from construction. When there were no regulations or bylaws requiring standard-quality construction, the buildings were often substandard. And when the building inspectors didn't do their jobs, the result was jerry-building.

Architecturally, these new suburban homes had a disconcerting sameness — brick houses in an orderly row, usually with the same brick, the same grey asbestos roofs, with concrete front porches and wrought-iron handrails and one-car garages. Often the lots measured less than forty feet across. Inside, the new occupants were at times challenged by this lack of space and poor design, trying to clear passageways from the dinette to the galley kitchen while steering themselves around the furniture. Appropriately enough, the houses were often called strawberry boxes. They weren't much sturdier.

One eminent architect whose annoyance flared every time he caught a glimpse of one of these squat, uninspiring structures claimed houses were springing up like toadstools, with no more attention being paid to design or community planning than there would be for a row of baseball bleachers. Another critic called them biscuit tins, unrelated to decent living. But they were bought eagerly by many people, tired of wartime housing shortages and anxious to have a family, who wanted houses of their own in the suburbs.

The industry was so poorly regulated that little protection was offered these new homeowners. With the exception of a national building code and a few city bylaws dictating the use of land, there were few rules to abide by nor government guidelines to adhere to. Real estate agents didn't require licences, nor did the builders and the subcontractors. And building inspectors were not always immune to the gifts or, in some cases, to the women that came their way as encouragement to pass a shoddy piece of work.

Dire warnings were issued by one planning consultant, Dr. Eugene Faludi, who commented at the time: "If we want a suit, we go to a tailor; if we want legal advice, we go to a lawyer; if we want medical attention, we go to a doctor. But if we want a house, we go to an ex-grocer who has found there is more money slicing up property than slicing up ham; or to an ex-stockbroker who went broke except for money to get into speculative building."

Many shortcuts to lower costs were found in the plumbing system or electrical wiring. Sometimes houses were not fully insulated or had inadequate heating systems. One homeowner discovered the hot water in the bathroom stopped running whenever the kitchen faucet was turned on. Instances were reported of mortar falling out of concrete walls; putty lifting around the windowsills; paint curling off the doors.

Everything that happened in the house-building industry revolved around money or the lack of it. Land speculators forced the price of land so high, so quickly that small builders couldn't afford the price of lots to build on. Unable to participate in the mass-scale homebuilding promoted by their new competitors, they began to close up shop. The inability to finance projects on a grand scale marked the failure of their businesses. Banks were reluctant to advance money to an industry considered a high risk and unlikely to provide a fast return on investment. The crisis deepened in the mid-1950s when money became tight owing to a monetary recession. These periodic dips in the economy nearly always hurt the small builders, whose assets were tied up in projects and equipment. Refused additional financing by banks and lending institutions that preferred quicker returns on their investments, the small builder had few places to turn for ready cash. Said one builder at the height of the 1950s money shortage, "If there is no improvement soon, we shall be laying off crews; if we lay off crews, we are out of business, and some of us will never get back in." Extraordinary as it seemed, by 1956 the demand for houses had never been greater, encouraged by new mortgage-lending policies to potential homeowners; but small homebuilders were repeatedly turned away from lending institutions.

Rarely did a builder have enough cash to buy a property and build. Usually a buyer would tie up real estate by using as little cash as possible. The seller agreed to accept a small initial cash payment of $500 to $1,000, with the promise of the remaining money later on in the form of a mortgage. These paper deals allowed land developers to gather property at relatively little cash cost to themselves while borrowing other people's dollars.

Money was also needed to develop this land. This second phase was costly and often unpredictable. A delay in construction caused by a strike somewhere in the construction or building materials industry could unexpectedly increase their cash needs. A delay in selling or renting homes and apartments would do the same. If approval of the developer's plans were stalled at City Hall, this too cost money.

There would have been fewer problems had these builders

been wealthy investors dabbling in real estate as a sideline; but many of these men were entrepreneurs, cash-poor, with the single ambition of making their fortunes in this business. They started out without much money of their own, and even when on paper they were doing well, they always had their cash tied up in projects. The risks were considerable in what was generally thought to be an unstable industry, vulnerable to economic recessions and a market that was often difficult to predict.

The smaller the builder, the more susceptible he was to sudden cash problems; however, as companies grew, they were able to weather difficulties with greater ease and locate cash from an increasing variety of lenders — finance companies, life insurance companies, trust companies and chartered banks.

Not all of Toronto's homebuilders were ruined by these periodic financial squeezes. One pre-eminent builder of the 1950s was the legendary Principal Investments Ltd., a firm that went from a modest portfolio of real estate investments in 1942 to a multimillion-dollar collection of holdings in 1949, then to become the largest single land developer in Canada through the boom years of the 1950s until its untimely demise in 1963. While other, less well-financed builders were concentrating on the construction of new suburban houses, which generated a relatively quick turnover and a cash profit, Principal was building shopping centres to service these rapidly growing communities. This required lots of ready cash and the financial strength to hang on for long-term returns, but during the Fifties Principal seemed to have the wherewithal.

Shopping centres were an innovation in the retailing field, and they were particularly suited to serving the needs of the new postwar suburbs. Once development of new housing was underway in an area, a company such as Principal anticipated the buying patterns of future residents and their need for groceries, clothing, drugs and other goods by assembling an appropriate site for a new shopping centre. Positioned near major highways and key intersections, a shopping centre captured much of the retail business of the people living in the area. The bigger the centre, the larger the territory where it dominated the retail business. The developers soon found that supermarkets and department stores would attract shoppers to a centre. Between these "anchor" stores, usually located at opposite ends of the mall, were a strip of stores rented to retailers who wanted a slice of the local trade. These malls, at first outdoors and later enclosed, were like main streets lined with small shops. As more people extolled the virtues of these centres, convinced of their convenience, small businessmen in the outlying areas were faced with little alternative but to rent space in a mall. Although the rents offered by the builder-landlords to the anchor stores were considerably lower, the small retail shops didn't complain as their own businesses began to flourish. In fact business was so good for the mall retailers that the developers were able to demand and collect from the retailer a slice of the action, a percentage of every dollar spent in the mall stores. This was known as a percentage lease.

The opening of a shopping centre was often vested with the pomp and ceremony of a ship embarking on its maiden voyage. At the opening of one Principal project, the Oshawa shopping centre, the mayor of the town claimed he had now seen convincing evidence of the scientific age in which everyone lived. Adulation also came from the attorney general of the province, who spoke of the project as a dazzling achievement. Then a cannon was fired and a crush of 10,000 shoppers pressed through the doors. The complex of sixty stores covered fifty-three acres. There were three miles of concrete strip parking dividers, 3,300 designated parking spaces, fifty sidewalk benches, a public address system playing music piped in from the local radio station and a total shopping frontage of 5,510 feet, nine normal city blocks.

The key to building shopping centres was, of course, money. And the important money was the up-front cash, the seed money, the initial investment that the builders had to put up to secure the land and help pay for the construction. It was much the same in the apartment business that began to boom in the late Fifties. With seed money from a syndicate of individual investors — $25,000 here, $50,000 there — the developers could get their projects going. For every investor's dollar, they could hope to borrow three or four dollars from a bank or trust company to finance construction. Once the project was up, they could collect their permanent financing, mortgage money equal to as much as 90 percent of the value of the finished project for high-rise apartment buildings. Since the buildings were often worth quite a lot more when completed than they had cost for the land and construction, the builders could often recoup the relatively small amount of seed money they had tied up in the project as soon as the permanent mortgage financing was in place. Sometimes they got all their seed money out; sometimes, in fact, the mortgage money came to more than the whole project cost them.

Though a developer could expect to recover all the cash put into a high-rise apartment project once the building was completed and fully rented, with its mortgage in place, it was difficult to predict how long all this would take. Equally difficult to predict was the amount of cash the developer would require to finance and carry construction costs. Whenever there was a tightening of credit in the banking system, the small independent builders felt it, as their lines of credit were cut back. Adding to the problem of tight money were high interest rates; in 1956 some residential developers were paying finance companies as much as 16 percent for money they were borrowing to complete projects.

Many apartment developers failed in this difficult period, but there were a number of Toronto builders who survived. One fledgling company, pioneered by an ex-navy officer named

Allen Ephraim Diamond, was to emerge as the largest residential builder in the city in just six years. A former engineer with a degree from Queens University, Diamond was employed for a time as project manager for Principal Investments. Then in 1953 he set up his own firm, Cadillac Contracting and Developments Ltd. Diamond had two partners in Cadillac, Joseph Berman and Jack Kamin. He hired Harbord Collegiate graduate Eddie Goodman as legal counsel. Goodman's practice in corporate land development expanded as Diamond and Cadillac prospered.

There were other new companies on the scene, such as Greenwin Construction Limited, incorporated in 1950, which began to specialize in building apartment towers. Eddie Goodman also acted on occasion on their behalf. Another success story was Belmont Construction Company, a firm set up in 1955, headed by Al Grossman, to build residential high-rises. Four years later, these emerging giants in the apartment field were joined by another Harbord graduate, Leonard Blatt, and his partner, Philip Roth, who incorporated their company, Meridian Property Management Limited, in 1959. Two years after this, the two businessmen were making plans for a $50-million high-rise village in a joint venture with developer Max Merkur and others.

High-rise apartments were built on quite different financial principles than houses in the suburbs. The developer often assembled the land by buying up a group of older houses. Then he went to City Hall to get the necessary rezoning to permit him to put up his apartment tower on the land. Under zoning regulations that allowed a developer to erect three or four square feet of apartment for every square foot of land he owned, an old house on a 25'-by-100' lot could be bought, demolished and replaced with ten or fifteen small units in a high-rise apartment. Under this arrangement the developer could afford to pay a fair price for the house and still find that his land cost per apartment unit was very low. The key element was the rezoning from City Hall, and then permission was sought to put as many apartment units as possible on a site.

Unlike houses, high-rise apartments were not built and sold by the developer. Instead, he built the building and kept it, renting out the apartments to tenants. Income from the tenants' rents was sufficient to cover all the expenses of owning the building, including the mortgage payments. Usually there was some cash left over every year.

There was another advantage for builders big enough to put up houses to sell in the suburbs and build high-rise apartments at the same time. The tax authorities allowed the developer to claim relatively high depreciation expenses for the apartment buildings he owned, and these expenses generated artificial, paper losses for the developer in his rental operation that he could use to offset the profits he was making in suburban housing. That way a builder-developer could pay little or no tax on the profits he made.

A.E. Diamond and Cadillac were using this approach as early as 1959. That year the company had 25 apartment buildings and built 154 houses. The houses were sold, but the 2,000 apartment suites were being rented out by a separate division of the company. Cadillac's ability to undertake these housing and apartment schemes, sometimes in partnership with a handful of other development firms, made possible its rapid growth in the high-rise apartment field.

A change in the city zoning bylaws in 1957 encouraged apartment developers to build higher structures. Thirty-five percent of any building site was to remain open space to ensure proper light and air circulation for the tenants. Where there was a complex of high-rise towers, buildings had to be at least fifty feet apart. This put an end to low, squat, flat-roofed tenements, separated only by sidewalks and narrow, dismal little canyons that offered little light or privacy to the occupants.

As the architecture changed, so did the use of certain construction materials. Tall, narrow buildings required more brick and steel, costly items that were soon to be replaced by a relatively new building system popularized by two Italian immigrants, Nicola DiLorenzo and Aurelio Bianchini. They promoted the use of concrete pillars reinforced with steel rods as an alternative structure for high-rise buildings, allowing developers to cut building costs considerably.

By the end of the 1950s the high-rise apartment was gaining wide acceptance among the new breed of developer, who knew how to combine money, land, construction and the rental market into successful projects. The activity attracted a little-known Montreal investment trust company called Cemp Investments Limited, which for a short time became involved in the reorganization of Cadillac Contracting and Developments, which changed its name to Cadillac Contracting (1959) Ltd. in 1959. Cemp was Sam Bronfman's family trust fund, designed by his lawyer, Lazarus Phillips, to shield the Bronfman family from succession duties and to perpetuate family control of the distillery business.

Buildings shot up, transforming the landscape. The ten-storey building was replaced with the twenty- or thirty-storey tower, which filled rapidly with new tenants, proving to everyone that the high-rise concept was a huge success. In some of the city's older neighbourhoods, meanwhile, houses were demolished as developers began to assemble land — indicating another housing boom, this time not in the suburbs, but within the city itself.

But why Toronto? asked the real estate experts. Why such a spectacular land boom here and not elsewhere? Land prices rose so high at one point that Toronto real estate commanded the highest price per square foot in North America. A spokesman for Bronfman realty interests provided several convincing answers. Toronto was strategically placed within a 500-mile radius of major urban centres such as Ottawa, Montreal, Washington, Detroit, Chicago and New York. As for political considerations, the government was exceedingly stable — the same provincial party had been in power for over a decade by the early 1960s. At the local level, planning was centralized through the new Metro Council; roads, expressways, public transit, water supplies and sewage disposal for the five boroughs came under the influence of this governing body, which achieved, if nothing else, an orderly pattern of growth.

But behind all this lay the increase in job opportunities for young professionals downtown; at the same time, various industries continued to centre on Toronto, providing work in their suburban plants. And ready to provide housing for the city's newest residents were the developers — businessmen who had successfully brought their financial expertise to focus on land and its development.

5
DIPPERS

After the war, particularly in the early Fifties, the dockyards in Halifax and Montreal were crowded with newly arrived immigrants, mostly Italians, usually with only a few possessions: a passport, some Italian money and a scrap of paper covered with the names and addresses of relatives or friends. Ignorant of the language, sometimes penniless and illiterate, these peasants and labourers had journeyed to the New World for only one reason: to make money and return home to their families and their villages. From the seaports, they took the train to Toronto, where there was a growing community of Italians who had made the choice that many of these new immigrants would — to stay in Canada.

Their arrivals were announced weekly in the *Corriere Canadese*, a Toronto Italian newspaper. From the issue of July 14, 1954:

168 Passeggieri del Saturnia Arrivano alla Union Station.

*Il 7 luglio sono arrivati a Toronto, provenienti da
Halifax dove erano sbarcati dal Saturnia 36 ore prima,
168 emigranti per la maggioranza destinati a Toronto.*

Crowded together under the towering arches of the railroad station, they stood with their hand baggage; years later, they would return to the same marble foyer looking for wives they barely recognized, some carrying pocket snapshots to help match faces to memories.

Bruno Zanini observed all this and later described the newcomers' attitudes: "These immigrants come over here thinking there's gold in the streets. That's exactly what these people thought. And no wonder, because most of the people who went to Italy from North America in the Fifties spent lots of money, so everybody wanted to come here. But when they got here, they found that the dollar was *dolore*. That means pain in Italian. 'Hey mister, you got work? Work? Me work cheap.' You know, they didn't know how to speak."

The Corriere, July 21, 1954:

*200 Emigranti Sbarcati dal Vulcania Arrivati a
Toronto.*

*Venerdi sera sono arrivati alia Union Station 200
emigranti Italiani sbarcati il giorno prima dalla
motonave Vulcania ad Halifax.*

It was nearly always the men who came first. When they found work, they saved their money to send to their families. They didn't mix. They kept to themselves, spending their evenings in billiard halls and espresso bars, often with men from the same home town. Their nights were spent in basements belonging to relatives or in rooms shared with one or two boarders. When their families finally came and there was enough money, they would buy a house, taking a room for their family and renting out the rest to help pay off the mortgage.

Dominic Moscone, illiterate and a father of two sons, was able to make the down payment for a house several years after he came to Canada. Like his relatives, he rented out most of the house, sharing the small 14'-wide residence with twelve people. The upper floor was rented to two families, with a room on each level set aside for kitchens. In the backyard, the sod was rolled and the earth turfed for a vegetable garden. Rarely did the family spend more than $5 a week on meat; mostly the diet consisted of macaroni or spaghetti, flavoured with tomato paste. As for clothing, Dominic had not bought a coat in four years. His most recent coat belonged to a neighbour who had died of a heart attack. He repaired all the shoes in the house himself; another man cut all the hair.

It was the desperate need for work that brought many of these newcomers to the country. With neither skills nor language facility, there was little opportunity for factory work; instead, these immigrants turned to construction, building homes — a sector of the industry that attracted the attention neither of unions nor of the government.

Dominic Moscone first found work as a labourer some fifteen miles from his lodgings. Often rising before 4 a.m., he walked the distance, returning home after dark. He was paid a dollar an hour. Later, he worked for a concrete slab company for 65 cents an hour, raised after a year to 75 cents. One day, he and three other workmen were grappling with a 30'-square concrete slab; it slipped and the weight shifted into Dominic's hands. One hand was so severely sprained he never fully recovered the use of it. Six weeks after the accident, he was laid off. He collected no compensation. Seven years later he finally managed, by working at a series of jobs, to save enough money to bring over his family. When they arrived, he wept openly.

The greatest fear for men like Dominic Moscone was of loss of work or an injury. This fear was so dominant in their lives that no one dared complain about the abuses that began to plague the housing industry. Unscrupulous employers, the disinterest on the part of unions and government, the lack of safety regulations all contributed to what Zanini once described as a jungle. The demand for sweat labour in this industry was met by agents acting as labour brokers, nearly all Italians who were making fortunes, both from the companies who needed work crews and from the workers themselves, willing to pay exorbitant prices for the privilege of having a job when they finally arrived in the New World. It was an echo of earlier times when the Chinese workers were imported to build the CPR; and as in the era of railway construction, the old practice of subcontracting had been revived. Back then, companies of different nationalities were pitted against each other. This time, however, it was Italians from one region pitted against Italians from another. Friulani worked for Friulani; Calabrese for Calabrese; Abruzzi for Abruzzi. As one labourer remarked: "You have to go to your own kind, and your own kind exploits you."

If there were problems — and there were — no one dared to complain. The jobs were unsafe, without scaffolding or shoring. Few housing inspectors came on the job site, saying, "Hey, you cannot do this, you cannot do that." Workers drank from the tap water used to mix their cement; the side of a block wall or a nearby bush was their toilet. They got up before dawn and got home after dark. Some tried to learn English at night school, but gave up after falling asleep in the classrooms. They were continually puzzled by Canadians and the grass they put in their backyards instead of vegetables. They knew little about the laws, the government or the monarchy. One worker described it this way: "You work from 7: 30 a.m. to 4: 30 p.m. and the contractors tell you that you will be paid only from 8 a.m. to 4 p.m. They say the rest of the time, you work for the Queen." One foreman on a big construction job forced newly hired workmen to pay him an initiation fee of $50 — and then kept the turnover high by firing every man after four or five weeks.

By the mid-1950s the conditions for the workers building homes had deteriorated to the point where men were being paid less than in previous years for the same work. Wages for bricklayers had dropped from $2.25 an hour to $2.00 an hour. Instead of $40 per 1,000 bricks, it was $30. Other trades also suffered. Carpenters and plasterers were reportedly being paid nearly a dollar less than what they had received before. And then there were some workers who weren't paid at all.

Some labourers, realizing that there was no money in manual work, tried subcontracting. In fact, a number of builders encouraged Italians to switch to contracting. There were not enough firms to serve their needs, so it was not uncommon for a builder to promise some bricklayer or carpenter money to buy equipment, if the man could find himself a truck and a work crew. As a former bricklayer put it, "These same builders — pretty foxy — created a surplus of contracting companies who cut each others' prices to get the job. This competition kept the builders' costs down. It was mostly Italians who got the contracts for these jobs because they knew how to build. But they didn't know anything about the contracting business. They would bid anything, even if they lost money, just to get the project. A lot of honest and legit subcontractors went bankrupt because they wouldn't cheat the workers by cutting pay. It was the workers who got hurt in the end, and this is why wages were going down instead of up." Some of these new companies were just agents for the builders, doing the job for next to nothing while accepting kickbacks to stay in business.

Bruno Zanini worked for some years as a bricklayer after his return from Italy in 1951, and he was one who complained bitterly about the drop in wages. He tried to join the Bricklayers, Masons and Plasterers International Union, whose members had higher pay and safer conditions. He was refused, even though he was skilled at fancy brickwork, doing corners, windows and chimneys. He recalled, "They refused hundreds and hundreds of people. I didn't know if it was prejudice or not but the men were bitter. We all wanted to join but somehow, the unions didn't want us Italians in there. It was like a private club. See, if you were Anglo-Saxon or from the British Isles, well, that was different. You got in."

At one point, Zanini was approached by one of the major housing developers with an offer to do the brickwork for 200 houses. The conversation he repeated some years later: "He says, 'Why don't you build for me? You can push them houses up like that!' I says, 'I haven't got a work crew to do all that.' 'Ah,' he tells me, 'Why don't you get yourself a whip and a bunch of dippers?' He was talking about Italians. Dippers! That means D. P. — displaced people. Which is not true because these Italians came here of their own accord. I looked at him and walked away."

The abuses continued and there was no one these people could complain to. No one talked because if someone mentioned a union, that worker was usually fired. Without work, he was a ward of the government, and some believed that if they didn't have enough money to keep themselves, the government would ship them back to the old country.

It was a situation quite unknown to those who lived outside the network of streets in Toronto known as Little Italy. Barred from unions, ignored by an Anglo-Saxon city, at times shunned by their own people, these immigrants had few places to turn. There were some sympathetic to their misery, like Joseph Grittani, a former busboy who ran the Italian Immigrant Aid

Society. There were also volunteers who acted as interpreters for immigrants in hospitals and courts. And there was Zanini's brother, Amilcare, a bricklayer who spent his spare time directing a choral group for benefit concerts to raise money for unemployed newcomers.

And yet, the exploitation continued unchecked. Worthless cheques, hours cut, injuries — legitimate complaints that were never raised out of fear of unemployment and deportation. It was this fear that silenced so many until the death of Gerarda Trillo. On October 21, 1955 this young Italian woman hung herself from the bars of a window in a deportation cell at the Claremont Police Station in Toronto.

Earlier that afternoon, she and her husband had left their Beatrice Street home, shared with relatives, to do some shopping. They were arrested hours later in a downtown department store, charged with shoplifting by police, who had been summoned by a cashier. Mrs. Trillo, who could not understand English, was separated from her husband and placed in a deportation room. Officials at the time thought it wise to leave Mrs. Trillo alone, ignoring her cries for help. Shortly thereafter, the mother of three climbed onto the small cot and hung herself.

Sometime later, Mr. Trillo was informed of his wife's death. A photographer took his picture, and a story about the incident was published in the *Toronto Star*. Mr. Trillo and his wife had been in Toronto for eight months. He had been working as a labourer, earning $20 a week.

When the news reached the local Italian community, money was collected, dresses for the three girls were sent by one garment store and a contractor hired Mr. Trillo for a better-paying job. There was some indignant talk among the residents, who blamed the officials for their lack of understanding. Surely the woman should have been released instead of being held for the alleged theft of an item valued at $10.

More questions arose. How could this woman and three children get by when her husband only earned $20 a week? What was the matter with the unions in this country? Why wouldn't they take in these immigrant workers? Why was there no law to protect these people and set a fair rate of pay? These were the questions asked by the Italian consul general and his wife a few days later at a benefit concert at the Brandon Hall — a centre of social activities for the Italian community — as they stood talking with Bruno Zanini and his brother.

The situation was not easily explained. And it was difficult to speak of prejudice. Yet it was true: Italians had been refused membership repeatedly during this period by construction trade unions dominated by Irish and Anglo-Saxon workers. The unions were tough, and they were run by tough bosses. These unions, represented collectively by the Toronto Building Trades Council, had achieved an orderly relationship with the construction firms who worked primarily on large commercial projects, such as office buildings and industrial complexes. By agreement, the builder hired his supply of workers from the unions. "But out in the suburbs," explained one labour reporter, "the houses were all of a sudden getting put up by people who were not commercial builders. New people had gone into the industry. And so the Italian was consigned out to the suburbs and everybody said, 'Well, the jobs are safe downtown — what [the immigrant] does, that's not our problem. He's not a tradesman.' So in the end, they organized themselves."

It was, in fact, Bruno Zanini who took up the task of organizing the Italian construction workers. Zanini was different from the other workers, partly because he had been in Canada longer. And he was a very odd mixture, with his streetwise background, his numerous criminal convictions, his on again, off again plans to become an opera singer and his knowledge of the construction business from his experience as an ordinary bricklayer. It was the death of Gerarda Trillo and the challenge thrown out by the consul general that triggered Zanini's initiative. Once he had taken the first step, however, he never looked back.

Zanini proved to be an organizer of rare skill. He began his work by frequenting Italian eating places, billiard halls and cafes. At times he drove out to the suburban construction sites, where he chatted with workers, taking a trowel in his hand as he spoke, explaining how they were going to have their own union since no one else was taking them in.

He expanded on this theme once, talking about how it had been in those years. "Those unions refused hundreds and hundreds of immigrants. Even I couldn't get in and here I was practically born in this country! There was no organization. Wages were being cut. How am I going to describe it? What is a jungle? If you walk two feet, the lion eats you. The whole thing was wrong! Safety — forget it! Don't even talk about it. The scaffolding, the shoring, if those things caved in on you — you've had it! I don't know how the hell to put it fancy. Nobody cared. The pay was what you could get. And who could they complain to? They were afraid: afraid of losing their jobs, afraid of being deported — and you'd better believe that!"

"It was the life of an animal," said one labourer, pinching his arm to indicate how his employers tested the men for muscle. Their day began before dawn and ended two or three hours after the sun had dropped. Few, if any, knew the name of their boss or the company they were working for, so even if government agencies received complaints, the employers were difficult to trace. "They tell us they work for Joe in Scarborough," said an official of the Unemployment Insurance Commission. "All they know about Joe is that he picks them up in a truck on Dufferin Street every day."

When Zanini first spoke of the union, there was some confusion, although nearly everyone wanted to join. Unions were operated differently in Canada than in the old country, where there were only large unions organized by industry. To join a union in Toronto was to become a member of the Toronto local of a union covering one trade: bricklayers supported bricklayers in different cities rather than aligning with other tradesmen on the same project. In addition, these unions were not Canadian but so-called "international" unions with ties to the U.S. Most head offices for these building trade unions were in the American capital, Washington, D.C. Regional headquarters for Toronto branches were in New York and Chicago.

Zanini's sole intention in the fall of 1955 was to organize a makeshift union for the immigrant workers. During those weeks, the men arrived at all hours of the night, after the jobs closed down. Inside the Brandon Hall, this small, defiant group of plasterers, bricklayers, carpenters — nearly all Italian immigrants — boldly declared themselves a union, and acclaimed Zanini as their leader.

This brief and daring attempt to organize an independent union for housing workers came to an end only a few months later, however. Zanini was persuaded to give up the idea of a Canadian union after an old friend from the Symington days set up a meeting with an international labour boss from Chicago who shared Zanini's interest in organizing immigrant bricklayers. Once the introductions were over, the white-haired Bricklayers' official, John McLeod, asked, "Can you get the signatures of ten men?" "A hundred," was Zanini's reply.

Zanini got the signatures and then the charter. McLeod's move was unusual. Overnight, he had created a second union local dividing a trade — bricklaying — in the same city. Zanini's territory was housing, where he was granted free rein to organize all the bricklayers. The Toronto Bricklayers' local, which had previously refused to include these men in their membership, began to protest bitterly, accusing this new local of raiding their potential membership. But where they had failed, the international bosses were to succeed by recognizing Zanini's talents as an organizer. Rather than infringing on the existing local's autonomy by ordering it to organize Zanini's men, the Chicago bosses simply set up another local. As a result the labour movement was divided between residential and commercial building. Divided too were the wage scales for workers in this trade, with immigrant workers in residential projects receiving less than commercial bricklayers. Apprenticeship programs were created to improve worker skills, with the intention of raising workers' wages in the future.

Backed now by this powerful international union, Zanini signed up more than 1,500 workers within the year. It was, Zanini believed, the greatest thing that ever happened to them. In the meantime, he urged subcontractors to form a housing association to facilitate bargaining for the bricklayers. Some of the contractors viewed the union with a mixture of enthusiasm and fear. While there was the stabilizing influence of uniform wages, some companies were willing to defy the demands. Higher wages and shorter working hours reduced the meagre profits made by these building firms. At the same time, housing developers refused to absorb the increased costs, preferring to deal with non-union companies using cheap labour. So the squeeze was on the subcontractor. To keep in business, many were forced to thwart the union and cheat their work crews. Many of those who found this unacceptable went bankrupt.

But the local ultimately failed because of the continued protests from the Toronto commercial Bricklayers' local and its boss, American-born Bill Jenoves, who saw no merit in dividing a trade between two sectors of the industry. When he threatened to pull his local out from the international set-up, the arguing ceased. Washington ordered the two locals merged in 1957, a proposal that was ratified by Zanini's members — the same immigrant workers who had once been rejected by this very local. Zanini got a job as a business agent, now under the watchful eye of Jenoves.

The gains made by Zanini were soon to deteriorate as Jenoves spent more and more of his time with the commercial builders. As was the custom, the union provided the labour supply to general contractors. For the commercial jobs, Jenoves sent his best men. For the residential, the rules for hiring union labour were less rigid. The union supplied half a company's work crew, while additional men were employed from the street. After fifteen days, the extra men were supposed to join the union. A number of subcontractors still refused to build with union labour. This left many immigrant bricklayers without work, sitting out their days at the union office, trying to cope with the growing frustration that they were paying dues to a union that was providing neither work nor protection.

It was at this time, in 1956, that a blunt-spoken Irish Catholic, James Francis Drea, took over the labour beat for the *Toronto Telegram*. Before that, he had worked for the *Buffalo Courier-Express* while a student at Canisius College, from which he graduated with high marks in English, history, philosophy and theology. There was a hint of the crusader in him, in the way he went after the stories, not working his beat but living it. There were a lot of stories and they nearly always hit the paper. He had his sources, most of them dead on. He once got an exclusive interview inside a washroom with labour boss Jimmy Hoffa, who refused to speak unless the shower was turned on. Another time, he hitched a ride in a paddy wagon when he couldn't find a cab.

As the years passed, he would become an authority on the national and international labour scene. But even then, at the age of 23, he had a brash instinct, predicting changes in the labour movement. It was the beginning of a new era, said Drea, where leaders stressed immediate goals in terms of wages, conditions and benefits. Unions were soon to operate like big business, using whatever power they had at their disposal to make deals.

Replacing the idealists in the labour movement were men such as Charles Irvine, who understood the utility of unions, with their vast resources of manpower, and who knew how controlling this labour supply directly affected industry at all levels. Irvine was a remarkable man. Born in the factory town of Glasgow, Scotland, he came to Toronto in 1907, quit school after Grade Four, earned 35 cents an hour on a West Indies banana boat, then enjoyed a brief career as a plastering contractor before he turned to unions. A tall, reedy figure whose poor eyesight required the constant use of glasses, Irvine was a union maverick who policed his meetings with a shillelagh, calling illegal strikes to raise wages and membership in the two locals under his charge in the Operative Plasterers' and Cement Masons' International Association: one group of plasterers and one of cement finishers.

Unlike his colleagues, Irvine was alarmed at the growing number of non-union workers in residential construction. As long as there was an alternative, cheaper labour supply available to builders, his own union would be threatened, and at the very time when the number of jobs was rising steadily, especially in residential work. It was Irvine's ability to grasp the significance of this situation that led to his visit to the office of Bricklayers' boss Bill Jenoves, one hot summer day in 1957.

Irvine issued a warning to the head of the bricklayers, who was also at the time chairman of the Building Trades Council, the umbrella organization of union locals in all sectors of construction. The plastering boss made clear his intention of setting up a separate residential local under the Plasterers' union. He would not brook any interference from Jenoves — this, at least, was the impression Zanini had; he overheard the conversation from his desk in the adjoining room. The door had apparently been left ajar, providing Zanini with his first glimpse of Irvine. "He had a dark suit on, very serious man," Zanini recalled. "He's telling Jenoves about this residential union he wants. But Jenoves argued, saying he didn't figure it could be done. The only trade that had been in housing with its own charter was mine and it was gone."

The incident apparently made an impression on Zanini. Some days later, at Irvine's suggestion, he agreed to assist in organizing this new local, handing over some workers' names and addresses he'd collected at the Brandon Hall. Irvine paid him $150 for his services. In addition, he made Zanini an honorary member.

No one would ever shake Zanini's faith in Irvine. Clearly, here was a foreigner attempting to organize immigrant Italians at all costs — a gesture Zanini would use to enshrine his alliance with Irvine. Irvine was among the few union bosses determined to expand his membership into housing. Though previous attempts had been less than successful, the initial success of a separate residential local under the leadership of Zanini intrigued Irvine. The fiery union leader had won an enormous following and it was Irvine who saw a chance to capitalize on it. "There were 1,000 plasterers to be organized and I went to the only man who could help organize them — Bruno Zanini," said Irvine later. "Every union in Toronto told me it couldn't be done, but we did it in three days."

The labour duet of Irvine and Zanini had its beginnings, then, in 1957. Schooled and moulded by Irvine's union tactics, Zanini flourished. This brand of unionism involved a number of tough organizing measures frowned upon by the majority of union officials. Irvine's bag of tricks included illegal walkouts, high wage demands and an uncompromising attitude to management. These techniques he passed on to Zanini, who remained indebted to Irvine's counselling: Irvine taught him how to be aggressive in the labour field, how to be bold, how to speak to people and bring them into an organization.

He once explained how well their partnership had worked. "At the meetings, Charlie would get up and put it to these men in English, and then I would get up and talk Italian. That's how it was done. I would use my own phraseology, translate in my own volatile way. Very scaffold language. I wouldn't talk dignified or very romantic to them. Simplicity! But I had my own way, too, of dramatizing, bringing out my voice so that when I come to something delicate like their families, I would use a murmuring voice. No other business agent ever done these things before. Then when I come to something tremendous, I would use a top 'C' of the voice that would just capture the crowd. I put it in their mouths. I fed it to them. Practically hypnotized them."

Within three days, the new residential local had a membership of 400 plasterers. Soon Irvine called a strike. Jobs were shut down on a number of housing and apartment projects; cars full of workers raced across the city; machines were smashed, walls perforated by bricks and bats, buckets of lime slashed. After five days, the company owners agreed to meet with Irvine. The forty-hour work week was established, welfare benefits were introduced and wages were upgraded from $1.75 to $2.68 an hour. So another residential union local was established by a spotty war led by Zanini, who for the purpose of history called it a minor immigrant uprising. The men, he said, were bitter.

Irvine's lack of concern about tactics raised some questions among other labour leaders who were less willing to condone this type of behaviour. Still, Irvine had his union and his contract, the only union in the city to succeed with these immigrants.

If there was any envy among other labour leaders, it was short-lived. The local fell into a snare; contractors refused to pay the increased wages. A number of companies had to change their corporate names to escape the new agreement, which threatened to bankrupt nearly everyone. As long as developers continued to force prices lower by accepting the cheapest bid, no one could afford to use Irvine's men. As a result, dozens of new plastering firms sprang up, hiring non-union men to work on the vast high-rise apartment projects that were beginning to appear in some parts of the city. The jobs went to these firms, leaving the members of Irvine's plastering local unemployed.

By 1958, the situation had deteriorated badly. Subcontracting companies voided their contracts with the plastering local and the bricklayers by either going bankrupt or changing company names. Unemployment for housing union members rose sharply, and unhappily, immigrant workers were forced back to work in the non-union jungle. A few dollars a week was better than no money at all.

Zanini succumbed to a mild depression, suggesting to close friends that in all probability he would return to his most beloved vocation — opera. But it was only a brief spell for some months later, he decided to form a Canadian union for the housing bricklayers, the Canadian Bricklayers' Association. His decision to break away from the international set-up turned out to be an unpardonable sin, arousing suspicion and mistrust among international labour officials. The exception was Charles Irvine, who had his own ideas of how the residential could be organized.

6
THE MOB AND ITS MONEY

The syndicate's program of expansion into legitimate businesses was well underway by the 1950s. The system that fed this new corporate giant, serviced by a battery of lawyers, stock promoters and accountants, was Lansky's innovative scheme to launder mob money through lending institutions. At the same time, mobsters found new ways to exploit union money, posing as investors or businessmen draining workers' pension funds for a number of dubious ventures.

As crime bosses prospered from their various rackets, the pressure to find new outlets for cash intensified. For Lansky, the challenge was even greater as gambling brought in by far the greatest revenue of all syndicate-related activities. The problem for Lansky was how to invest the millions of dollars in unreported income from his casino operations without arousing the curiosity of the Internal Revenue Service.

The answer was simply to wash the money clean. This procedure to disguise the source of money — what Lansky called the laundry business — involved three phases: the skim, the run and the wash. The skim was the cash set aside before the nightly gambling profits were tabulated and recorded for income tax purposes; this money was then bagged for the run, when it was carried by courier for deposit in some foreign bank. The last stage, the wash, was the return of the money through a lending institution to finance syndicate-controlled business ventures. This method of banking mob money established a flow of cash independent of legitimate money markets and of a fickle economy.

The origins of this scheme were described some years later by a close Lansky associate, Doc Stacher: "It sounds complicated but it wasn't. Meyer had decided long ago that we had to reinvest the money that had been coming in ever since we made fortunes in bootlegging. Arnold Rothstein [a mentor of the old Lower East Side gang] originally taught us all the lesson: take the money from these various activities and use it in an intelligent way. Rothstein spent a lot of his on high living, but that wasn't the way Meyer chose. I don't know who it was who first decided to call the system 'laundering' but that's what it was: to wash clean — by that I mean make legal — these vast cash flows, particularly from gambling."

The skim was removed from casino profits each night after the gambling tables closed. Lansky and a few trusted associates would count the cash, then set aside a percentage of the take before the bookkeepers made their reports. The amount of money skimmed in a nightly take from one casino often amounted to well over $100,000. The skimming procedure was described by one casino accountant who testified before the Kefauver committee. The accountant's statements referred to a casino operation at the Club Boheme in Florida where Lansky and George Sadlo were partners: "At the end of each night . . . after they close each table, they take the money and put it in the cashier's cage and count it."

"Who counts it?" asked a committee investigator.

"Mr. Lansky," replied the witness.

"Personally?"

"Yes or Mr. Sadlo or whoever is with him."

The skim represented millions of untaxed dollars, a private income that increased every time a new casino opened where Lansky was a partner. Already there was a string of gambling joints in the U.S. but none that met the vision Lansky entertained for Cuba.

Though he'd gone a long way with his post-Prohibition scheme with Batista, built his casinos and watched them flourish, everything had fallen apart when war came. An additional loss was Batista himself, who got into trouble after he legalized the Communist party as a move to help himself in an election campaign. Although these leftist overtures gave him the presidency in 1940, they earned Batista the hostility of the American government. Meyer Lansky later told this story: "I was told at one stage that President Roosevelt himself asked his intelligence men to get me to speak to Batista. It was made quite clear to me: the American government wouldn't let Batista go on running the island if there was any danger it might go Communist. I explained this to my good friend Batista who was very reluctant to get out of politics."

Batista was finally persuaded by the Americans to find a front man to replace himself, and to leave active politics. He chose a well-known doctor, Ramon Grau San Martin, and those unaware of the behind-the-scenes manoeuvring considered his election a defeat for Batista. After this, the Cuban leader left for Florida where he remained in political seclusion with the permission of American authorities. In 1948, Carlos Prio Socarras replaced San Martin. Prio Socarras was also a Batista man, although he resisted Lansky's renewed efforts to return Batista to Cuban politics in the early 1950s. Lansky won over Prio Socarras by opening a bank account for him in Switzerland. The Cuban official then graciously agreed to retire to a newly built $2-million home on the island, opening the way for the return of Batista.

Lansky wanted a secure political ally in Cuba before he invested additional millions of dollars to build super-hotels in the unsurpassable gambling spa planned for Havana. Batista took control of the capital by force on March 10, 1952. Fearing that he might not win an election, he chose to reinstate his regime militarily. Lansky then reaped the rewards of his longstanding friendship with the Cuban strongman, who proceeded to force through laws that would guarantee Lansky full autonomy to run his own show in this complex of super-hotels, complete with chandeliered gambling halls. Never was any tax levied on the casino operations, nor did Lansky pay import duty on expensive building material. Even his own hotel personnel from the U.S. were exempted from paying Cuban taxes. In return for this cooperation, of course, Batista received a generous cut from the gambling profits.

The Havana seafront became a monument to gambling with its glittering hotels. There was the Riviera, built at a cost of $14 million. Then there were the Sevilla Biltmore, the Havana Hilton and the Hotel Nacional. Invited to share in some of these ventures were other syndicate bosses, such as Moe Dalitz from Cleveland. Once the rooms were furnished and the equipment set up, the croupiers arrived. Training programs were set up to groom Cubans as casino operators. Lansky called it a "kind of social experiment," intended to offset some of the unemployment he saw on the island.

More casinos meant more money. There were plans to use the cash to open casino-hotels in London. A Christmas trip to inspect the territory was made in the early 1950s and recalled by Salvatore Luciano some years later: "That was the time gamblin' still wasn't legal in London, but it didn't hurt none to get a feel for the place."

From every casino that opened came the nightly skim, wads of bills, counted, packaged and locked in suitcases or stuffed into satchels for the courier pickup. None of this money was reported to the tax authorities. As he did in all his operations, Lansky kept neat, well-documented accounts of the profits — minus the skim. His U.S. books were inspected by the Internal Revenue Service; taxes were always paid. In fact, there appeared to be nothing illegal about his activities. Lansky told tax agents his main source of income was as kitchen manager of the Riviera hotel, and he paid income taxes accordingly. As Doc Stacher once recalled, "We used to kid Meyer about his abilities as a chef, and he would smile a little when we asked him, 'What's on the menu today, cookie?'"

The only time Lansky ever went to prison was during this period; he was arrested in 1952 as a common gambler. He and Doc Stacher had been gambling illegally in upstate New York at the Arrowhead Inn. Stacher was fined $10,000 and given a suspended one-year sentence. Lansky received a ninety-day jail term.

"I'll tell you a story about those ninety days." Lansky said some years later. "I asked the guards to bring me a dictionary and a Bible. I thought I might as well use the time to improve my mind and study the holy book. A few days later, I was astonished to see in the newspapers that I'd turned religious and was going to become a Christian." On July 21, 1953, Lansky was released from prison. He moved to Florida, closing up his New York apartment forever.

Lansky's scheme of laundering money was kept secret for some years. The first tip police got came in March 1957, when they found Frank Costello bleeding from a gunshot wound in the lobby of the Majestic hotel on Central Park West in New York. Officials discovered a note in Costello's pocket that disclosed the amount of money received in a nightly take at some unnamed casino and the remaining profits after someone had skimmed about $200,000 off the top, a sum unreported to income tax authorities. Costello, who survived the attempt on his life, refused to comment on the note, which read, "Gross casino win as of 4-26-57: $657,284. Casino win less markers (IOUs): $434,695. Slot wins: $62,844. Marks: $153,745." These figures matched the turnover of the casino in the Tropicana hotel in Las Vegas, one of four hotels Costello shared an interest in with Lansky. Even after this discovery, the system continued to operate without much difficulty for at least another decade, owing largely to the secrecy provided by Swiss bankers and their numbered accounts.

The skimmed cash still had to be flown out of the country to complete the laundering process. This task was assigned to couriers, hand-picked men whom Lansky trusted with his fortune. Among the select few was John Pullman, by this time a close friend who had travelled with Lansky on his honeymoon with his second bride, a manicurist he married after his divorce in 1948. Pullman made frequent runs, hopping around the country by plane, collecting money earmarked for the wash in numbered Swiss bank accounts. The discretion of Swiss bankers assured the mob anonymity, protecting this secret flow of cash for years. In time, the bulk of syndicate cash went to the International Credit Bank of Switzerland in Geneva. Between these international flights, Pullman claimed to be a merchant carrying on business in Toronto under the name of Pullman's Shoe Mart, according to a declaration filed in an Ontario registry office in 1950. A Toronto resident until 1960, Pullman banked at the Canadian Imperial Bank of Commerce at Bay and Queen.

Pullman's role as courier for mob money went undetected for nearly a decade. However, evidence did surface to document his involvement when U.S. airport authorities found a scrap of paper carelessly dropped from the pocket of another Lansky courier as he was loading suitcases of money into his car. The note read: "This is to acknowledge this 28th day of December, 1964, the receipt of

$350,000 in American bank notes for deposit to the account of Marel 2812 with the International Credit Bank, Geneva; the said sum was turned over to me in the presence of the names signed below." One of the signatures was John Pullman's.

The flight of cash was a risky business. Eliminating the need for couriers, a number of new banks opened in the U.S. and later in the Bahamas, where two more casinos were to open. A Florida bank opened in 1955, and the Union National Bank of Newark (New Jersey) also became a depository for gambling funds. Some years later, Pullman himself became a banker, joining the board of the Nassau-based Bank of World Commerce along with other Lansky associates, and soon becoming the bank's president. Just as the money was washed through Swiss banks, so too were the funds flowing in and out of the Bank of World Commerce.

Lending institutions were essential to the wash. From these reputable sources, loans were made to corporations and businesses in the U.S. The directors and owners of these borrowing companies might be legitimate businessmen, but Lansky and his associates worked from behind the scenes and controlled the company stock. This was explained by Doc Stacher, who elaborated: "We would borrow the money from Swiss banks, which really meant we were borrowing our own money. Interest was paid in the proper way and this interest went straight back to Switzerland. So we were paying interest to ourselves for our own money. There was another advantage to this system, too. This interest was tax-deductible in the United States. We were paying taxes and avoiding problems, and of course the interest was helping to cut down our tax burdens. Real estate was of course an excellent place to put newly laundered cash. Affiliates, subsidiary corporations, numbered bank accounts and lawyers acting as trustees were devices that could be used to disguise a property's true ownership. In addition, real estate investments offered continuing opportunities to bury cash gained from gambling operations. "You can make improvements on your property and pay cash for it, and get the money back when you sell the property for a higher price. That way you can turn black money from Las Vegas into clean capital gain," said one analyst of mob financing. With dummy real estate corporations, fronts or shells of companies to buy and sell land with money whose source could never be traced, the system worked flawlessly.

In essence, the syndicate created its own respectable banking apparatus, a system of financing that remained immune to high interest rates, tight money, recessions and stock market slumps. The syndicate had a guaranteed flow of cash, generated by gambling and other enterprises, which it then invested to generate further profits and control in legitimate businesses. Access to cash was a considerable advantage in an industry where money was a means of competing. As one U.S. academic expert on organized crime explained: "A cash-rich position at times when legitimate interest rates are high, or when funds are unavailable at market rates for all who would like to borrow and could normally obtain credit, may lead to relatively large investment by organized crime groups. Capital would be provided where it would earn the highest return, specifically in those areas where interest rates are differentially high, such as they were in real estate and mortgage lending in the mid-1960s."

One active investor in mortgages and real estate was John Pullman, who invested privately in a number of deals involving Toronto real estate. Pullman money later found its way into a number of development and construction companies. Pullman apparently also lent to nursing homes and companies in the food business, and he himself became active in shopping centres as owner of the Yonge Street Arcade in downtown Toronto. According to one of his lawyers, Sam Gotfrid (once a legal partner of Pullman's nephew by marriage), the investments made by Pullman were small. He was usually involved with two or three partners in the deals he got into. The money Pullman used for investment purposes was, again according to his lawyer, his own.

Borrowing Pullman money on one documented occasion was the giant shopping centre development company Principal Investments. Principal had a long history. It had been incorporated by three publicity-shy brothers in 1936. One of the brothers was Archie Bennett, the former editor of the *Jewish Times* and colleague of Sam Bronfman in the Canadian Jewish Congress.

In 1942, Principal was still a very small company. In a filing with the government, it reported holdings of just five real estate properties, valued at a total of $12,870.33. But Principal's next statement of holdings, filed in 1949, showed real estate holdings that the company valued at $3,370,952.59 in land and $7,585,700.16 in buildings. There were choice sites along Bloor and Yonge Streets in Toronto, and real estate in Brantford, Chatham, Dundas, Gait, Niagara Falls, Ottawa, Orillia, Owen Sound, Port Arthur, Peterborough, Sarnia, Sault Ste. Marie, Windsor, Woodstock, St. Catharines and Waterloo. It was clear that Principal had access to a lot more money than its directors, Archie Bennett and his brothers, were earning.

One source of cash for Principal was John Pullman. Pullman helped Principal finance the completion of one of their early shopping centres, Dufferin Plaza in Toronto, when they didn't have enough money to finish it. Another Bennett company, Food Chain Properties Limited, was incorporated in 1956. John Pullman lent money to Food Chain, and a tax department listing showed Pullman was earning a steady income from those loans in 1971 and 1972. In the 1960s one of Food Chain's lawyers was Sam Ciglen, who some years later was disbarred and convicted of defrauding a public company of $1.8 million.

During the 1950s Principal Investments was considered the largest shopping centre developer in the country, assembling land for plazas in fourteen Toronto locations and other centres in

Burlington, Hamilton, Kitchener, Oshawa, Ottawa, St. Catharines, Kingston, Brantford, Peterborough, Windsor, Sarnia, Fort William, Regina and Saint John. It also had properties in Toronto at Yonge and Bloor, Yonge and St. Clair, Yonge and Eglinton, and Yonge and Sheppard.

It had grown fast. By 1958, the value of the company's ownership in these centres was expected to be more than $100 million. Principal was able to continue its plans to build its fourteen Toronto centres even when a monetary recession came in 1956.

However, in 1958 the company ran into trouble. It was overextended, and many of Principal's most valuable projects and land assemblies were acquired by Cemp Investments, the Bronfman family trust, for $18 million. Cemp trustee Leo Kolber put these properties into a real estate subsidiary of Cemp, the Fairview Corporation. Principal Investments went into receivership in 1963 and was eventually liquidated.

Pullman was charged with stock fraud several years later, but was acquitted. Pullman has repeatedly denied allegations that he invests money for the mob. What cannot be disputed is his role as a courier in washing syndicate funds. And it was precisely this wash that would supply money to be reinvested into legitimate businesses acting as fronts for the syndicate.

The prime source of all this cash was gambling skims, but there were other activities where the syndicate made money. The labour field was a highly attractive prospect: once a union fell under mob control, it was effective as a tool for extortion; employers who refused to pay for labour peace were confronted with a continuous round of strikes. Other payments were made for protection to minimize the risk of arson and sabotage.

It wasn't always easy for the mob to get into unions. The initial move was often to place a syndicate member within a union local by either paying off a top business agent or shooting him; the new union official then proceeded to extort money through strikes and labour interference. A bonus to supplement the income was the collection of monthly payments or dues check offs from companies under contract to the union. With the contract as leverage, sweeter deals could be made. Business agents often agreed to keep wages low in return for money under a kickback scheme. Some of those firms who refused to negotiate a sweetheart contract became victims of arson and sabotage. If the mob failed to buy off a union leadership, a rival union was often formed, offering lower wages to employers to induce them to cooperate. Competitors paying workers higher rates were eventually unable to compete and were forced out of business.

Labour rackets were more easily established in the industries where continuous delays threatened to ruin a business — in construction, for instance, where time was money. The infiltration and control of the building trade unions by syndicate members in a number of U.S. cities began in the 1930s. In Chicago after Al Capone's arrival, approximately sixty trades and professions came under his rule. Apparently one reason why building costs were relatively high in Chicago was the early control by the mob of the trade unions, which wrecked legitimate contractors through work stoppages and violence. New York also had a substantial contingent of labour racketeers working certain businesses. Detroit was not much different.

One of the classic examples of the delicate alliance between unions and the syndicate was found in the business activities of the International Brotherhood of Teamsters. Labour boss Jimmy Hoffa, who remained the backbone of the union for years, worked hand-in-hand with a number of dubious characters.

Hoffa's own involvement with unions began in 1932. Late one night he refused to load strawberry boxes for a warehouse worker at 32 cents an hour. He handed the night manager a list of grievances and in a short time won a one-page agreement including a 13-cents-an-hour raise for his fellow workers, nicknamed the

Strawberry Boys. It was the start of a one-company union, earning Hoffa respect and a reputation in Detroit as a skilled negotiator. From there, he was offered a job to organize a Detroit local for the Teamsters trucking union. Their first citywide strike in 1937 was staged successfully by Hoffa. Key to Hoffa's success was a deal he struck with an ex-convict hired frequently by Detroit companies to bust unions. This local mobster, Santo Perrone, agreed to remain neutral in the union–management battle.

Hoffa's trucking union became so powerful in time that it acted as an enforcer for other unions on strike, for a fee. Once the Teamsters were called in, management quickly came to heed union demands. Hoffa's colleague and business agent, Frank Fitzsimmons, used a Teamster local to exact money from companies. In 1953, Fitzsimmons was indicted on charges of bribery and extortion, as were several other officials. The charges against Fitzsimmons were dropped, but not until a court had heard that Fitzsimmons had received $500 as a personal gift from a trucking company owner wanting a favourable union contract.

Fitzsimmons's skills as a negotiator were clearly shown in a deal he made with a Detroit firm that delivered films. The owner, Howard C. Craven, was promised a monopoly over the business in return for 90 percent of his current net profits. Craven paid several thousand dollars to Fitzsimmons through a third party, but there was no appreciable increase in his business. When Craven complained, Fitzsimmons called a strike. Insurers cancelled a $50,000 policy on Craven's trucks. The strike destroyed Craven financially, and he was forced to sell the company. The new owner turned out to be none other than Frank Fitzsimmons, who put the new company in Hoffa's wife's maiden name, with Fitzsimmons's own brother-in-law, nephew and son as partners as well.

As the years passed, more sophisticated methods were used to derive income from the labour rackets. The growth and popularity of union pension funds created a natural well of financing for syndicate-related ventures. Borrowing money from these funds, held in trust by union officials, was an uncomplicated and largely unregulated procedure. There were few legal fetters on union trustees that limited where they placed their members' money for investments — few, at least, compared with the restrictions imposed on other finance-lending institutions. Little public disclosure was required, except for a barrage of monthly or annual statements to union workers, explaining how and where the money was being used. Frequently businessmen lacking credit with traditional lending firms sought loans from union trustees.

This led to a new era of business unionism and for Hoffa, a mesh of friendships and obligations he would never be free of. It was Santo Perrone, the union-buster, who became Hoffa's contact with the syndicate, introducing the union leader to a number of his associates. It was through Perrone that Hoffa met Paul Dorfman, business agent for the Chicago Wastehandlers Union. After some persuasion, Hoffa agreed to transfer the Teamsters' welfare funds to a newly formed branch of a company called Union Casualty Agency, owned by Dorfman's wife, Rose, and his stepson, Allen. Money from a second union fund was directed to the same firm, the two accounts making up 90 percent of the branch company's business. Through its control of these funds, Dorfman's Union Casualty Agency expanded into twelve insurance companies and ten non-insurance enterprises, including banks, a resort hotel in the Virgin Islands, oil wells, slum real estate and the buying and selling of tax liens. A 1957 U.S. Senate committee investigating labour rackets named Dorfman as a "major figure in the Chicago underworld."

Before Paul Dorfman was expelled from the Wastehandlers Union for misusing funds, he enjoyed a close relationship with the union's major employer, Theodore Shulman, president of Sanatex Corporation. Dorfman compromised some of his own union members by agreeing to a sweetheart deal that allowed Shulman to continue paying certain workers at a lower rate than stated in the new union contract. In return, Shulman put two people on his payroll to sell insurance for the Union Casualty Agency. Named as the union's only pension fund trustees were Dorfman and Shulman. The sum of $150,000 from the health and welfare funds was diverted by Dorfman into a bank owned by a friend, George Sax, where the money was held without accruing interest. Sax owned a Miami hotel where Hoffa, Shulman and Dorfman often stayed when they went to Florida. Dorfman's career with the union ended when it was learned he was paying personal bills with membership money.

In 1958, Hoffa and the Teamsters purchased control of the Miami National Bank, whose manager was a man named Lou Poller. Poller's significance as a banker was emphasized later by a U.S. syndicate figure turned government informer: "Poller worked for the Miami National Bank, and his specialty was taking money that had been gotten illegally and washing it — cleaning it up and legitimizing it. Whatever money you'd put with Poller, he'd take 10 percent. It might take him a year or two, but if you gave him $10 million or $1 million, that money would be invested for you in something legitimate. You'd be able to pay taxes on it. No one knew how he did it — he had his own ways — but he was a master at it. Hoffa offered to write me a letter of introduction.

"Poller, I found out later, was one of Meyer Lansky's men, and he washed the mob's money through the bank. It came out in the form of real estate, apartment buildings and business ownership, like motels or hotels or mobile-home companies. The government could trace all day and never find anything illegal."

As the Teamsters' membership grew, expanding across the country, so too did its power and its pension fund. There is considerable documented evidence, the result of the U.S. Senate's

1955 McClellan committee inquiring into labour rackets, that makes clear how the syndicate operated labour power. On occasion, it was used to extort money, arrange kickback schemes and destroy competitors who refused to cooperate, while managing the investment of pension fund money through a union racketeer or a business agent fearful for his own life. The strong-arm tactics used by extortionists in the heyday of Al Capone and the Lower East Side gang were rapidly becoming a thing of the past, as emphasis shifted from terror to money to accommodate the growing interest in business on the part of both unions and the mob.

It was precisely this change in attitude that nearly split "the Organization" during one of its rare conferences, at the Waldorf hotel in New York in 1956, called to discuss the fate of Frank Costello, heir to Luciano (who had been deported ten years earlier). Costello's disorderly conduct during the Kefauver hearings had put him behind bars, and syndicate chiefs from across the U.S. argued heatedly about Lansky's proposal to pension him off. The Italian faction wanted Costello silenced permanently. Lansky finally won the support of the majority and Costello was saved, though an attempt was later made on his life. However, this turn toward refined corporate conduct prompted one Italian syndicate boss who favoured pulling the Mafia out of the syndicate to comment bitterly, "The traditions of the Honoured Society have been forgotten. The old days were bad, but at least we could hold up our heads in pride. We had respect then; now we're a bunch of fucking businessmen."

The move by mobs and unions into the corporate affairs of North America had its own significant consequences. Some believed it would in time corrupt politics, the courts and the free enterprise system — not with guns but with money.

PART III
The Brandon Group Campaign

7
BOOMTOWN TORONTO

There was so much building excavation going on in 1960 that it was hard to believe what economists were saying about the country. Costs had spiralled and people talked about inflation. Warnings were issued daily, urging measures of restraint in public spending. The governor of the Bank of Canada, James Coyne, raced about the country pleading with Canadians to "tighten their belts," to use credit more wisely and stop living beyond their means. He advised temporary measures to clamp down on the unrestricted flow of foreign capital buying into the country's natural and industrial resources. He also called for a reduction or easing off in construction starts.

All this cry and fuss about tight money came at a time when builders were gearing up for an unprecedented boom in urban development. The apartment developers who had made their fortunes in the 1950s were scanning opportunities for greater growth. Instead of merely one or two neighbouring apartments, high-rise villages of six or seven towers were on the planning boards. Miniature towns within huge residential parks were proposed, with churches, schools and shopping malls conveniently placed near the apartment towers.

One such developer's plan that became a reality was U.S. developer William Zeckendorf's Flemingdon Park. Some 350 acres of land had been assembled for it in northeast Toronto. By 1961, the first apartment tower, with 325 suites, was under construction. It was said to be the largest residential building in Canada. In time, the project would accommodate between 15,000 and 20,000 people.

In 1961 another private apartment developing firm, A.E. Diamond's company, did more than $10 million in building, fully expecting to exceed this amount by a further $2 million within twelve months. Al Green of Greenwin Construction was soon to be at work on another high-rise village, called the Village Green.

That same year a consortium of apartment developers announced their intention to build yet another high-rise village in the downtown core. The land had been assembled in the 1950s by a group of speculators known as the Parliament Syndicate. Eventually the project was sold in 1961 to the group called Howard Investments Limited, involving a partnership of Max Merkur, Phil Roth and Al Grossman of Belmont. They were preparing to build sixteen high-rise towers on the thirty-two-acre site; the project was called St. James Town. This neighbourhood, just south of Bloor and west of Parliament, was not far from several public housing projects built by the government to provide improved living conditions for the poor. In fact, the city itself was one of the first major developers of large-scale projects in older neighbourhoods; it was the city that had first assembled large tracts of land, demolished the houses and put up high-rise apartments.

But the boom in land development and apartment high-rises was clearly in the hands of private developers by the early

1960s. There was little commercial construction owing largely to the monetary recession. Coyne refused to change the Bank of Canada's restrictive monetary policy, deepening the crisis while embarrassing John Diefenbaker's Progressive Conservative government, whose finance minister, Donald Fleming, strongly believed expansion was the better policy. The feud ended with Coyne unwillingly submitting his resignation, accusing the government of trying to undermine the independent role of the bank. His immediate successor, the shy, brilliant economist Louis Rasminsky, briefly expanded the money supply to get out of the 1961 recession before returning to a tight-money policy.

The expansion helped commercial construction companies and renewed interest in downtown development. Soon a Toronto bank announced its intention to build a $100-million bank plaza. Partnered with the Toronto Dominion Bank in the TD Centre project was the Bronfmans' Cemp Investments, which agreed to help with some of the financing. The move to stake a claim in valuable city real estate reflected the Bronfman philosophy, as Cemp's president, Charles Bronfman, explained: "If you're going to make a profit, do something that is useful to others at the same time. We won't buy land just to sit on it. We buy, build and provide a service that adds something to the community. We are not," he added, "interested in residential property." Cemp and its subsidiary, Fairview, had already put some $50 million into real estate across Canada. Cemp was connected to another active developing firm, William Zeckendorf's Trizec Corp. Ltd., through family lawyer Lazarus Phillips, a director of an insurance firm that was one of Zeckendorf's partners. Trizec was eventually taken over in 1962 by this insurance firm and the third partner, a British firm, after Zeckendorf ran out of cash. This gave the new owners control of Place Ville Marie, Flemingdon Park and Toronto's Yorkdale, destined to become Canada's most profitable shopping centre. Numerous other developments were acquired as well.

Yorkdale was more extravagant in design than the plazas built by the pioneering Principal Investments. Located next to an expressway and right on an intersection with another proposed route, the Spadina expressway, the centre became a nucleus for shoppers living in the northern suburbs of Toronto. The financing to complete Yorkdale came largely from the British partner, Eagle Star Insurance, indicating the growing interest on the part of insurance firms in the mortgage-lending business.

Many Canadian builders dependent on traditional bank financing were less fortunate during the tight-money squeeze and as a result were slower to make a recovery in spite of the easing of credit under Rasminsky. Some firms who had been unable to meet their short-term financing needs, their money tied up in equipment and half-completed projects, had already declared bankruptcy.

For all but a few construction companies, 1961 was a disastrous year financially. There was a shortage of money, strikes and the ever-growing red tape at City Hall, where building plans were approved or discarded after lengthy deliberations. All this cost money, both to carry a project and to retain a work crew. One developer who had nursed an $85-million downtown waterfront residential scheme through three years of delay by city politicians finally got approval but lost the project, because he was unable to refinance the development after the original investors withdrew.

Certainly politics played a key role in the land development business. Every high-rise project, big or small, depended on approval and rezoning from City Hall. Although reaction to the sudden growth of the Fifties and Sixties was mixed, there were a number of politicians who looked approvingly on the prosperity associated with all this new construction. One outspoken fan of developers and their projects was Phil Givens, whose boyhood political ambitions were coming true. The former Harbord schoolboy and Osgoode Hall graduate opened his law practice in

1949. Next, he ran for City Council and was elected in 1951, the same year his high school classmate and friend, Eddie Goodman, also a lawyer, became active politically with the influential backroom boys of the Progressive Conservative party.

A buoyant, talkative man, Givens loved politics. An entertaining debater, he also had a flair for publicity. During one all-night council session, he posed for photographers at City Hall dressed in a nightgown and cap. In 1961 he won a citywide race for comptroller. When Mayor Donald Summerville collapsed suddenly and died one evening in 1963 while attending a civic function at a hockey rink, the city politicians chose Givens to serve out Summerville's term. Givens had said he had always wanted to be a politician, but not necessarily the mayor of Toronto. Nevertheless in the 1964 election, he was on the campaign trail, with Eddie Goodman acting as his adviser and part-time fundraiser.

Goodman's face was well known around City Hall. He was to be seen up in front of civic committees, speaking on behalf of clients of his such as Cadillac and Greenwin who needed re-zonings and planning permission from the city. On one occasion Goodman negotiated the purchase of 10,000 square feet of city-owned land needed for a development. The price at which Goodman got the land for his client turned out to be $65,000 less than its market value. A number of Goodman's clients also favoured Givens as a mayoralty candidate; Cadillac kicked in $500 for the campaign.

Having won election in 1964, Givens remained as enthusiastic as ever about development of the city, applauding projects like St. James Town. During his tenure, the city finally approved the scheme, which resulted in the demolition of 300 homes, the relocation of 700 families and the closing of a number of city streets, which were to be sold to the developers. Other projects met quick success, assuring Givens that progress was being made to transform boomtown Toronto into the urban showcase of North America.

The new City Hall also fitted in well with Givens's vision of the new Toronto. For the reflecting pool in the square in front of the twin curved towers, Givens ordered that another $5,000 be spent so that it could be used as a skating rink just in time for the 1964 election. Then there was the controversial sculpture the city was to buy from the artist Henry Moore. When the local citizenry failed to see an "Archer" in the piece of bronze with that title that Moore delivered, Givens defended it — and raised the money for its purchase privately.

Givens ran into some criticism from community leaders who decried his lack of interest in more public housing, which they claimed the city badly needed. Nor would he support an independent authority to build such housing. As one reporter said, it seemed that Givens was not so concerned about the housing itself as about who would build and own it. Givens's preference was often stated: he preferred the private builders.

Mayor Givens's most severe critics were city homeowners who balked at the prospect of apartment towers rising twenty or thirty storeys next to their property. Apartments, they claimed, lowered the value of real estate in the surrounding neighbourhood. Some said tenant living attracted only transients to the area, people who paid their rent and came and went, adding little to the quality of the neighbourhood. Others complained of pressure to sell when developers began to buy up real estate for their projects in existing neighbourhoods. Houses bought early on the proposed apartment site were leased to tenants and middlemen and often neglected for some time before demolition. Givens remained loyal to private development on most of these issues, and in the 1966 election he ran on a boomtown platform. Toronto was growing, he said, and residents should take pride in the new city building. He had two opponents, one of them a former CCF-NDP comptroller, William Dennison, who criticized the "beanpole" apartments and the proposals that the city expropriate homeowners on behalf of private developers. Givens lost; Dennison won.

While Givens was mayor the flow of approvals for high-rise apartments had gone largely uninterrupted. The builders had survived the tight-money squeeze, and they were popular enough with certain politicians at City Hall to get most of the decisions they needed to build their projects. But the militancy of city residents, opposed to the changes that were coming to neighbourhoods across the city, was something they hadn't expected.

8
ZANINI AND IRVINE

From 1960 on, Toronto was a city in transition, as more and more high-rise apartments appeared in residential neighbourhoods. For the men building these imposing structures, however, conditions remained less than satisfactory. Wages for residential workers continued to drop. Building inspectors were rarely seen on project sites. Safety was ignored. If a man was injured, he was laid off. If he died, he merely became a statistic. Few of the international unions had cared to organize this sector, and those who did met only limited success. There was one exception: Charles Irvine and his plastering local, which was barely hanging on in 1960 as membership dropped. The only other organizing effort with a sizable membership was Bruno Zanini's new Canadian association for bricklayers.

The lack of union organization was apparent not only in the housing sector. Workers building roads and subways were not fully organized. Hundreds of non-union men were employed at this time as transportation routes were being quickly built, above and below ground, to service the fast-growing city. Roads were blocked with equipment, and everywhere there seemed to be squads of men drilling holes in the asphalt, ripping apart roads, crawling in and out of pits at a frenetic pace. The unpleasant noise and inconvenience to local residents drew a few complaints, but the work continued.

Then on March 17, 1960, five Italians working on the Bloor-Danforth subway project died in a tunnel underneath the Don River, when a fire broke out in the main shaft. Four of the trapped men — called sandhogs in the construction industry — were discovered five hours later at the end of a 250-foot tunnel half-filled with silt and river water.

This was the second cave-in in the same tunnel in five months, and two more men would die in a third tunnel collapse before the line was completed. Safety inspectors were generally unqualified and rarely seen, particularly on the sections where the Italians were employed. One worker said that conditions varied according to the nationality of the work crew. The Irish had the fewest complaints.

There had been other incidents of neglect that often went unreported to authorities. One day more than a dozen men were hauled out of a Florence Avenue sewer project, twisted and crippled by the bends, a condition caused by inadequate precautions for below-surface work.

As yet, no union had effectively organized the subway tunnellers. Within the International Hod Carriers, Building and Common Labourers Union, which generally organized unskilled construction workers, there had been many disputes over which of the Toronto-based locals should represent these men. The internal squabble was finally resolved when Washington gave the bargaining power to Gerry Gallagher, the militant Irish organizer who had already bargained for a Labourers' local of Ontario Hydro workers. But the Italians who died that day were non-union workers.

For the small group standing around the tunnel shaft at Hogg's Hollow late that March night, their feet stiff from the cold, there was only an ounce of hope, and that vanished the moment a rescuer scrambled over the lip of the shaft muttering in Italian. One relative who was wearing only a thin windbreaker collapsed. "They're dead — they're all dead," said a fireman. Identified by their families were John Fusillo, 27; John Correglio, 45; Alessandro Mantella, 25; and his brother, Guido, 23. The body of Pasquale Milantoni had been found earlier in the tunnel corridor.

Reporting the death of these five men, *Telegram* reporter Frank Drea told how these immigrants were being treated. In a series of news reports, he portrayed the dismal life of Italian workers, carted daily in the back end of pickup trucks to housing and apartment sites; recounted the complaints of men who had worked long hours without any pay; chronicled the stacks of worthless cheques issued by subcontractors who had since fled the country; noted the absence of safety inspection officials, leading to numerous accidents for which there was little compensation.

Drea made several proposals. Builders and contractors should be licensed. There should be a return to the tender system, as was the practice in the construction of commercial buildings where union labour was used. The subcontracting system used by housing and apartment developers who wanted to cut costs led to the hiring of the cheapest subcontractor, who in turn, working on a very narrow margin, had to find the cheapest workers. And it was the workers who were cheated out of decent pay and the decent life that nearly everyone in this country claimed as natural right.

The series of stories sparked by the Hogg's Hollow disaster won Drea an award for crusading journalism. For several days, the editorial writers of the city's English newspapers wrote angry articles deploring the abuses of nearly a decade. There was talk of exploitation of fellow human beings. Some called the whole affair a slave trade, where employers had forced workers to accept starvation wages. Others accused the government of gross neglect and the public of indifference.

Meanwhile Bruno Zanini was busy signing up immigrant bricklayers for the new Canadian union he had created in 1959. This he had done following his disenchantment with the international union, which had taken in Italian members from the residential sector in 1957, but appeared interested only in collecting the dues of its membership. No effort had been made to improve conditions for these bricklayers. When Zanini quit and created his own association, 400 bricklayers followed. The rebellion provoked the Washington-based unions. Stories began to circulate that Zanini was a "gangster" trying to destroy unionism by defying his international brethren.

For some months Zanini went without a salary, drawing on his own savings at times to keep open the office over a variety store. Then one day in the early spring of 1960, a short time after the tunnel deaths, Charles Irvine paid an unexpected visit. He had a message, said Zanini: "'See! You people are always getting killed,' he says to me. 'It's a crime what's happening to your people. You should be helping them.' 'I know, Charlie,' I says, 'but I'm only one person. Everybody is calling me a crook with this Canadian union. The Toronto unions are fighting me but they don't realize this is what the workers want! The workers don't understand why all these unions aren't Canadian. And they can't understand why there can't be just one big union like in the old country.'"

Zanini nearly always grew exasperated whenever he dutifully explained those things he learned from the workers. Irvine nodded as though he understood, pursuing in the meantime another line of reasoning. Clearly, something had to be done in residential construction to organize the workers. The situation was an embarrassment to Washington and a number of union officials, who were now seeking Irvine's counsel, he said. Their sympathy was with these immigrants, the plastering boss added.

The alternative Irvine suggested was to accommodate both the internationals and Zanini. Why not form some kind of umbrella organization to organize all the trades? The umbrella group would be named after Brandon Hall, where immigrant workers often held their meetings. Under this scheme, separate residential locals would be organized for all the key trades. They would exist side by side but independent from the already existing building trade union locals that represented workers on commercial construction projects. Both Toronto groups of locals would be affiliated to the international building trade unions in the U.S.

And so, some weeks later, Zanini told a crowd of nearly 2,000 immigrant workers packed into the Brandon Hall how he and a few others intended to remedy all the injustice that had been going on for the past ten years. "Because someone made a buck over your sweat," he began, only to be interrupted by shouts from the audience in Italian: "Over our bodies!" Then from all sides of the auditorium, men began to stamp their feet while others rose halfway in the seats, clapping wildly; here and there, workers shared cigarettes, nodded their approval, turning toward the stage where Zanini stood, leaning over the podium, his arms raised to silence the room: "Italy sent Canada its best men, not people from the jails," he said as the room fell silent. "You work 18 hours a day now because you are single men. You can't expect to get married and raise a family under these conditions."

When he asked those who had not received vacation pay to stand, nearly two-thirds of the men jumped to their feet. There was one man who reported he hadn't had a vacation in ten years. A father of three children spoke of how he had been fired from his job when he asked for a raise. The next day, the meeting was reported by the press as the largest mass rally in 14 years. As Irvine predicted, a union came out of it within two weeks.

Zanini and Irvine's unexpected move ran counter to the efforts of the Toronto commercial locals and William Jenoves of the Bricklayers, who remained convinced the answer was to negotiate contracts with the apartment builders directly. Since the commercial locals had not organized the residential workers and brought them into these unions as members, the builders had little reason to pay heed to Jenoves and his ideas. Now adding to the growing frustration of the commercial sector's union officials was this announcement of a rival campaign led by Zanini and his bricklayers, who now returned to the international union of their trade. Irvine's residential plastering local joined, and Washington officials added a new local of cement masons, as did the Labourers and the United Brotherhood of Carpenters and Joiners. The rationale for a separate residential drive eluded Jenoves, who viewed it solely as a deliberate attempt to divide the labour movement and prevent these residential construction workers from proper union representation and, it would appear, equal wages. These were spirited words from a man who had so many years earlier ignored the same abuses in his own backyard.

At a second meeting a few weeks later, some 1,800 workers applied for membership with the newly formed Brandon Union Group. When the subcontractors working for the apartment builders learned how their men had been organized, they treated the whole affair as a joke. A shorter work week, higher wages, more safety: where, they asked in mild amusement, was the money to come from? But the laughter died shortly. Already, Irvine was deliberating his next move, conversing with Zanini daily, questioning the mood of the men. If there was a strike, would these workers walk out? Had they enough money to live on? Was there any hope these men would come out and fight for their rights to bring in laws? So many families depended entirely on their meagre pay. Would they make this sacrifice? Zanini gave his assurances.

A month later, on the long, hot holiday weekend of August 1, 1960, 3,000 residential construction workers met at the Lansdowne theatre, an old brick movie theatre in the west end of the city. Inside this dark, dank hall the men gathered to plan a strike, their heads bowed briefly for a silent prayer. As they stood shoulder to shoulder, the men knew that in all probability they would lose their jobs. Some still believed they would be deported. But no one left the hall. It was in every sense a sacrifice, particularly for men who had never complained or missed a day's work.

Speeches followed. At one point, an Italian immigrant who had been overwhelmed by what he heard jumped onto the platform waving a cheque for $392, which he said had bounced. The cheque was grabbed by Zanini who waved it at the men. "This is the sort of exploitation that has to be stopped. Canada is a free country and immigrants should be treated the same as Canadians," he said, pulling out another handful of worthless cheques. There were shouts of support from the audience. Then Irvine spoke: "All you men have a brain. I can't stop you from going and pulling men off the job, but I can't tell you to do it from here." Again, there were cries: "*Carte bianca, si*?" Interpreting this, Zanini said they meant carte blanche — the workers were to settle things their own way.

The next day, men stood on street corners, ignoring the pickup trucks on their daily shuttle out to the apartment sites. When some workers refused to stay off the job sites, squads of strikers arrived, ten, twenty carloads of men at a time armed with bricks and two-by-fours. At one site, fifty unionists bearing placards, with tools and wrenches in their hands, pushed workers off the job. One man was hit on the head with an axe. At another project, strikers shouted hoarsely at workers until the police were called. Walls were knocked over and cement bins dumped as workers still on the job dodged flying bricks and stones. Meanwhile some $50 million worth of apartment and housing projects were stalled due to the tie-up. Forty-five of the fifty-two high-rise apartment projects in the city were shut down. For developers operating with little or no cash and subcontractors without any resources, the strike meant more than a delay on their projects. It cost them money in extra interest charges, and threatened them with bankruptcy if it went on for long. "Yeah, they stopped almost every job," said Zanini. "It was something that had been built up for years in these immigrants. They were pushed and beaten. They had no way of letting off steam. The subcontractors never seen the men like this before. They were frightened! 'Cause the men were excited, see? They were like animals — they had to be. It's unfortunate, but there were no laws in them days, so we had to use baseball bats — the men had to do these things."

To end the fracas, Irvine sent telegrams to the subcontractors disclosing his demands. About 400 of the employers met one night, arguing with the Brandon Hall union officials that there wouldn't be any jobs at all if the walkout continued. Some companies were close to bankruptcy, starved by the strike. Others complained about the wage increases. One bricklaying subcontractor who acceded to the demands, doubling his wages, said: "Okay, I agreed to higher wages. But on three jobs I asked the builders for increases to cover the new wages and they laughed at me. Now what happens?"

Irvine, apparently unmoved, told the subcontractors to appear for the next meeting in groups according to their trades. Coming this time to settle wage demands, the companies began to bargain as separate residential trade associations. Wages were doubled in some cases. The work week was set at forty hours instead of seventy. Adequate safety measures were to be mandatory.

In the midst of some of these negotiations, Zanini was at one point called to the phone. As he stood there listening, he grew somewhat agitated, then motioning to Irvine, his hand capped over the mouthpiece, he uttered something inaudible. He left the room without another word.

A few hours later, on the curb of a quiet street near St. Clair Avenue, as arranged, he spotted a car and an old friend waving at him. Within minutes, as Zanini was to recall years later, "I was sitting in this guy's Cadillac when he says to me: 'Listen you bugger, you're still the same. Remember when we used to go out together? Like the time we got shot at getting the gas coupons? And you went across the Humber?' I says, 'What are you getting at?' 'Listen,' he tells me, 'you know that big builder on that subdivision, one of the biggest in Canada? Well, you got 'em by the balls. There's a hundred grand there — fifty Gs for you, if you put the men back to work.' I told him, 'Look, those days are over. How can I do that when the men don't have any agreements yet?' 'Talk it over with Charlie,' he says."

Zanini dutifully gave Irvine the message. The plastering boss apparently blackballed the proposal and gave Zanini assurances that the men would not return to work until they had agreements.

So that was the end of that. The men stayed out until the contracts were signed, four days later. Irvine estimated the drive resulted in 6,000 new union members. To celebrate, the union officers called a victory rally. Thousands of workers pressed into the Lansdowne theatre to honour Irvine with a portrait of himself, the frame laced with stella alpina, a flower said to inspire leadership. Zanini's wife, Mariella, accepted a bouquet as another token of the workers' gratitude.

The same week the men returned to work, Zanini heard that some mob syndicate had tried to extort money from the builders during the strike. He was standing in front of the Medical Arts building on Eglinton Avenue when a big fat man known in gambling circles came at him, wheeling his fist in the air. "'Whatsa matter for you?' the guy says to me," Zanini remembered later. "'What did you put the men back to work for? Some of the boys had these builders on the muscle and they said they could get the men back for $200,000.' And he's telling me how they were going to twist arms, force us to put the men back and give us an end. Extortion! Get it? I was shocked. 'Give me an end,' he says. Like hell."

But it all proved to be another illusory victory. Less than half of the residential subcontractors had signed agreements to pay higher wages; the remainder continued to hire cheap, non-union labour. They were awarded more and more contracts by the apartment builders as jobs for the Brandon Group union members dwindled.

Nearly half a year went by, and Brandon Group residential locals were losing members as subcontractors paying the higher rates went bankrupt. In the interim, their competitors, employing non-union workers, cornered the majority of the apartment work. To save their operations some employers either refused to pay the new wages or changed their corporate names to void the contract they had signed. For a time, companies were discarded like shells. By April 1961, with more than 1,000 complaints filed by immigrant workers to union officers at the Brandon Hall, there was talk of another strike.

Clearly this time the provincial government would be forced to act. Laws were needed to protect the worker, to establish at the very least a minimum wage scale and set a safety standard. By now Toronto's residents had long since forgotten their indignation of the previous summer at the treatment of these immigrants and the stories of families trying to live on $40 a week, sharing homes with eight or nine boarders, subsisting on a diet of macaroni and bread to meet their payments. Somehow it was generally believed that the organizers of the residential unions, Irvine and Zanini, had matters in hand.

Toward the end of May 1961, there was a renewed sense of urgency as rumours flew about another summer walkout. Irvine was seen frequently discussing strike possibilities with some business agents from the union locals representing commercial construction workers in the city. The rift between the two labour groups was apparently past history. New instructions from the parent international unions in the U.S. had been to form an alliance among the Toronto-based residential and commercial unions. The idea was to tie up the entire residential field in a campaign to organize every immigrant worker into some kind of union. The new strike date was set for May 29, 1961.

Irvine promised the industry a "long, hard, dirty fight" to collect the estimated $500,000 in back pay owed to the workers. The action began that morning at the Brandon Hall, as 2,000 immigrants tried to press inside the auditorium. Some found space in the basement while others stood outside in the parking lot, listening to the platform speeches carried over loudspeakers. Hours later, 200 squads of men sped across the city in cars and trucks borrowed from friends and relatives. Their aim was to close down every apartment project in town. At one site, twenty cars arrived shortly before noon. Shouting and screaming and waving, strikers raced to the foundations where a dozen men were still at work. "Get out of here," they yelled, grabbing the reluctant men by the arms and shoving them aside. When the police arrived, the strikers scattered, their cars fishtailing up the road to another site. In the north end of the city 200 strikers hurled bricks and boards at workers who refused to walk out. One carpenter was struck on the ear with a flying brick while a unionist was hit on the head with an axe. Both men had to be sent to hospital. On another site, fifty carloads of men arrived and began to harass a small group of carpenters who had escaped to a clump of bushes. Three men later ran out screaming, "I quit, I quit!" Their faces were bruised and bleeding from the flying stones pelted in their general direction by the strikers.

On the second day of the strike, police were called to disperse crowds on various projects. Six men were arrested; this number rose to twenty-seven five days later.

Nearly all the authorities blamed Irvine for the violence, but the 53-year-old plastering boss retorted: "It all depends on who defines violence. There is another kind of violence that cuts the hearts and souls out of men: long hours, low pay, hungry children. If that isn't violence of the worst kind I don't know what is. It's killed more men in this city than any two-by-four." He went on to criticize the excessive bail set for the immigrants now filling up the jails. Bond was set at $1,000 cash or $2,000 property. Other labour leaders took up this cry, denouncing the authorities for making unwarranted arrests for loitering and unlawful assembly. Italian shop-owners began to complain about the lack of business and the absence of window-shoppers. One merchant basking in the sun outside his store said police told him to clear off the sidewalk or he would be considered a vagrant.

The violence continued. Cement bags were slit open, walls knocked down, machinery smashed. And more arrests followed. One man was charged with pulling a telephone off the wall on a site and sent to jail. Meanwhile, government officials were unavailable for comment. The labour minister was vacationing and his deputy was out of town.

Some response came from newspaper editorials demanding reform for these workers and laws to protect them. Once again public sympathy began to swell, and funds poured in from all parts of the U.S., raised by twenty major American construction unions in areas heavily populated with Italians. On the sixth day, the Home Builders Association called for deportation proceedings to begin against these immigrants.

But jailing men and deporting them were measures that many found loathsome and unjust. So there was some relief when the provincial government reluctantly intervened on June 9 with a three-point proposal to end the illegal walkout. The premier of the province, Leslie Frost, agreed to set up a temporary board to hear all labour complaints. According to his suggestion, a team of inspectors would examine abuses while appointed government officials were to create a commission of inquiry with the ultimate goal of establishing maximum hours, minimum wages and safety conditions for the industry as a whole.

Union leaders spent a sleepless night studying the plan before it was finally accepted. Irvine called it a milestone in Canadian labour, while urging strikers to continue the fourteen-day-old walkout until contractors had signed the agreements proposed by the premier. "We like the premier's plan," said his labour colleague Zanini, "but the boys aren't going back until we get it in black and white from the contractors."

Experience had taught Irvine that as long as fly-by-night subcontractors continued to hire non-union men, the housing unions would fail. By withholding labour, Irvine made clear his determination to force these companies to hire union workers. He also called on builders to take some action to rid the industry of speculators and "fast-buck" promoters who were erecting apartments with "little more than gall." It was these operators who were ruining the industry, driving prices down through cutthroat bidding techniques while forcing out of business some of the old-line subcontracting firms who always paid their workers a decent wage. Irvine wanted the entire residential sector organized first with the workers, then the subcontractors; the ultimate goal was to win an agreement from developers.

On June 26, putting into full operation the new-found alliance with the international union locals controlling the city's commercial construction sector, Irvine shut down the entire industry. For twenty-four hours every construction project in the city was idle. Irvine called a mass meeting attended by 16,000 construction workers, who poured into the grandstand at

Exhibition Park in one of the largest labour demonstrations ever seen in Canada. It had the desired effect of underlining the power of the men — and of their leaders.

From a podium glistening with microphones, Irvine spoke not of specific goals but of the importance of winning the strike: "We could settle this tomorrow and go back to work. But next year the war would be on again. When we go back, we stay back because the mess in Toronto has to be cleaned up once and for all."

Hours later, talks resumed with some trades, but these failed when the press released details of the pending settlement prematurely. There were some critics who claimed this stalling indicated the union leaders were not interested in ending the strike. Negotiations were halted, as Irvine extended his battle from the subcontractors to the developers they worked for, demanding now a master agreement from all these builders agreeing to use only union subcontractors. On July 3, the immigrant strikers voted overwhelmingly to continue their walkouts as Irvine reminded them, a small child held in his arms, that the fight was now for the right of their children to live as Canadians. "We will fight the builders and contractors in the courts, the sewers, the ditches, the fields and on the streets," he said.

A number of concrete and drain companies continued to operate with "scab labour" while refusing to negotiate or meet Irvine's demands. If the delivery of concrete to sites could be halted, Irvine knew he could then press for some action. As Irvine told the strikers: "They don't seem to know what they want — they are just opposed to anything. Any time you see any building with concrete, you can put your foot in it. It's okay with me."

The week after the rally, the plastering boss flew to Miami to discuss the Toronto situation with Teamsters president Hoffa. If the trucking boss could be persuaded to stop the flow of concrete and supplies to non-union firms, Irvine would then have an unbeatable hand in his bargaining with the builder-developers. Hoffa was sympathetic and immediately ordered his Teamsters to honour picket lines. Details of the agreement reached between the two union leaders were never made public; one union spokesman said at the time, however, that Hoffa had pledged money as well as men to organize the entire housing field.

It was casually termed a mutual-aid agreement. Irvine's request offered Hoffa the opportunity to increase his own membership as well as to obtain some influence with the Toronto residential unions. His business agents were experts in the labour field, always on the alert for new areas for expansion. And the Teamsters had resources. Although the striking immigrants received no strike pay, Teamsters officials could guarantee payment of lost salaries to any of their drivers fired or suspended for enforcing the building trade unions' picket lines. A spokesman for the concrete industry mused, "I guess Hoffa must have figured out some way for these fellows to make a living without working."

As the weeks of the strike turned into months, many workers and their families were suffering badly. One woman had tried to keep her family going through the strike by ironing shirts on a piecework basis, receiving 4 cents a shirt. Then, almost without warning, on July 17 the strike was over. Some 2,500 workers at the Lansdowne theatre cheered and embraced each other as Irvine announced the end of the forty-eight-day walkout. He spoke vaguely about the contract settlements: "We got everything we wanted plus the machinery to enforce it." Instead, he emphasized the objectives accomplished through the strike, forcing the government to take a hard look at the industry and enact laws to guarantee minimum wages, fair hours, safe and decent working conditions — laws that would in effect end the exploitation of construction workers, immigrant or native-born.

The Ontario government had finally stepped in to create a special board to speed up arbitration of grievances and contract violations. Investigators from the provincial labour department promised to inspect contractors' books. And a one-man royal commission was established to investigate labour–management troubles in the industry.

Slamming the shillelagh he always carried against the table, Irvine shouted: "We've won! But this is only one battle. We still have to win the war." This was an apparent reference to the need to secure an agreement with the housing and apartment builders to use only these union firms. As the meeting ended, the crowd moved forward to surround Zanini, who was hoisted over their heads and carried out of the theatre. Broke but expecting that the government would back up these guarantees, they marched into the street, believing that at last they had a future of fair treatment and reasonable wages ahead of them. The immigrant workers had at long last broken their silence and taken advantage of their own power by organizing into unions, firmly convinced that it was the end of an era of abuse and exploitation.

Scarcely was the summer strike over when the court trials began for 106 immigrants who had had charges laid against them. Some were there for such unruly behaviour as throwing bricks and stones while others had been taken into police custody for refusing to clear sidewalks or leave construction sites. Fifty-three were sentenced to jail terms, including one business agent for the Labourers. Nine men were fined, nine more were awaiting trial and the remainder were acquitted or had the charges against them withdrawn. While their cases were being discussed, the government began to accept briefs from the industry to determine what changes should be made to correct the abuses. H. Carl Goldenberg, a labour mediator of some renown, was appointed as the one-man royal commission to investigate the industry.

At a sacrifice of $5 million in lost wages, these immigrant workers had achieved more for themselves in a six-week battle than the entire labour movement in Canada had achieved for them in 20 years. Nine homebuilding contractors had been charged with violations of the *Labour Relations Act*. Other firms were still under investigation. New laws were to be enacted following the inquiry to set a minimum wage and improve safety standards. Wages had improved but were still lower than the commercial rates. The commercial locals benefitted too, increasing their membership in some trades through residential affiliates. The Brandon Group with its separate residential locals made strong inroads as well. So successful was the campaign that a string of new business agents were hired and trained to oversee the housing sector union locals.

But the real importance of Irvine's victory was the control he had acquired over the apartment builders' labour supply. With a fleet of residential locals firmly entrenched, he had acquired an extraordinarily powerful device that had twice brought the industry to a standstill at a time when the developers were committed to costly high-rise projects.

9
THE SPLIT

Organizing immigrant workers into so-called residential unions — separate locals from other construction workers, with their own lower wage rates — was a new wrinkle in the labour set-up. The existence of this separate structure, where men working for residential subcontractors were paid less for the same work than men on the commercial projects, precipitated dissension, union rivalry, raiding of memberships and finally violence. As long as it lasted, however, this disunity between the two sectors of the industry meant the apartment developers were ensured of a cheaper source of labour. Not only did residential unions prevent wages from climbing to commercial rates but these locals also made it impossible to organize all the workers in any trade into the same union local.

Residential unions were better for builders than a single, unified union bargaining for the same wage rates across the board in a particular trade. But residential unions were better than no unions at all for the workers. Or so it seemed. Control of the new residential locals was in the hands of the tough-minded Scotsman Charles Irvine. Largely through his efforts and those of Bruno Zanini, the immigrant workers were now organized; however, Irvine remained unsympathetic to the apartment builders, who were justifiably wary of his new-found power. Gouged twice by his summer strikes, they had no reason to believe that his bargaining methods would change. Added to this was the rumour that a few local extortionists had gotten into the act again in 1961 and that there had been a big pay-off by some builders during the last strike to get the workers back on the job. When the men then stayed off, the builders became incensed, convinced that the money had found its way into the strike leaders' pockets. When questioned about the alleged double-cross, Zanini said: "These builders were coming to me as if we'd collected the money, asking why the men hadn't gone back to work, but we never took any of their money." Still, the accusations were far less worrisome than unexplained incidents that began to trouble Zanini's personal life. On several occasions his car wouldn't start. There were threatening phone calls. Two or three times, his tires were slashed. Then without warning, late in September 1961, someone fired a shot at him, nicking the rooftop of his car while he waited at a stoplight. When the police gave up their investigation after finding nothing, Zanini conducted his own search. Eventually he learned through an informer that some builders had hired two gunmen, German boys, on a $2,000 contract. As a result of these disruptions, Zanini grew convinced that his organizing work was over. He wanted to quit the union business, and the two residential locals he now directed for the Bricklayers and the Labourers. But for one reason or another, he stayed on, continuing to inspect jobs and record workers' complaints.

Meanwhile, there was an extraordinary amount of activity down at the Brandon Hall union offices, although Irvine was not always involved on a day-to-day basis. Scores of new business agents were hired to handle the Brandon Group's expanding activities. Then a contingent of U.S. labour experts arrived and proceeded to educate the local recruits. These labour boys, in their custom-tailored suits and silk ties, lent an aura of sophistication to the tiny, cramped union quarters at Brandon Avenue. Smoking expensive Cuban cigars, they chatted and joked, mostly in Italian, crossing and uncrossing their feet on the desks as they sat in comfort throughout the day. Finding the conversation at head office more interesting than policing jobs at the apartment sites, more and more business agents neglected their duties. Safety was not enforced. Workers' complaints were shelved. Meanwhile, the American business agents took control of the group, recommending a number of innovative practices used by the more successful union locals in Detroit and other U.S. cities. Toronto business agents were instructed to pull workers off certain jobs. Two or three times, men were pulled off the same project. More and more sites were hit by rotating strikes even though the subcontractors concerned were paying the men fair wages. Indeed, a number of honest and legitimate firms were faced with a continuous round of walkouts.

Harassed by illegal work stoppages, many of these companies were forced out of business while some of their competitors continued to work without any labour interference. To many, there seemed to be a pattern in this business of withholding labour from reputable subcontractors who had always paid their crews a decent wage. As companies folded, it became more apparent that an extortion ring was at work. Those firms refusing to pay for labour peace or failing to hand over a percentage of the company profit to a racketeer were soon left without crews, their half-completed projects barricaded by picket lines. Squeezed financially by builders at one end and new unions apparently operated by labour racketeers at the other, many subcontractors found themselves mired in debt. Despite the bankruptcies, no one complained to the authorities although there was now talk of how greed and force had come into the industry.

Nothing was done to interfere with the activities of these new business agents. Sharing power at the top with these Americans may not have been entirely what Irvine had in mind; nevertheless, he went along with the arrangement whether or not he agreed with it.

Another small but steady source of money for the unions was the monthly dues checked off and deducted by the employers from the payrolls. This money was forwarded directly to the union offices at regular intervals. Unfortunately for the workers, little emphasis was placed on bookkeeping. For nearly a year money was collected, including pension and welfare benefits; then a fire of unknown origins swept through the Labourers' office in the spring of 1962, destroying all the records of where and how this money was spent. Not even the Fire Marshal's office could uncover the cause of the blaze.

The next disaster to befall the Brandon movement was the breakaway of two of the five residential locals in the group. The withdrawal of the Bricklayers and the Labourers late in 1962 came as an unpleasant surprise to Irvine, who had clearly not anticipated this sudden desertion of two of the group's most powerful housing trades.

At the request of a regional boss for the Labourers, Washington officials cancelled the charter for the Brandon Group local. Zanini, as its president at the time, was later instructed to re-sign the men into membership in a newly chartered local. Deserting the Brandon Group at the same time was the Bricklayers' union. Members of that local's executive wanted to remove themselves from Irvine's influence. After their departure, Irvine was left with only the Carpenters and his own Plasterers and Cement Masons as separate residential locals.

The split within the residential ranks was yet another division, removing further the possibility of labour unity in the city while destroying Irvine's brief and mighty grasp of control of residential construction workers.

Irvine's own grief and subsequent bitterness could not be disputed. What inspired even greater ill feeling was the inexplicable and impetuous behaviour of his old labour crony, Bruno Zanini. Irvine began to suspect that Zanini had made some sort of private deal that had effectively undermined the residential locals. The only beneficiaries of such a collapse, he felt, were the apartment builders. Still, he refused to confront Zanini, ignoring his repeated phone calls. "Oh, Charlie was against me, I could see it," Zanini said some years later. "But they were going their way and I was going mine. See? I was ordered to go in and assist. See? They cancelled the charter. It was a hell of a job for me. Because you're dividing these workers. Charlie felt that I made deals with people, certain subcontractors and builders and stuff like that. Which I did not! I didn't have no money."

It was, however, Zanini's acceptance of the split that sealed the fate of the Brandon Group. Impressed by authority, he obeyed his orders, not realizing the damage that would extend to his friendship with Irvine, a man he had followed almost like a faithful dog. In fact, he was puzzled by Irvine's wall of silence. But despite this setback, he continued his work with the two breakaway unions, aware now that at times he was being followed.

Some weeks after the split, Zanini was called by a man who identified himself as Paul Volpe. The exchange was polite but brief. The two men agreed to meet that afternoon in the west end of the city.

The presence of Volpe casts a whole new light on the complex affairs of the Brandon Group. A Toronto businessman, Volpe claimed to have an unspecified interest in the labour field, describing himself as a labour consultant. His greatest attribute was a physically imposing stature, a thick neck and wide, generous cheekbones. His features were well defined, and he moved like a boxer, giving everyone the impression he was a man of unmeasured strength. His credentials were just as impressive. He moved in and out of careers with ease, turning his talent to whatever opportunity arose. For a time, he ran a car wash; later he tried selling real estate. At one point he was in partnership with his brother, operating a casino in Haiti. Albert Volpe was an antique dealer whose reputation was momentarily tarnished in 1963 when a U.S. Senate investigating committee claimed he was a member of the Cosa Nostra, with ties to a Buffalo syndicate. Albert Volpe denied this continually, blaming the press for the bad publicity that often surrounded his activities. Paul Volpe blamed the police for similar harassment. Since the time he was 16, Volpe complained, the authorities had found one excuse or another to mingle in his affairs. Some years later, he was convicted of trying to extort money from a business partner.

But it was as a self-described labour consultant and fellow Italian that Volpe made his approach to Zanini. The meeting took place on a curb several feet away from Volpe's parked car, where two or three men were standing around. Describing the stocky Italian as a jovial, sporty type, Zanini related the incident without comment on Volpe's motives. "'What the hell you screw the men around for? Why are these unions fighting each other? Did you take payoff?' he's asking me," recalled Zanini, his own voice rising. "I says, 'I been promoted. That's all. Orders came down for me to assist and I just done my job. But jeezus, it's very nice of you to be so concerned.'"

Volpe then left to make a phone call. Soon Irvine arrived. Zanini repeated his story of how he had been instructed to take the Labourers out of the Brandon Group by the bosses. Zanini assumed from Irvine's lack of response that nothing could sway his suspicions that Zanini had made some kind of deal.

When questioned some years later about his integrity as a union leader, Zanini said, "Let's get this straight. What I did before the labour movement and what I did when I got out, that's different. But when I was a business agent or union official or any part of a union, I didn't take one penny for one little deal — and I suspect and I know deals were being made — but I never made any deal and I never got any money."

Shaken by the visit, Zanini made every effort to persuade Volpe he had told the truth. Some weeks later, he asked an old gambling friend to help allay any misgivings Volpe might have. The two met Volpe one lunch-hour, the friend elaborating on Zanini's past, praising his character and emphasizing how Zanini was a man of his word. He had served his prison term like a model inmate, hadn't he? Occasionally, Volpe would grin, said Zanini, and then nod courteously. "'Listen,' he says to me, 'we were led to believe that you destroyed the Brandon Group.' Then he told me not to worry, that they had no bad intentions; so I filled him in on how people were trying to divide me and Charlie and how they done a good job of it. Say what you want about the man — Volpe was really concerned with the men and how the Italians were getting the shit kicked out of them."

Volpe's active interest in the fate of the residential unions was shared by a number of different groups. First there were the apartment builders, who suddenly saw their source of cheap, unorganized labour threatened by unions; then the uneasy alliance of the local Building Trades Council, its affiliates and what remained of the Brandon Group, and thirdly, there were different mobs trying to move in and carve an empire out of the spoils. Pushed around in the power grab were the immigrant workers and their unions. And so was Zanini, as he would tell nearly everyone. It was his theory that someone was trying to divide Charlie Irvine and himself by splitting the unions. The next move was to get him out of the union business entirely, he believed. This was achieved — through a promotion that left

Zanini virtually isolated from the workers, as a consultant and conciliator for the Labourers in the new local.

Despite the fact that his restaurant meeting with Volpe had ended amicably, there was another attempt to knock Zanini out of unions. Apparently, a union business agent had tried to hire a gunman who was in fact an acquaintance of Zanini's. "Watch out," the friend told him, "there are people out to set you up because of your activities with unions." Needless to say, the gunman refused the contract.

As a result of all this, Zanini's health began to fail. His condition he once described as *nevrastenico*, or neurasthenic — a state of feeling fragmented with only the body wanting to come together. At this point, he started to buy protection, paying two men to act as bodyguards whenever he had the extra cash. "Understand now," he explained years later, "when I was seen with these type of people there were no more phone calls or slashing of tires. But still, there was an uneasiness about it when I used to be with these fellows, always the two of them would say, 'Hey Bruno, what do you know?' That means, do you know any scores or tips on who's got cash stashed away and where? I'd say I didn't know anything. Well, then they'd say, 'How about driving us around, then?' So I used to drive the guys here and there, and word was getting around that I was involved with them. But I wasn't. I just needed protection. The thing is, when you're hanging around, if you travel with those type of people, people start to think you're part of that element. If you hang around long enough, you become like them, too, eh? What I did was just the odd favour for them. It's a choice, eh? You want to get your legs shot off or do you want to get killed, or do you want to be with these people once in a while, so you got some protection?"

How many enemies he had, and who they were, Zanini himself was not sure. But it did seem quite clear that some people wanted him out of circulation one way or another. The sad reality of it was that Zanini had become expendable. His brief and glorious moment in history had been organizing immigrant workers, and now this was done. His promotion in the new local of the Labourers appeared to be nothing more than a move to pension him off. After this, he had no more contact with the workers — nor was it necessary. New business agents taking his place showed a considerable lack of interest in policing the jobs and reporting workers' complaints. In fact this new local eventually disappeared.

For Zanini, the life of a consultant was not satisfying. But he remained in the job until the end of December 1963. His employment was abruptly ended following his arrest on a charge of theft. It was this incident that finally put him on ice. It was a puzzling turn of events since Zanini had now gone for fifteen years without arrests and, to all appearances, had left his criminal past far behind. Though his arrest was undoubtedly as much a surprise to his enemies as to himself, it effectively removed Zanini from the union business during a crucial five-year period.

The sequence of events leading to his conviction started late one night in December, when Zanini agreed to drive his two paid escorts to a doctor's house in Forest Hill, a wealthy part of Toronto. For some weeks, word had been about that this doctor kept a large amount of cash in the house, earned from an illegitimate trade with drugs and wayward girls. Zanini's companions decided to try their luck even though, at the last moment before they left Zanini's car, one of the men got nervous. He suspected it might be a trap set up by police. Several minutes later, while parked on a side street near the house, Zanini was arrested by a carload of plainclothes policemen. There was more questioning later at the police station. Zanini was disheartened when he caught sight of his two friends there.

"What have you got him here for?" said one of the men. "He's a good Samaritan. He drove us there."

"You shut up," said the sergeant. "You say that again, bastard, you get eight years."

"But he . . ."

"Shut up!"

"It was wrong, yeah," Zanini admitted as he told this story from his past. "But I was grasping at straws. I was so vulnerable then, with a sick wife and two small kids at home, no money and that's the way it was. Oh, it was a set-up all right. The cops were just waiting to see who'd they catch. Here they thought I was some kind of mastermind, and I didn't have two cents. You couldn't explain this to people. They figured I was worth $100,000 because I was a leader in the unions, that I was Jimmy Hoffa, they figured. Maybe I got a million put away. Christ! I had to get legal aid in the end. Well, if I was a crook and a mastermind, I would have a lot of money. I could have took those bribes, eh? I could have made deals with the subcontractors to get 20 or 30 percent of their business like some of these other business agents done. If this was true, that I was this and I was that, why, then, would I want to drive these guys in windbreakers on a score?"

At the time, Zanini was $4,000 in debt. He and his family lived in a $105-a-month apartment. Following his arrest for possession of burglary tools and housebreaking, he lost his $10,000 job with the Labourers, and until the trial, the only support he received was a $142 welfare cheque each month.

His defence lawyer spoke of him as a Moses leading his people out of the wilderness by triggering a royal commission on industrial safety. The Crown prosecutor argued the man was a master of criminal affairs. At the time of the trial, the incident was reported in the press:

> *Bruno Zanini, 43, of Dufferin Street, a former labour organizer among immigrant construction labourers,*

is charged with taking part in a break-in at a doctor's house where four 50-cent pieces were stolen. He pleads not guilty.

The evidence introduced by the police to demonstrate Zanini's alleged involvement in the break-in consisted of a wallet, left behind in the car by one of the two thieves. A mistrial occurred on the first hearing, but Zanini was convicted after a second trial in 1965.

It was an unfortunate incident for Zanini, who clearly had made an effort to stay away from this type of activity. He steadfastly maintained that he had no direct involvement in the break-in. This charge was eventually dropped. The second charge of possession or knowledge of burglary tools led to his conviction and a two-year sentence. Convinced he had suffered a miscarriage of justice, Zanini twice appealed his conviction. Only after ten months in a Toronto jail did he finally give up his efforts to reverse the conviction, and he spent another six months in a minimum-security prison in Joyceville. He was released in 1968.

The arrest, the trial, the appeals and the prison term succeeded in keeping Zanini out of union activities for nearly five years, all because a policeman had found a wallet in his car. There were people behind all this, he said. Big people, who didn't want him around any more.

During Zanini's absence, the remnants of the Brandon Group continued to lose members to the swelling ranks of non-union workers doing the majority of apartment construction in the city. In spite of the earlier organizing efforts, conditions for the workers by the mid-1960s were again worsening as wages continued to fall. Subcontractors were also hurt as prices fell in their trades, owing to the highly competitive market and the persistence of apartment builders in shopping bids openly and taking the lowest building estimate. It was an unhealthy situation that prompted this comment from one subcontractor: "The builders got no allegiance to anybody except the dollar." After all the organizing, all the strikes, and the sense that the workers had finally won the right to reasonable wages and working conditions, things had gone back to the way they'd been before Zanini had got involved in union organizing.

Futile attempt to save five Italians trapped in the Hogg's Hollow tunnel cave-in.
Photo: Toronto Sun

Nick DiLorenzo made a fortune as a concrete forming subcontractor in the apartment field during the 1960s.
Photo: Toronto Sun

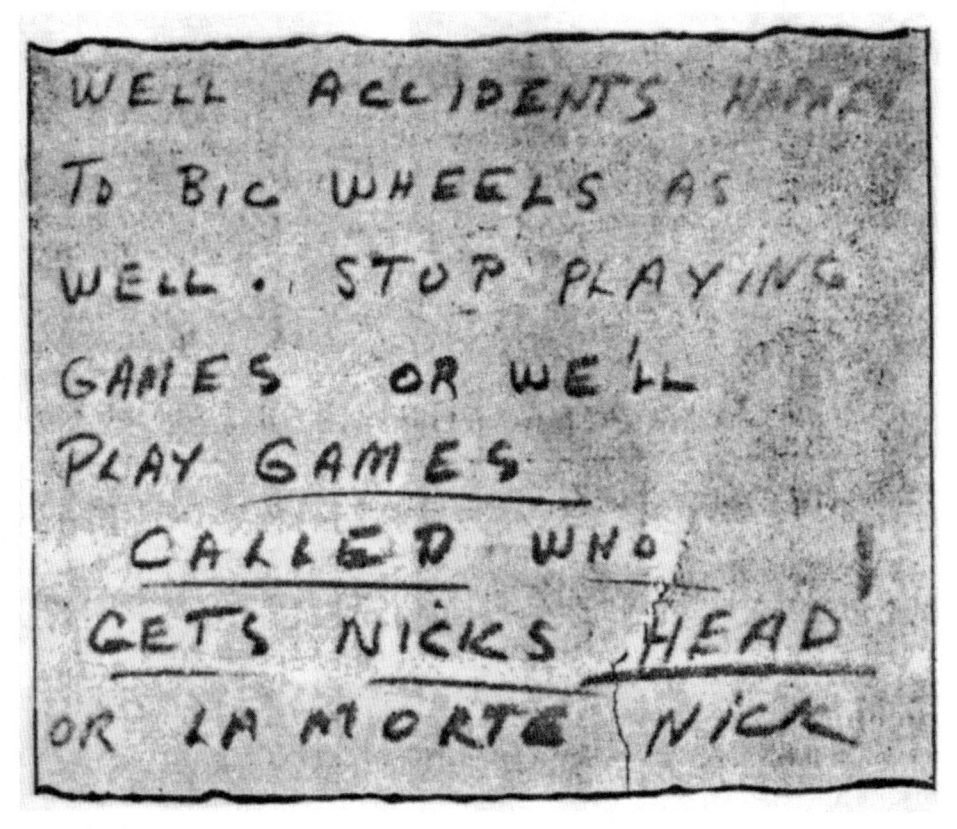

> WELL ACCIDENTS HAPPEN TO BIG WHEELS AS WELL.. STOP PLAYING GAMES OR WE'LL PLAY GAMES CALLED WHO GETS NICKS HEAD OR LA MORTE NICK

Part of a threatening note sent to Nick DiLorenzo.
Photo: Toronto Star

Paul Vope, a real estate businessman and self-described labour consultant.
Photo: **Ontario Government**

A controversial figure on the labour scene, Brunno Zanini organized a number of immigrant unions.
Photo: **Canadian Press**

Agostino Simone played a significant role as a business agent for housing workers.
Photo: **Toronto Star**

Architect Eric Arthur compared these Toronto houses of the 1950s to "strawberry boxes."
Photo: Maclean's

Immigrant strikers give Bruno Zanini a rousing welcome in the final days of the 1961 campaign.
Photo: Globe and Mail

John D'Alimonte, affectionately known as "Big John," helped organize a union for his employer, Nick DiLorenzo. Photo: Toronto Sun

Meyer Lansky, "The Little Man," reputed to be the head of organized crime in the U.S.

Union maverick Charles Irvine dominated the residential labour scene for nearly a decade.
Photo: Toronto Star

PART IV
The Gambling Connection

10
THE BAHAMAS ADVENTURE OF C. POWELL MORGAN

The syndicate continued to refine its methods for laundering money and investing it in legitimate enterprises. From its inception, the practice of washing money clean to disguise its true origin gave mobsters a growing competitive edge over their business rivals. It wasn't long before the mob began to experiment with a more sophisticated method of laundering money that had the desirable side effect of generating windfall profits at the same time. The best illustration of the new approach in the 1960s was a Toronto story, the collapse of Atlantic Acceptance Corporation and the role it played in providing money for the syndicate's lavish new gambling resort in the Bahamas.

The proliferation of new kinds of moneylending institutions offered new opportunities to mobsters to legitimize the loansharking business. Not only could trust companies, finance companies and insurance companies lend money legally but they could also raise money from legitimate investors anxious for a good return on their investments. Reputable investors' money could be mixed with mob money in some of these lending institutions, and when the money came out in the form of a loan it appeared legitimate. The further twist the mob gave to this scenario was to induce these institutions to invest in risky ventures that had no hope of success. In this manner, money in the financial institutions was siphoned off in loans to a money-losing company under syndicate control. If the lending institution were to run out of money because of loans that had gone sour and was about to default on its obligations, the syndicate got its cash out early, leaving the legitimate investors to swallow the losses.

One institution that moved into this moneylending field in a big way in the Sixties and illustrated this new approach to laundering and investing was Atlantic Acceptance. Atlantic was based in Toronto and Hamilton, and some of the same characters who played a role in syndicate financial activities in the Fifties were active in ventures with Atlantic in the Sixties. The beginnings of the story of Atlantic Acceptance and its Bahamas hotel project lie in the failure of the Cuba plans of the mob's financial wizard, Meyer Lansky. That roulette and slot machine spa had cost the Little Man millions in investments. The money-making machine that was a vital source of mob money had come to a sad end. In 1959, Lansky himself was forced to leave Cuba, a hurried and unscheduled departure that left him with three painful ulcers that required medical attention for years. He fled on the heels of the island's military dictator, Batista, boarding one of the last planes leaving Havana for Miami. His legacy to the natives: a seafront strip of gambling hotels and $17 million in cash, which just missed being shipped out and distributed to his partners in Switzerland. Just hours later, out of the hills of the Sierra Maestra came a little band of revolutionaries, some carrying their guns crosswise to chests that were pinned with religious medals. Some were on foot while others drove, entering Havana in cars as small groups gathered in the streets, waving, at times cheering. In a number of casinos, looters smashed slot machines; some shops were vandalized and every parking meter in the city was broken and emptied.

A week later, on January 7, 1959, the bearded leader of the Cuban guerrillas arrived in the capital, the streets this time thick with Cubans cheering him as he drove to the presidential palace, where he was embraced by President Prio Socarras's successor, President Manuel Urrutia Lleo. Someone in the crowd outside released a flock of white doves. The campaign to rid the island of Batista and his six-year military junta was over, and the casino halls fell silent.

Lansky did not accept this defeat easily. In fact, he used every political connection he could to try to rid the island of Fidel Castro. At one point he approached the U.S. Central Intelligence Agency, volunteering to finance and assist in an attempt to assassinate Castro. When this offer was refused, he became bitter and depressed, consoled temporarily by his long-time friend George Smathers, a Florida senator, who agreed to appeal directly to the Eisenhower administration to take some action. Some years later, Smathers was still at it, making every effort to persuade John F. Kennedy to destroy the Castro regime by an armed invasion.

Lansky always refused to elaborate on his brief but discreet role in international politics: "I'm not going to discuss my relationship with Castro. Now or ever. But you'll appreciate that I was opposed to him both from a personal point of view and also because of the danger to America if his regime got a stranglehold on the island. A number of people came to me with a number of ideas and of course I had my own suggestions to make."

While Lansky was rueful over his Cuban experience, it convinced him that the methods of operation of the syndicate had to change. His friendship with Batista, a political alignment essential to the establishment and operation of the island's gambling casinos, had been poorly disguised. In the end he had lost millions with little hope of recovery. He had underestimated the fragile nature of politics, so Lansky began to develop new approaches. The direction he favoured was the increased use of legitimate businesses and professionals to screen his operations and the vital movement of illicit funds acquired through various syndicate-related enterprises. Lansky had the cash flow; what he needed was more legitimate covers for his money so that it could finance apparently respectable enterprises without tainting them with any hint of mob involvement. This entailed the employment of professionals in the corporate/financial structure: lawyers, accountants, bankers, stock promoters and real estate investors. With this drapery to cover its activities, the mob became a success as a syndicate of businessmen and investors.

Gambling, of course, was a key factor, generating the enormous flow of cash profits to sustain legitimate ventures. When Lansky lost Cuba, he sorely needed a replacement. He chose the Bahamas. Just seventy miles off the coast of Florida, this string of islands, barren and thinly populated, was ruled by a small group of merchant-politicians who ran the British colony from Nassau, the capital, on New Providence Island. The most powerful branch of the government was the select nine-member Executive Council, which basically ran the affairs of the colony in a manner reminiscent of the Family Compact that had ruled Upper Canada more than a century earlier. Islanders believed government officials should give freely of their service without pay. Many were confident no government could pay what they would earn privately, so those who possessed the greatest wealth held public office.

The most dedicated government official was Sir Stafford Sands, minister of finance and tourism, whose previous endeavours to make the island prosperous had been less than spectacularly successful. Sands had the good fortune to make the acquaintance of a New York entrepreneur named Wallace Groves. A former Wall Street operator convicted of mail fraud in 1941, Groves envisioned a duty-free port in the Bahamas to attract industries seeking a tax-free haven. To accommodate this vision, Sir Stafford drafted a bit of legislation that permitted the sale in 1955 of 211 square miles of Grand Bahama Island to Groves, at $2.80 an acre. The development company, Grand Bahama Port Authority, got the cash to finance the scheme from two sources: a Wall Street brokerage and investment firm, and a British holding company.

But it was evident by 1960 that the project was faltering, reviving Sir Stafford's earlier belief that the only practical approach to stir the dormant economy of the island was to attract tourists, not industry. This line of reasoning was welcomed by a Toronto stock promoter whose interest in assembling land for a hotel and resort development on Grand Bahama eventually led to a series of long chats with Sir Stafford in 1960. Shortly after his arrival in Nassau, Louis Arthur Chesler, a Toronto broker dealing mainly in Canadian mining stock, persuaded the government to sell him more land, at prices comparable to the previous deal with Groves. The land owned by Groves and originally allotted for industry was rezoned as residential, permitting Groves to sell the land to future homeowners or build on it himself. In return, the Groves-controlled company agreed to build a first-class hotel with 200 rooms by December 1, 1963. The Grand Bahama Development Company Ltd. was then set up as a subsidiary of Grand Bahama Port Authority, which held a 50 percent interest. Other investors included a Canadian uranium mining company, a development firm called Seven Arts Co. Ltd. and financier Louis Chesler.

Born in Belleville, Ontario, and a graduate of the University of Toronto, Chesler had been active in Canadian mining deals, investing for a number of clients, on occasion working with Meyer Lansky. At one time, he was a partner in a Miami nightclub with Lansky associate and one-time Toronto resident John Pullman. But his main expertise was in stocks and more recently in land. Three of his developments in Florida had been successful. And now he was expanding into the Bahamas.

A financial news report made public the extent of the new company's involvement on the island. Some 89,000 acres of land with thirty miles of beach frontage had been acquired by Grand Bahama Development. An additional 115,000 acres was under option from the government for purchase on favourable terms. The company promised to stimulate the lagging economy by constructing resort hotels, private residences, clubs, marinas and golf courses as well as mounting a fully organized campaign to sell some of the land once developed. Money was raised from private investment companies and finance-lending institutions, particularly Atlantic Acceptance.

It was, however, the American entrepreneur Wallace Groves who remained the dominant figure in the Bahamian enterprise. His business ties to Nassau politicians proved that private enterprise and government could operate in mutual accord. At least four members of the government's Executive Council supplemented their income as paid consultants to Groves and his companies. To earn his $14,000 a year, the premier's son was asked to advise on marina construction. The dentist who operated Hobby Horse Hall, the Nassau racetrack, also received $5,000 a year as a consultant. The premier himself, though hotly denying payments as a consultant, did admit he had a road-building contract at one time with a Groves-controlled company. Corporate records indicated that Sir Stafford Sands received more than $1 million from a Groves-controlled company for his services.

Meanwhile pressure mounted to legalize gambling on the island. Promoting Groves's interests on the Executive Council was Sir Stafford Sands. As a Groves consultant, Sir Stafford was to receive some $50,000 a year for ten years or as long as the proposed casino was in operation.

Construction began in 1963 on the luxury hotel called the Lucayan Beach. Money was poured into an extravagant interior, its walls covered with gold paper and ceilings studded with crystal chandeliers. The hotel itself was Chesler's project, financed largely by an $11-million loan from Atlantic Acceptance to a construction company headed by Chesler. In return, Atlantic received as security a minority interest in the shares of the hotel. It was more like a gift than a loan, commented one accountant who assessed the transaction some years later.

The hotel was half built when its gambling licence was issued in April 1963. The casino monopoly was handed to Groves after the Executive Council had deliberated the issue in a secret session. The decision to exempt the operation from the penal code to permit gambling was made by this powerful group of merchant-politicians. As plans were made to convert the convention hall at the Lucayan Beach into a casino, members of the Council continued to receive their payments as consultants from Groves-controlled companies. One reluctant recipient was Sir Étienne Dupuch, whose newspaper had opposed gambling on the island. A letter from Dupuch to Sir Stafford acknowledging receipt of a consulting fee from one of the Groves-controlled companies indicated the Bahamian editor and publisher's stressful position: "You had talked with me briefly on this proposal but I did not realize that it had been finalized. I am sure you know that I am not happy about having casinos in the islands but since a casino has been established at Grand Bahama, I am concerned to see that a high standard is maintained. If you think that my services in this way might be helpful I shall do my best, but I want you to feel that it is an arrangement that can be terminated at any time by either side. I told you at the time that this arrangement must not in any way be considered as influencing my decision in the Senate or the policy of the *Tribune*. You agreed to this condition.

"I would have readily given my services free of charge but since you insist on paying what you say is the normal fee for this kind of service I shall deposit the money to a special account I have in the Royal Bank of Canada for helping children and for other charitable purposes."

Sir Étienne Dupuch's lack of enthusiasm for the casino operation was not shared by others residing in the island community. At least four members of the Executive Council, all of whom at one time or another acted for Groves as consultants, viewed criticism of the project as excessive and ill-founded. Gambling, they claimed, would boost the economy. Their prediction came true when a record 800,000 tourists arrived in Freeport during 1966. Still there were Bahamians who looked warily from their balconies and spacious verandas at the distant Lucayan Beach hotel. No one cared to believe this "offshore Las Vegas" had been infiltrated by the syndicate, but nearly everyone agreed there was a remote possibility that someday this might occur.

A balding, 61-year-old New Yorker named Frank Ritter became the casino's credit manager. He had been indicted three times in the U.S. for tax evasion and other offences. Max Courtney, alleged to be a New York bookmaker, was given the job of chief supervisor. Both men helped in setting up the casino operation, as did Dino Cellini, a Lansky crony. All three men, according to one insider, spent some months in England grooming a European staff of croupiers in the American game of craps before returning with their trainees to Grand Bahama. The finishing school cost the casino $250,000.

The doors opened. Tailor-dressed men in double-vented suits passed between the roulette wheels and blackjack tables, pausing, nodding quietly to a dealer, reaching into pockets full of $100 chips while the roll and click of slot machines turned up lemons and plums. After the last gambler had departed, the boxes were taken from each table and carried into the counting room. There were three sets of keys to the boxes, but none were used in the absence of either Cellini or his associate, George Sadlo.

The imperative presence of these two men, as described by one witness, probably explains exactly how Lansky protected his interest in the offshore gambling spa. If Sadlo was performing the same duty as one casino consultant described to the Kefauver Committee in 1950, a percentage of the take was set aside every night for a courier run to one of the syndicate's banking deposits. But any suggestion to the Bahamian police that skimming profits was part of the casino operation at the Lucayan Beach drew bitter rebukes and denials. Access to all the casino operations, including the counting house and records, had been given to two security officers, hired on the recommendation of the island police force. In addition, the company's books were audited by the esteemed firm of Peat Marwick Mitchell & Company.

Soon after the casino operation got underway in 1964, a new bank opened in Nassau called the Bank of World Commerce. John Pullman joined a number of known Lansky associates in this enterprise, becoming a director, and later president. The opening of a bank on the island with ties to the syndicate would relieve the pressure on courier runs to Europe, where syndicate gambling profits were handled almost exclusively by the International Credit Bank of Switzerland. This bank also opened a branch office in the Bahamas, which facilitated the movement of funds earmarked for investment into legitimate enterprises.

Bank manager Tibor Rosenbaum had already displayed a rare form of banking genius, attracting a number of moneyed clients seeking a tax-free shelter for their millions, including Lansky, who kept his own account under the code name of "Bear." Money raised by Jewish charities was also deposited in Rosenbaum's deep vaults in Geneva, beyond the gold and marble entrance. On one occasion, tens of thousands of dollars raised by Edmond de Rothschild from Jewish patriots around the world found its way into Rosenbaum's bank, where it was used to shore up some of Rosenbaum's collapsing property deals. There was a scandal, of course, when Israeli officials and Rothschild learned some years later that the money held in trust had been transferred to the Rosenbaum bank in a secret deal. However, in the mid-1960s there was no reason to suspect any illicit dealings, especially among Bahamian bankers whose profession was regarded with proper respect by the islanders.

Rosenbaum's branch office in Nassau was set up in time to absorb the expected millions once a new casino was established on a second site, Paradise Island. An American firm called the Mary Carter Paint Company had already purchased 1,300 acres and developed a subdivision in the Bahamas. Mary Carter Paint then invested with Groves in a scheme to build a casino-hotel on Paradise Island, owned by an eccentric millionaire, Huntington Hartford. When Sir Stafford Sands filed for an exemption from the penal code to permit gambling there in 1965, he met with success that had eluded Hartford, whose repeated requests to open a casino had been denied. Within the next two years, a bridge from Nassau to the island was built and financing for the hotel was provided by a consortium of interests, reputedly including funds from Rosenbaum's International Credit Bank, Edmond de Rothschild, Bernie Cornfeld of the Investors Overseas Service and Major Louis Mortimer Bloomfield, once a legal partner of Lazarus Phillips, who on occasion represented Bronfman interests in Canadian land deals.

The Lucayan Beach hotel was the first to open, and it was not the success it was expected to be. After four months in operation, it reported heavy losses. The cause was hotel mismanagement. The staff remained indifferent to complaints of poor service;

some wore soiled uniforms; others pilfered items they found while cleaning guests' rooms.

The question now being asked was how Atlantic had gotten mixed up in such a mess. The company's apparent prudence and skill in handling other people's money in speculative investments had made it one of the fastest-growing institutions in Canadian history. Its expansion was due largely to the efforts of a relatively new but highly successful private New York investment firm, Lambert and Company, which bought the finance company in 1960. Jean Lambert, once a son-in-law of Sam Bronfman, had received $1 million from the Bronfman family as an investment in his firm. Although the Lambert–Bronfman marriage ended, Bronfman money remained in the company. The spectacular growth of Atlantic Acceptance in the years following the Lambert purchase was the result of the firm's ability to attract as investors in its notes and debentures a number of prestigious U.S. investors such as the United States Steel Fund and the Carnegie Foundation Pension Fund, Morgan Guaranty Trust Company, the Ford Foundation, Princeton University and others. On Wall Street, Kuhn, Loeb and Co., one of the most reputable U.S. investment banking houses, placed more than $20 million in Atlantic securities with investment institutions.

Atlantic Acceptance was run by its president, C. Powell Morgan. The company was in constant need of fresh transfusions of capital, and it depended on raising funds by selling common stock and borrowing from the market. It did not have the large credit line with banks that was customary for U.S. finance companies. The expansion-minded Canadian firm, whose paper sales rocketed from $24 million to $176 million in three years, usually made loans primarily to individuals and small businesses.

It was through some of Atlantic's subsidiaries that loans were made to a number of companies, which in turn advanced some of the money to the Lucayan Beach hotel and its resort complex.

Louis Chesler, the promoter of the hotel, was an associate of one of the small group of shareholders who controlled Atlantic. One accountant claimed the loans were nothing more than gifts, as he attempted to trace the source of money used to finance the construction of the Lucayan Beach project. In total, Louis Chesler received almost $11 million from Atlantic to build the resort hotel.

This large outflow of money to the Lucayan Beach project tied up a lot of Atlantic Acceptance's money. Financial experts nearly all agreed it was this unsound lending that triggered the company's inability to pay maturing notes for investors on June 15, 1965. Shortly after 5 o'clock the day before, a cheque for the required $5 million in payments was refused by banking officials. The company was then officially in default.

The sudden collapse of Atlantic Acceptance stunned the financial world. Newspapers called it one of the biggest speculative crashes in history. Said one bankruptcy trustee: "Atlantic is probably the worst blow the free enterprise system in Canada has suffered in many years. It perhaps could not have been prevented, because it is next to impossible to recognize easily a criminal conspiracy when the partners have the roles that they did in the Atlantic situation. A small group of people made a monkey out of a very large segment of the financial community."

Most of Atlantic's financial troubles arose from its subsidiary companies, which gave loans to a number of dubious promoters with all sorts of dubious products. Hundreds of thousands of dollars were advanced to a used-car salesman whose credit rating, as one reporter put it, "would have had them rolling in the aisles at a bank managers' convention." Money was also lent to Racan Photo-Copy Corp. Ltd., whose copier had never worked. In return for the $11 million invested in the Lucayan Beach hotel, all Atlantic got was a minority interest in the shares of the hotel, not a mortgage on the building that would have protected its investment.

Investors saw further evidence of Atlantic's deterioration the same day in 1965 when forty-one New York brokerage houses received orders on the letterhead of a non-existent Bahamian bank, along with phony certified cheques, to purchase shares in a number of small companies including Racan. The apparent purpose of buying shares was to inflate the price of the stock of a company whose product didn't work anyway. Toronto lawyer Sam Ciglen, who had acted at times for a number of subsidiaries of Principal Investments (including Food Chain Properties, later a borrower from Lansky courier Pullman) now turned up in the Atlantic story as a director of Anglo-Overseas Capital Corp. Ltd., a Bahamas-based company that was said to control Racan. Like the money that went to the Lucayan Beach, the money that went to Racan was lost to Atlantic.

The two men who audited the accounts of the Atlantic subsidiaries making these dubious loans, which lost the firm millions of dollars, were later expelled by the Institute of Chartered Accountants of Ontario and sentenced to two-year terms in penitentiary for conspiracy to defraud an Atlantic subsidiary. In addition, poor judgment and bad investments made by Atlantic subsidiaries had allowed certain ventures to receive loans that turned out to be gifts, never paid back to Atlantic. Chesler's loan for construction of the Lucayan Beach hotel was an example of Atlantic funds being funnelled into a project in a way that offered the firm little hope of getting its money back.

Estimates of losses for investors in Atlantic Acceptance's crash ran from $50 million to $75 million. Some investors claimed they had been misled by their illustrious institutional partners or by Canadian banks. Others blamed Atlantic directors and auditors. And many were convinced they were victimized by fraud. The government agency with responsibility to investigate mismanagement of securities in Ontario, the Ontario Securities Commission, was removed from the case. Instead, the government appointed one man to inquire into the company's failure, Chief Justice Samuel Hughes. His assistant was a lawyer from London, Ontario, Albert Shepherd.

Unfortunately one of the key witnesses scheduled to testify — the senior partner of Atlantic's auditing firm, Deloitte, Plender and Co. — died after his plane blew up in mid-air between Vancouver and Whitehorse. The Hughes inquiry was also hampered somewhat in the early stages by the death of a second key witness, Atlantic president C. Powell Morgan, who succumbed to leukemia in 1966. After four years' work the Hughes inquiry produced a report. Several chapters were devoted to Morgan under the title "The Guilty Knowledge of C.P. Morgan." Wrote the judge, "Morgan and Morgan alone drove Atlantic forward to catastrophe and like all well-known swindlers of history, he did so with a fatalistic and cynical disregard of those principles of fair and honest dealing which have been generally accepted and adhered to for generations in both the civilized and the savage world."

The Atlantic inquiry report's references to Morgan were uniformly unflattering. Throughout his denigration of the dead man, Hughes failed to place much emphasis on the fact that Morgan's success was due largely to enormous investments placed with his company by a number of U.S. blue-chip institutions who were initially attracted to the Canadian company by the Lambert firm. However the report concluded: "It is clear that the Lambert partners were deeply and genuinely involved in the fortunes of Atlantic Acceptance."

Some of the money raised by Atlantic from investors was apparently mingled with money from less reputable sources to wash it clean, then siphoned away through money-losing ventures or projects that had avoided high interest on loans. How this was done was not always clear in every case. C. Powell Morgan took this knowledge to his grave. But it was the company's ill-starred adventures with the Lucayan Beach resort complex that toppled the empire. One witness testified that he once told Morgan, "They're stealing you blind."

So the entrepreneurs of Grand Bahama had not only managed to buy land cheaply but had built the resort development at little or no cost or risk to themselves, largely through money obtained from Atlantic Acceptance. It was a very sweet deal.

By the mid-1960s, there were those on the islands of the Bahamas who had come to believe that the Lucayan Beach hotel and its casino had been an error in taste and political judgment. The man they blamed was Sir Stafford Sands, named in a 1966 news report by two Wall Street journalists about the politicking that had led to the granting of a gambling permit to Wallace Groves. A year later, Sir Stafford told a royal commission convened by a newly elected Progressive Liberal government that he had once been approached by Meyer Lansky, whose offer of $2 million for a permit had been refused. Soon after his testimony, Sands made a hurried departure, leaving behind his Nassau estate, "Waterloo," with its private lake, and an island community reeling from the disclosures of how gambling came to the Bahamas.

This shakeup and the political roasting of Sands and the merchant-politicians served Lansky's new plan to merchandise gambling as a source of revenue beneficial to governments, not just private individuals, as had been the custom. The defeat of the United Bahamian party, which had ruled the islands for some years, was half expected by the Little Man, who wisely secured his holdings there, it was believed, through a public company among whose shareholders was U.S. crime-buster Thomas Dewey. The casino on Paradise Island would now operate without the shadow of private entrepreneurs like Chesler and Groves, whose pasts were open to scrutiny.

Wallace Groves sold his interest in the new casino partly constructed on Paradise Island and left. The public company owning controlling interest in the casino, Mary Carter Paint, changed its corporate name to Resorts International, broke its agreement to hire casino managers from the Lucayan Beach hotel and immediately placed on staff two specialists in organized crime, a former attorney with the U.S. justice department and a former police chief, to screen applicants for jobs at the roulette tables. These measures were taken by company owner James Crosby, whose inner fears were expressed in this public statement: "I don't want it on my headstone that I went to bed with the Mafia." But when the casino opened in 1968, one of the new club managers was Eddy Cellini, the brother of Dino Cellini, who was well acquainted with Lansky and his business procedures.

As opposition leader, Lynden Pindling had publicly denounced the Bahamian government's practice of awarding government contracts to businesses run or owned by its own ministers. But he made it clear that if his party came to power, as it did in 1967, he would not carry his campaign of eliminating conflict of interest so far as to shut down the casinos altogether. Pindling kept his word. Casinos continued to operate, paying taxes to the government that provided sorely needed revenue for the islands' administration. Only native Bahamians were forbidden to gamble there — a regulation Pindling insisted upon.

Meanwhile, several hundred miles away on the island of Haiti, shipments of gambling equipment, dice tables with built-in electronic devices and roulette wheels began to arrive in 1968, coinciding with the upsurge in the political fortunes of the country's dictator, Dr. Francois Duvalier. Following the election of U.S. president Richard Nixon, a change in American foreign policy reversed a decision to withhold aid to this military strongman, who relied on revenue from legalized voodoo. A U.S. government official, Nelson Rockefeller, was flown into the country, where he stood smiling for a photographer with "Papa Doc," whose distaste for Communism had won him a fresh infusion of American dollars to aid the economy and the military. This buoyed the image of Haiti, which had been shunned by tourists for years.

During an earlier lapse in foreign policy under President Lyndon Johnson, a $2.6-million loan from the Inter-American Development Bank had been made available to this Caribbean dictator, self-proclaimed president for life. Influential in this advancement of funds was Florida senator George Smathers, whose wide circle of friends included both Lansky and Nixon.

The Haiti casino, which had remained almost idle since 1958, when the Cleveland syndicate and Moe Dalitz took over its operation, was a sore point with Lansky. Sporadic raids by mountain guerrillas had made the island ever less popular with tourists in pursuit of peace and rest. Adding to the island's bizarre history was an invasion financed by members of the syndicate during John F. Kennedy's presidency in an abortive attempt to replace Papa Doc with a puppet leader willing to conform to American policy.

A variety of promoters had tried to operate the casino despite the political uncertainty. One Canadian group was so optimistic that a chartered plane service was organized to fly directly to Port-au-Prince. This brief foray into the tourist business came to an abrupt end after Lansky arrived in Toronto, counselling the promoters on the prematurity of their scheme.

Elsewhere, the former entrepreneur of Grand Bahama Development, Louis Chesler, became the new owner of a hotel on the lush island of Jamaica. Efforts to legalize gambling were reportedly in progress. In the U.S. Virgin Islands, a Hilton hotel had been constructed with a convention hall the size of a casino. Land there had been bought by Allen Dorfman, an investor for Jimmy Hoffa and the Teamsters' union.

Haiti's Casino International opened in 1969. American travel writers filed in and out of its doors, invited to inspect the splendour of the gambling hall and the beauty and stability of the island. The revitalized casino apparently had its most profitable season in a decade that year. This precipitated a boom in the price of real estate along Haiti's shoreline, as a land development company bought and sold choice waterfront lots to a number of Americans.

The proliferation of casinos in the West Indies boosted the income of the syndicate immeasurably, adding untold millions that were refinanced into legitimate businesses, securing their foothold in a wide variety of enterprises, which now included banks and brokerage houses, insurance firms and lending institutions. It was precisely their ability to provide financing and lots of it that widened the gap between the syndicate and its more conventional business competitors, who paid high interest rates on the money they needed in their business. And it was Meyer Lansky's success in keeping the flow of profits coming from gambling through the 1960s that pressured the mob not to continue its endeavours to find safe havens for its laundered money. As the story of the Bahamas and its gambling resorts shows, the world of mob financing had become far more sophisticated by the 1960s. Atlantic was a complex manoeuvre, one that involved many financial operators from many parts of the world. Atlantic was Hamilton- and Toronto-based, but the people who used it were from many corners of the financial world. The loan and trust company business in Ontario, like the land development business, was poorly regulated and offered many opportunities; sophisticated operators were quick to take advantage of the possibilities for fraud.

PART V
The Union Business

11

THE BARGAIN BUILDERS

The unprecedented growth of Toronto in the late Sixties continued to puzzle real estate analysts, who could never make up their minds why this city had such an easy time of becoming the third-fastest-expanding centre in the world. There seemed to be an unlimited supply of money to finance real estate development as tower after glittering tower rose out of ground.

Since the unfettered land boom of the 1950s with its suburban sprawl, the government had taken measures to ensure more orderly growth. For this reason, politics began to play an increasingly significant role in the land development business. Government-appointed agencies were to determine how and where the land would be used and developed. Decisions affecting all developers were made at two government levels: the province made all the big decisions dictating routes for water and sewer facilities and expressways that would service the properties, while local town governments or municipalities made the small decisions. But bureaucracy was slow-moving, costing developers money through delays in zoning changes and building approvals. To speed up the whole operation, the province set out in 1969 to redraw the map of Ontario and create regional governments. Appointed to oversee this was the lanky, handsome Darcy McKeough, minister for municipal affairs and a wholesale plumbing and heating supplier in private life, who made his own first major investment in land in 1968. A number of other politicians, including several cabinet ministers, were also to put money in land for speculation or investment during these boom years.

It was these same cabinet ministers acting as policymakers who gave the final decision on appeals by developers, residents or city governments attacking or defending new development proposals, if the decision made by the provincially appointed Ontario Municipal Board was not satisfactory. The undisputed final power lay in the provincial cabinet — in the late Sixties, in the hands of a Conservative government that had ruled the province for nearly two decades.

It was precisely the province's political stability, as well as the good climate, that attracted such enormous investment to Ontario and Toronto. The greatest and most rapid change was in Toronto's residential areas, where high-rise villages began to dominate neighbourhoods. But as the city projects grew in size, so too did the controversy among Toronto politicians; people were divided between reformers and developers, those who saw unlimited growth as destructive and those who claimed it was productive.

The debate was often sparked by groups of local residents who began to complain about apartment towers and the inferior quality of life they associated with high-rise living. On the other hand, high-rise builders argued that there was a need for alternate housing. The price of real estate and city homes had gone far beyond the reach of many young couples, who would rent and save until they had enough money for a down payment on a house. Joining them were a growing number of young professionals who also needed temporary accommodation.

In 1967 the first 32-storey apartment in St. James Town was completed and opened. Fifteen more towers were planned. The developing company, Howard Investments, became a member of a newly formed group representing the interests of residential high-rise developers, called the Apartment Developers Association. The membership was surprisingly small considering the activity in this sector. Among the most active were Cadillac, Meridian, Greenwin, Belmont, Heathcliffe Developments Limited and Del Zotto Enterprises Ltd., a relatively new competitor in the league.

Building apartments on such a grand scale meant enormous expenditures on both materials and labour. In order to maximize profits and to limit increases in building costs, apartment developers began to experiment with new building techniques that required less-skilled labour and used cheaper materials. This approach to the industry prompted one insider to quip: "They ought to call it the Bargain Builders Association."

The apartment developers did manage to cut costs on materials by discarding costly, time-consuming crafts. One trade that fell victim to the developers' changing tastes was plastering. Replacing it was an interior building system called drywall.

Until the mid-1960s, the interior construction of buildings was done almost exclusively by plasterers, who applied wet plaster to metal frames or laths erected by tradesmen known as lathers. But the cost of labour in the plastering trade was extraordinarily high. In order to avoid using this time-consuming and costly craft apartment builders began to favour the use of gypsum board lath, which was cheaper, cleaner, easier and faster to apply. Here wet plaster was placed between thick sheets of paper and dried to make a board, then attached to wall units.

As before, the developers shopped for bids, accepting only the lowest price. It was easy money for those who knew how to cut corners. Eager to make a quick fortune, the residential lathing business was suddenly flooded with new subcontractors bidding irrationally for the projects. The sudden increase in competition upset a number of long-established firms, who tried to end the pricing warfare by agreeing to set up a bid ring, allotting jobs among themselves. The outgrowth of this bid ring was a price-fixing combine established some years later when these subcontractors began to take over commercial work.

Another new trade that helped keep the costs down was concrete forming. The extensive use of concrete for the shells of high-rise apartments created miniature empires for a handful of immigrant Italians familiar with the system used in postwar European construction. The invention of the flying form, a method of scaffolding that could be reused from floor to floor as the building progressed, greatly helped to improve efficiency. Its promoter, Nicola DiLorenzo, once a $35-a-week labourer, was soon to become the apartment developers' favourite in this field, low-balling his rivals to grab the enormous projects that in time netted him a $7-million fortune.

The residential concrete forming industry was crowded with DiLorenzo companies that employed hundreds of immigrant workers. Most of his labour was semi-skilled, newcomers who had barely stepped off the boat before they were turned into concrete forming teams. His competitors found DiLorenzo's appetite for power formidable. A former employee who later worked for a rival company gave this description of DiLorenzo's operation: "Well, Mr. DiLorenzo made a lot of money in the early stages of his career in the forming business . . . He had labour at, oh, unbelievably low rates — less than a dollar an hour in some cases. This was when there was a large number of immigrants coming into Canada and they would work at anything, any type of job. So that he was quite successful for three or four years.

"Well, then competitors started coming, people like Bianchini and some other people . . . and you get what you call 'Dutch auction' bidding. The builders were just having a field day, because when you submit a price it isn't done as you normally do on commercial work, where you submit a sealed tender and it is opened and the lower man gets the job. What you do is, there's about three rounds of negotiations to put in a price. Then the developer would show that to every other forming contractor in town and ask them if they could meet it . . . They just kept beating the price down."

Despite DiLorenzo's claim that he was the only man who knew how to do the job, there were other successful forming companies. One of his major rivals, at least in size, was a group of companies partly owned by another immigrant Italian, Aurelio Bianchini. Unable to operate profitably at DiLorenzo's prices, Bianchini moved into commercial construction where, through his expertise, he managed to dominate the industry for some years. However, Bianchini's costs were substantially higher, because commercial general contractors required him to use union labour from the commercial building trades locals for all his projects. This meant dealing with the five separate trades involved in the concrete forming process.

DiLorenzo kept the costs of manpower to a minimum in residential high-rise construction by discouraging any attempt by labour to unionize his men. His labour force alone represented nearly 60 percent of the concrete forming done in residential construction in Toronto. The plain fact was that he could not afford to pay his workers higher wages in spite of the number of projects that came his way. Pressed to outbid his rivals to retain control and provide steady work for his men, the cherub-faced DiLorenzo beat the prices in forming down so low that nobody — including himself — could make any money. In his discomfort, he lashed out at the growing number of forming companies, some now headed by former employees, accusing these new companies of trying to copy his technique and of trying to steal his jobs. To save his rapidly diminishing empire, DiLorenzo sought the aid of a private investigator, Norman Menezes. This thin, spidery man had a number of unofficial functions, and became actively engaged in trying to destroy other forming companies contracted for residential work. On one occasion, according to Menezes, DiLorenzo asked Menezes to damage a building under construction by a former employee, Kiriakos Vlahos, who had set up his own firm. When this didn't work, DiLorenzo contacted the subcontractor by phone. "He wanted a share of my company, 50 percent," Vlahos later testified. "I said I would give him one-third, provided he put some money into the company. He said he didn't have any. 'If you haven't got any money, forget about it,' I said. He was upset."

Nearly a year later, Vlahos received another call. This time it was from a woman. The name — Marianne — was familiar to Vlahos, who was aware of her friendship with DiLorenzo. On several occasions when he had worked for DiLorenzo, Vlahos had carried envelopes for his boss to the woman's apartment on Roehampton Avenue. Holding the envelope to the light once, he could see there was a cheque inside. After this, he inquired about her services and agreed to pay the $20 for each assignation. So he returned her call that week in February 1968 and made a date for Friday afternoon at 2: 00 p.m. When he arrived, the two went to the bedroom and got undressed. Then the phone rang and the woman answered, saying, "I'm busy right now." Minutes later as Vlahos was stretched out naked on the bed, the door flew open and Menezes's brother George and a friend rushed in with a flash camera, took pictures, then darted out again, handing the camera over to the private investigator waiting in the next apartment. A tape recorder hidden in the chesterfield by Wayne Rastorp, the head of Fact Finders Ltd., a private investigation agency where Menezes worked, was later recovered.

The photographs were hidden by Menezes's wife, who was concerned her children might see them. It was learned that DiLorenzo wanted the snapshots to be sent to Vlahos's wife if Vlahos didn't meet a payment of $3,000 or give up a half-interest in his business. Vlahos refused but the photos were never sent. The woman, Marianne Lundszien, was promised $5,000 for the extortion set-up, but she claimed she never received it.

Menezes continued to work full-time for DiLorenzo until his arrest in 1969 on two counts of threatening his boss. The charges were dropped when Menezes volunteered information that enabled police to lay eleven charges against DiLorenzo, including counselling Menezes to assault a journalist, a union organizer and a competitor. DiLorenzo was also charged with counselling Menezes to set fire to an Ottawa apartment building. Seven of the charges were withdrawn, and DiLorenzo was acquitted of the remaining four after a lengthy trial. But Menezes was one reason for the repeated failure of unions to organize DiLorenzo's men. In 1965 he posed as a labour official, questioning the workers about unions, noting down the names of those who wished to join. Days later, the men were discharged. The fear of dismissal soon outweighed the merits of unionism.

These company skirmishes and inter-union battles for control of the concrete forming trade left the big builders unscathed. When DiLorenzo later became party to a sweetheart contract, aiding union officials in the organization of his own men, the builders were already working on a new building system that would not only displace concrete forming but would give them direct control over this aspect of construction. The threat of increased wages, the escalating costs of materials and speculation-inflated costs of real estate hastened their decision to experiment with an alternative construction method called system building. Concrete wall and floor slabs were poured into multiple moulds at a factory, then transported and placed as completed units in high-rise towers. Making the units required the minimum of labour skills and fell under the jurisdiction of the lowest-paid organized trade, the Labourers.

The apartment developers involved in this scheme formed a company called Modular Precast Concrete Structures Ltd. in 1969. The firm was jointly owned by subsidiaries of Belmont, Cadillac, Greenwin, Heathcliffe, Meridian and Wates Ltd. of England, a firm experienced in this field. Prefabricated forms had been used in Europe and England in postwar construction. However, controversy developed over the method in England when one of the buildings erected by this system partially collapsed in 1968.

Although the system promised to save the developers untold amounts in labour costs, the whole venture ended prematurely. The prefab concept could not compete with the efficiency of on-site concrete pouring. And time, as always, was money.

For the builders, the period from about 1967 to 1972 was the peak of Toronto's postwar high-rise housing boom. Projects had progressively increased in scale, from small suburban houses and three-storey apartment buildings in the mid-1950s to large land assemblies on the outskirts of the city and high-rise buildings containing several hundred apartment units in the late 1960s. The larger the projects, the larger the land development companies required to finance and build them. By the late 1960s, the handful of major high-rise builders in Toronto were no longer faced with the same problems finding financing for their projects as had been the case a decade earlier. Still, they were just as concerned as they always had been about putting up their buildings as inexpensively and as quickly as they could. The introduction of the two major innovations of the Sixties — drywall as a substitute for plaster, and concrete forming as an alternative to steel construction of high buildings — greatly helped the builders keep costs down. And the lower the construction cost of a new apartment building, the greater the profit margin on the rents that the builder-developer would collect from his tenants.

The largest single cost component in the apartment construction business was not cement or drywall sheets or steel or any other building material. The largest item for the builders was labour, which amounted to 40 or 50 percent or more of the final cost of an apartment building. In the boom times, the builders' first concern was finding the men they needed to put up their buildings. But their overriding worry was how much they had to pay for that labour. The lower construction wages went in the residential field, the better the builders liked it.

Once again in the second half of the Sixties, the builders were faced with attempts by labour unions to organize the workers on their jobs. By far the most feared organizer was Charles Irvine, whose union had already been linked to a combine of plastering contractors that had effectively kept plastering prices high. It was later learned at a provincially appointed inquiry that both Irvine and business agent Ed Thompson took an active part in the formation and conduct of this combine. Companies not part of the association were unable to get union workers and were harassed by labour trouble. The association allocated the job to a contractor, and the chosen contractor was entitled to estimate his price at cost plus 30 percent, together with an extra profit known as a "kicker." A fund provided for the payment of wages to the men, who were pulled off jobs in order to harass non-conforming contractors. For this purpose, Thompson received large sums of money from the contractors that were unaccounted for.

This scheme kept the price of plastering so high that commercial builders began to switch to drywall. The apartment developers eventually made the same move. There were some unkind enough to suspect that Irvine had influence in the drywall business as well as in concrete forming, through his paternal relationship with yet another popular labour organizer active in both these areas.

As attempts to organize these two new trades on apartment projects began in earnest in 1968, the real battle was between Irvine and the developers. Again, it was Irvine's union organizer underlings who would cause him to fail by breaking away from his influence. Zanini and the Labourers had broken up Irvine's previous effort in the early Sixties; this time in the drywall field it would be another Italian organizer and another international union, the Lathers.

It didn't take long for the builders to find that they could live with the new union that was organized for the drywall trade. In concrete forming, however, there were four separate attempts to set up a union for the workers until finally an arrangement was arrived at. Once again, everybody's problem was Bruno Zanini. It took blackmailing, bombings, denunciations, sabotage, explosions, fires and finally the shooting of Bruno Zanini before a *modus vivendi* was reached in the concrete forming business.

12

GUS SIMONE, ORGANIZER

Drywall had been such a relatively insignificant trade in the Forties and Fifties that nobody paid much attention to it. This material was really quite inferior to plastering and had previously been used primarily for temporary wartime housing. Its growing acceptance and popularity, favoured at first by commercial builders and then by apartment developers, was largely due to its low cost and efficiency. The real savings for builders came in labour. The plastering trade by the mid-1960s had outpriced itself as a result of improper practices. Through illegal work stoppages in this key trade, the plasterers' international union representative, Charles Irvine, pushed wages to unprecedented levels; added to this was the occasional operation of a price-fixing combine among eleven plaster and lath contractors doing commercial and occasional residential work.

So the builders began to use drywall for their projects. It soon accounted for 80 percent of interior wall construction. Picking up the trend were scores of new subcontracting companies, mostly plastering and lath firms who moved easily into the drywall business. For the unions, however, the move was more difficult. Most of the workers hired to erect these drywall sheets were semi-skilled immigrants. Jurisdiction for these so-called boardmen fell between two unions, the Carpenters and the Lathers. As early as 1963, the Carpenters had organized the boardmen and signed a contract with commercial drywall contractors, doing mostly office towers, but the story in residential construction was quite different. Here the bulk of drywall work was done on a piecework basis. Boardmen were employed as independent contractors rather than employees of a company. As a result these men were left completely unprotected, stripped of any worker benefits such as injury compensation, insurance, pension and vacation pay. Companies hiring pieceworkers were not required to make income tax payments for these men since, by definition, they were not considered employees. Safety on the job sites was virtually non-existent. The abuses inherent in this system were perhaps the worst of any in construction.

When the apartment developers switched to using drywall, the scramble was on to organize the boardmen. Carpenters certified for this work began to move into housing but with little success. Next the Wood, Wire and Metal Lathers' International Union tried. The small and little-known trade had an unimpressive history of repeated failures in the residential field. On two occasions, in 1951 and 1961, they attempted to organize immigrants through residential affiliates. Now the Lathers would try again. Their eventual success was the result of the efforts of a remarkable Italian organizer named Agostino Simone. An immigrant from Pescara, he arrived in Canada in 1954, penniless and without any formal education. In appearance he was rotund, a good-humoured man with a penchant for whiskey. For a time he worked as a lather, erecting wall frames to which plaster was then applied. It was tedious work but in time he improved his skills, rising through the ranks from journeyman to foreman before he left for New York, returning to Toronto in 1965.

Simone tried to get work through the local Lathers' union. But the only jobs were in the apartment field, where there was no union. So he volunteered to become an organizer. In eight months, Simone signed up several large lathing firms, increasing wages from $2 to $2.85 an hour. It was an extraordinary success story for a youngish man barely able to speak English, but Simone was a man of unusual talents. He had a flexible approach to the industry. He didn't mind bending rules.

The officials from the Lathers' local representing workers in commercial construction were unpleasantly surprised by Simone's freewheeling approach. This led to arguments and squabbles between the two groups. Finally Washington stepped in and granted Simone a separate residential charter so that he could run his own local's affairs. By this time the only other residential union locals still active were Charles Irvine's Plasterers and a new independent Bricklayers' union, formed in 1965, when the men in the group originally organized in the early 1960s by Bruno Zanini voted to become a Canadian entity.

Unlike other residential locals, Simone's was not restricted to organizing housing. His charter allowed him to expand beyond the residential sector as a rival to the existing commercial local while offering cheaper union rates. The wage differential was substantial. Companies doing developers' commercial work using Simone's labour paid from 50 to 70 cents less per hour.

By undercutting wages, Simone had no trouble signing a contract in 1968 with the association of lathing subcontractors for their residential work. In the new contract Simone not only cut wages but also provided a longer work week and less vacation pay. He agreed to permit piecework contracts to continue since there was a shortage of boardmen and the lathers were still inexperienced. He also offered certain subcontractors the right to use his cheaper labour supply on developers' commercial construction projects. In all, it was such an attractive proposal that it had the desired effect of sewing up a residential union for lathers and drywallers, shutting out the competing Carpenters.

From this point on, Simone became the sole supplier of labour in this trade to apartment subcontractors. He was in an excellent position, as a business-oriented labour broker, to make money not only for the union but also for himself. This became apparent the night the employers in the new association threw a party at the Conroy hotel to celebrate the contract. Simone made it known that all those who planned to attend were to bring $1,000 with them. This canvassing confused a number of employers but nearly everyone who came felt the need to contribute something. The donations were placed in an open envelope by the entrance and by the end of the evening an estimated $11,000 or more had been collected. One owner of a small lathing firm said: "I knew the money was for Simone, but I didn't know why."

Simone's behaviour was considered unusual but then, people argued, the union was still in its infancy. But as the months passed, Simone's attitude hardened. The bookkeeper who looked after the union's records was fired and not replaced; Simone began to pull men off job sites for no apparent reason; certain companies were always sent the best workers, while their competitors faced a labour shortage or strikes. One man experiencing labour trouble soon learned how to deal peacefully with the union after he bought Simone a freezer. Another contractor who lost $18,000 on a job because of labour strife began to make payments to Simone amounting to $5,000 over some years. Seeing his competitors lavishing gifts on Simone, a subcontractor decided to offer the union leader 20 percent interest in his firm. When the copy of the partnership agreement was shown to Simone, he refused to sign it and tore it up, insisting "he wanted the shares hidden under the table." Then there was Antonio

Riolino, who helped pay for Simone's trip back home to Italy after the union had ordered the lathers off various jobs his company was doing. "What was the matter, we didn't know," said Riolino. When he tried to pay Simone by cheque, it was refused. Simone only wanted cash.

While the union received cash for labour peace at one end, the subcontractors were squeezed further by the big developers who continued to play the old game of shopping for bids among competing companies. Sometimes builders lied. If a subcontractor put in a bid, they would convince him someone else had submitted a lower bid. This forced the subcontractor to lower his own bid and operate with a very small profit just to keep working. Sometimes cash went the other way, as subcontractors tried to buy their projects through bribes. As one man said: "It was like a merry-go-round, and when the subcontractor looked around, he found he couldn't make a living."

In self-defence, a number of lathing subcontractors took measures to control the price warfare. They began to operate a bid depository in the late 1960s, arbitrarily allotting jobs to one another. The union was essential to the bid-rigging as muscle to enforce the rules. If a company became greedy, taking too many projects at lowball figures, the jobs would be picketed. The scheme worked well for a couple of years; Charles Irvine later explained how it operated to a provincially appointed inquiry.

The extent of Irvine's influence over Simone was difficult to determine; however on numerous occasions Simone sought his advice. All this ended in the summer of 1969 when Simone decided to go after the residential drywall workers alone. He did not share Irvine's sentiments about the revival of plaster and lath; he was convinced his own future lay elsewhere, with the potential offered by a union in the residential drywall trade.

Simone's star then began to rise. In 1970 his union got a boost when apartment developers began to move their operations into commercial projects, building office towers and mixed-use projects. Under a new contract signed with the Building Trades Council and its affiliated commercial union locals, these builders were allowed to use residential rather than commercial unions for office or industrial building if they owned the land being developed. This meant, of course, enormous savings in labour costs to the developers. In the drywall trade alone, companies saved up to 90 cents an hour per worker by using Simone's union instead of the commercial union.

The same year, a new association of drywall subcontractors was set up to deal with Simone apart from the lathing trade. The union was also used to regulate the industry for this association as companies continued to allot jobs among themselves. Simone still allowed the companies to use pieceworkers to supplement his own labour supply, which was running short as more and more projects came his way.

All this new-found work in commercial construction for Simone's union local began to take jobs away from its higher-paid sister local. Resenting Simone's invasion and his exploitive tactics, the commercial lathing local fought bitterly to keep commercial contractors and their work. But it was evident that these companies could not remain competitive when they had to pay higher wages than the firms contracted to do apartment developers' work. As a result, one of the largest lathing firms in the commercial field changed its name and signed a contract with Simone. The firm, which employed between 500 and 600 men, began now to use Simone's union members instead.

The next startling event was Washington's decision to merge both locals in 1971, with all workers earning the cheaper residential wage rates, and to grant Simone jurisdiction for all the drywall work done in the city. It was hard for some to believe that a commercial local could be destroyed so easily. Its members tried to stop the merger by applying for an injunction to the Ontario Supreme Court. They won and the merger was dropped. But Simone continued to benefit from the backing of the Washington boys who had thrown the drywall jurisdiction his way. It subsequently emerged that the decision came from a lathing boss who had no official authorization to make such a decision.

The drywall subcontractors' combine first ran into trouble when an outsider tried to seek new work. Cesidio Romanelli had worked exclusively as a residential drywall subcontractor for a development company run by the Del Zotto brothers. When he decided to expand his operations to bid on other developers' jobs, he found he had to bid so low there was hardly any profit. When he won a job, other subcontractors sometimes tried to buy him out. At first he refused to cooperate with the combine but some months later changed his mind and began to take an active role. In May 1971, Romanelli became the conduit for newly authorized monthly payments by the contractors of $1,000 each for the union. This led to a formalization of the arrangement. With this money Simone was to hire "inspectors" to pressure uncooperative or greedy firms that stepped out of line.

About the time Romanelli began to seek jobs independent of the Del Zotto interests, he made a number of new friends. Among these acquaintances was the amiable Paul Volpe, the sometime labour consultant and convicted extortionist. Volpe's friendship with Romanelli blossomed. In fact, when Romanelli incorporated in 1972 a new drywall company that did not include Del Zotto work, Volpe persuaded him to do the incorporation through Volpe's longtime friend and lawyer, John M. Rosen.

Volpe was also eagerly finding work for other friends. Romanelli hired a man named George Bagnato to scout for contracts for the new drywall firm from some of the larger developers, such as Cadillac. Romanelli also added another Volpe associate to his staff, Nat Luppino, who acted as a chauffeur. Luppino was also selling coin-operated laundry machines to apartments at the time.

Shortly after Simone learned through Romanelli of threats made against him by his former labour crony, Charles Irvine, he agreed to hire a bodyguard and so-called drywall organizer. The man Simone employed was a long-time friend of Volpe's, Joey Bagnato. Simone's fear of Irvine was easily aroused; when he betrayed Irvine in 1969 in connection with the Labourers' bid for the concrete formers, there had been a nasty exchange between the two, ending with a threat from Irvine. Since that time Simone had paralleled Irvine's earlier success in plastering with his own new trade, drywall, the very trade that knocked plastering out of the picture.

Bagnato became a constant companion of Simone's. He was a thin man, with an elfin face, a former lightweight boxing champion. Joey Bagnato's employment with the union lasted fifteen months. During this time, in 1971–72, the union's financial records showed a number of discrepancies. An accountant cited several examples of abuses. Business agents took out small personal loans; petty cash receipts were recorded on scraps of paper; there was no inspection of the books and no reporting of the local's finances to its membership. But the biggest shortage was the loss of some $15,000 to $50,000 in union dues and $12,000 to $100,000 in checkoffs (money deducted from paycheques by the subcontractors for the union).

At the same time there was trouble among the subcontractors. The bid ring wasn't operating smoothly. In the spring of 1972 one company, Acme Lathing, bid on two phases of a big project, winning both. The awarding of a second contract to the same company upset other contractors. This defiance of the combine rules led to a visit by Simone to the company owner, Naftali Kanner. Kanner later described the incident, saying the union leader had taken him to lunch and during the meal "had more than his share of alcohol. He talked as if I was his best friend and asked, 'Would you do me a favour?'" The favour was the withdrawal of the bid. Kanner said Simone had engaged in "double talk" and made references "about my family and kids. I don't know whether I would have taken it as a threat, because he was drunk."

The incident disturbed Kanner, who had previously enjoyed Simone's favour. The union boss, apparently, had always sent Acme his best men when the union got its agreement in 1968. Acme was one company allowed to perform commercial work for developers and to let piecework contracts. Now the company refused to withdraw its bid. It also picked up two more big jobs, from developers Meridian and Belmont.

Some months later, the company's premises were hit, the windows shattered by bullets and the offices by a dynamite blast. The damage was estimated at over $4,000. Some believed the violence was directed against Acme to prevent a merger of this company with two smaller firms. Others claimed it was the work of an extortionist. A lengthy police investigation turned up a number of suspects. Some years later, a judge at a provincially appointed inquiry decided that it was reasonable to infer that one person involved was Charles Yanover, an associate of Paul Volpe. The violence was a form of intimidation to prevent the merger; however, the attacks on the company may well have been the work of so-called inspectors, hired to discipline the combine. The union had failed to work as a regulator, in any case, as Acme continued to pick up jobs belonging to others in the combine, so there was some reason to suspect enforcers had been called in.

Even though this violence was minor and localized, it undoubtedly added to the impression that something peculiar was going on in the residential construction industry. People began to demand a royal commission to investigate the matter. Some weeks after the shootings and bombings Bagnato was dismissed by Simone's treasurer, who crouched behind a desk in the union office when he gave the boxer the news.

A reshuffle of subcontractor associations took place that summer of 1972. The lathing association and the drywall association merged to form a new employers' organization. The following year Simone negotiated a new collective agreement with the whole group, establishing his union as the most powerful bargaining agent for drywall workers in the city. The union certified to bargain for these workers, the Carpenters, fought to hang on. Joining them were members of the commercial lathers who refused to take a cut in wages. Both commercial locals accused Simone of raiding their membership with the intent of destroying a sister local.

At the root of all this dispute was the growing worry among commercial union locals that they too, like the Lathers' commercial local, could be scuttled out of existence. It happened in drywall. It was to happen in another new trade as well.

13

THE CONCRETE FORMING CAMPAIGN

The tale of another important new trade in the residential construction industry in the mid-1960s is a strange one, often bizarre.

As the price of materials rose, more and more apartment builders made the transition from costly brick and steel to the less expensive method of using poured concrete reinforced with steel rods for the exterior shells of their buildings. The power of concrete formers in labour–management relations derived from the fact that the shell so constructed was the first part of a project to get above ground; no other work could get done unless the formers were content. But the great appeal of forming was the saving to developers in labour costs. Immigrants and semiskilled workers could perform the work. Although the forming team used five separate skills, none required an accomplished craftsman. Rod-setters placed steel rods to reinforce the concrete; carpenters built the wooden forms for the concrete pour; crane operators hoisted the buckets of concrete into place, cement finishers completed the job and labourers cleaned up the site.

The problem was that the work spanned five unions, which all claimed jurisdiction for the trade. A forming contractor doing commercial work had to bargain with all five; however, in the high-rise apartment field, the workers were non-union. No union had been able to organize these men, hired mostly by Nick DiLorenzo and his fleet of companies, who dominated the business. A reputed union-buster, DiLorenzo discouraged unions repeatedly. By keeping wages down, he managed to hang onto his residential empire, doing most of the concrete forming work for major apartment developers.

To grasp the importance of concrete forming to international unions requires an appreciation of the amount of money generated by union dues and pension funds. Of all the construction trades forming had the largest number of workers; manpower was the essence, overriding skill and equipment. For both the builders and the unions, concrete forming was of paramount importance. The battle was drawn between builders, who wanted to keep costs down in labour, and unions, who fought to raise wages while fighting among themselves, often bitterly, to gain control of the labour force. In five short years, the residential concrete forming workers were shuttled from union to union, bought and sold in backroom deals. A secondary battle took place among the forming subcontractors, as competitors resorted to blackmail and sabotage to gain control of the industry. And at yet another level, the developers, keeping a watchful eye on the proceedings, managed finally to sign with a union that neither had the jurisdiction nor was certified to bargain for these men.

Nearly all the action took place in residential concrete forming where most of these men were employed by 1968. High-rise apartments were reaching a construction peak, as builders continued to press out their buildings at an increasing rate. Previous sporadic attempts to unionize concrete formers had been disasters. In an attempt to consolidate, the five international unions involved in forming agreed to create a council for the organizing drive in the residential trade. By the spring of 1968, contractors were already meeting with this Forming Council.

That same spring Bruno Zanini was released from prison. He tried unsuccessfully to get a job with a number of unions, offering himself as an organizer for forming workers. All the residential unions had been built through him and he believed concrete forming would be no exception. Still, nobody wanted a man with such a recent criminal past involved in the delicate business of grabbing one of the biggest trades in the construction industry.

For a time Zanini got a job singing at the Cooksville Inn. Then he campaigned for a local politician. It was through this contact that he eventually learned of a Lathers' union boss who shared his interest in unionizing the formers. The two met in the dimly lit Mona Lisa restaurant in the west end of the city. In the far corner, sitting with his back to the wall, was Gus Simone. It was their first encounter. Zanini later described the conversation. "We get introduced and he speaks broken English to me. 'I hear . . . you thousands of people down at the Exhibition. You know how to organize people. I think I better be straightah witha you,' — they talk that way, you know! He didn't speak good English but he was sharp, the little bugger. 'You know,' he says, 'when I see my people working hard, no organization.' 'What are you talking about?' I says. 'The concrete forming. There's no union there,' he says. 'Yeah, Mr. Simone, but I hear the contractors already got something going with the commercial unions and a forming council. They haven't got the men yet, though,' I says. 'Anyway, Mr. Simone, it isn't your jurisdiction. You're a lather. You got nothing to do with these trades.' 'Never mind,' he says to me. 'You organize these people and I buy you a Cadillac.' 'Forget the Cadillac!' I says. 'I'd be happy with a $500 car. I just come home and nobody give me a job.'"

Simone's attempt to organize men into a union totally unrelated to his trade sounded peculiar to Zanini, but he took the job. It was nonetheless an ill-disguised raid on the jurisdictional claims of other unions — and not just one, but five at that. Not only did Simone have no legitimate claim to organizing these men, he was also willing to swim upstream against all odds, to grab the men before the Forming Council made any inroads. In effect, he was challenging the system of labour union jurisdiction and regulation set down by Washington.

It was a bold move for a labour greenhorn who had entered union politicking only two years ago. But Simone had the optimism of an entrepreneur and little regard for ethics. Clearly Zanini, despite his jail record, was the one man who could organize these workers. Zanini the organizer was an old tried-and-true formula, used first by Irvine and then the Labourers. Why not by Gus Simone?

The arrangement, of course, did not give Zanini any official status with the union. He was a freelance organizer with the sole function of getting the men to sign into Simone's union. Everything was left to Simone. The biggest hurdle was creating a legal vehicle to bring the men into a division of the Lathers. This was set up by a lawyer in concert with Canadian law, unrelated to the rules from Washington and to usual labour policy.

Once the legal machinery was set up, the next step was to induce forming contractors dealing with the Forming Council to recognize this residential union instead. Simone's biggest drawing card was his plan to set up forming as a single trade, eliminating the five unions by simply reclassifying the men into categories commensurate with skills. Another attractive feature of the contract he proposed to the subcontractors was its five-year no-strike guarantee. It was an extraordinarily long agreement that promised to freeze workers' wages for an unheard-of length of time. While Simone met with contractors at one end of the deal, Zanini spent his time scurrying around the job sites, calling on workers he'd helped back in 1960 and 1961. Most of these men were now foremen; their key positions made it easier for them to organize, as they spread the word among the work gangs that a new union was starting up under Zanini.

Simone's method of gaining voluntary union recognition from contractors apparently did not vary from his earlier success with lathing companies. He simply made his offer so attractive to employers that few of them could afford to say no. His low wage rates undercut the commercial locals, offering companies substantial savings. In fact, the deal Simone proposed to the forming subcontractors' association was so sweet that its president gratefully offered to help Simone organize his own men by handing over a list of employees from his company and several others. This of course encouraged workers to sign with the union; they would have to be concerned about keeping their jobs if they didn't. It was a strange reversal of usual employer policy.

Certainly, Simone offered a sweetheart deal. Strictly speaking, it was not the way a union should be organized; however, Zanini didn't complain. With the cooperation of employers, his job was made much easier. Still the residential concrete forming trade was hard to crack. No union had ever been successful with these formers. Irvine had tried once. So too had the Carpenters. And now here was Simone, offering something no one else had: a five-year contract and a union that promised to keep wage rates low by eliminating the five trades and reorganizing the men into lower-paid categories.

At first, Zanini refused payment for his work. As he told Simone, "Look, I don't want any money from you. Let me show you what I can do. I'll go out there and you'll see." But the next time Simone offered him money, Zanini accepted. The pay was cash: $200, with half coming from Simone and the remainder from Charles Irvine. The news of Irvine's financial involvement came as a surprise to Zanini. He had not seen Irvine since the day they had met in Volpe's car. Questioning Simone about Irvine's role, Zanini was told the lathing boss felt the campaign would fail without Irvine's cooperation. Irvine still had control through his plastering union over the cement finishers, one of the trades active with the Forming Council.

Irvine's link with Simone and this rival campaign was financial. There is some reason to think he had his own designs on forming once the men were organized. The immediate problem was to gather the men up into a union — any union. From there, he could at least negotiate from strength, if not manipulate all the workers into his plastering union. He later admitted giving money to Simone in order to gain control of a key trade, with the hope of forcing developers into a trade-off: a return to the use of plaster instead of drywall in their apartments.

Another labour boss connected officially with the Forming Council, Frank Giles of the International Union of Operating Engineers, threw his hat in with Simone. This crane operators' union was by far the most important trade in forming, as no work could proceed without the hoisters of concrete who did the actual pouring. But Giles's involvement with Simone at the union was considerably more complicated. In fact, Giles soon became the chief negotiator for the contract, sewing it up for Simone. The truth is that without Giles, the union could easily have been a failure.

The only obstacle that snagged the campaign was the reluctance to sign of the largest forming contractor in apartments, Nicola DiLorenzo. DiLorenzo loathed unions; certainly he felt he could not afford to have his men organized. He had cornered the apartment developers' market through low bids, and it was only by hiring cheap labour that he could float his empire from project to project. He had employed a private detective to discourage men wishing to join unions. The rest of the contractors refused to sign the proposed contract unless DiLorenzo did so too.

Simone approached DiLorenzo on several occasions. The only common ground between the two was the belief that concrete forming should be organized as a single trade. But DiLorenzo refused to be persuaded. Meanwhile, pressure began to mount as word leaked out to the rival Forming Council of the campaign by Simone and Zanini to steal their workers. Zanini wanted to call a meeting and sign the men up before it was too late. He badgered Simone daily. "'Come on, Gus,' I says. 'Are you a man or a mouse?' You know, he always fancied he looked like Al Capone. 'But,' I says, 'you don't look like Capone. You look like Frank Nitti, the guy that gives the orders,' Boom! I'd slap him on the back and he'd laugh. He got a kick out of that. And every Thursday night, when *The Untouchables* was on, he'd invite me over to his house and we'd watch it. Ooh, you shoulda seen the drive he got out of that!"

After a number of heated discussions with Simone, the contractor finally had a change of heart. If his men were going to be organized, it may as well be into a union of his own choosing. Besides, wages would be frozen for five years once the contract was signed. So he instructed his foreman to go and make him a union. Appointed to this task was John D'Alimonte, a beefy character who filled the door frame whenever he entered a room. D'Alimonte's first job was to sign up all the crane operators. Said the blunt-spoken Italian some years later: "I told them, 'You'll have to join the union or I'll have to let you go.'" That organizing campaign took half a day. The rest of the workers were signed up a few days later.

With the majority of residential concrete formers mopped up into a division of the Lathers' union, Simone felt the time was ripe to finalize the contract. He called a meeting of all the subcontractors at a hotel. Dictating the terms of the agreement, he left the crowd with the impression that those who refused to sign would have their jobs stopped. Men would be pulled off their projects. Saying this, Simone nodded toward Zanini, who recalled the incident this way: "It was right there, they left me as a tough guy. Made it look to the contractors that I represented the Organization, sort of left the implication that I was the guy with the muscle. Either sign, or we got Zanini here with the mob. So anyways everyone was a little frightened about me. I played the part in a half-assed way, not realizing that I was being taken, being used. Listen, I could play the real part too if I really wanted to. But I felt it wasn't needed. You didn't have to resort to this strong-arm stuff. But I guess Frank Giles and Gus just wanted to make sure the thing was wrapped up."

And so with Zanini grinning and nodding in the corner, as though he were the enforcer — a part he had in fact played in 1960 and 1961, when he was instructed to pull workers indiscriminately off projects —everyone signed. There were only a few companies that refused to go along with the deal. One builder who did his own forming, Elvio Del Zotto, walked out. Two other forming contractors whose work was primarily in commercial construction — Kiriakos Vlahos of Fran Kiri Forming and Aurelio Bianchini's Leader Group — also indicated they didn't want to sign with the union for residential work. As well, they undoubtedly didn't want to belong to a union that DiLorenzo controlled by the sheer numbers of men he employed. Everyone else signed the contract.

Two days later on November 4, 1968, a party was thrown in Simone's customary style to celebrate the contract at the Mona Lisa tavern. For their assistance in organizing the union, employers now had a five-year agreement with a union that promised to lower the men's wages, in effect, by placing nearly all the workers in the lowest-paying category. DiLorenzo, of course, was the key to signing the contract. At no time were any of the men consulted about the terms of the agreement. It was, as Zanini said, a sweetheart deal. Against all odds, Simone had now organized two emerging trades, drywall and concrete forming, placing the men into residential unions and blocking any attempt by commercial locals to organize the entire field. By perpetuating the split between residential and commercial, the labour movement continued to be divided with men working on residential projects paid less for the same work than their commercial counterparts.

Vlahos's and Bianchini's residential companies signed with the Forming Council. An agreement that gave their workers substantially higher wages than Simone's union members was reached a few days later. Jurisdiction for concrete forming rightfully belonged to this Council. Simone and his lathers should have had nothing to do with the trade. But to avert a split in wages and the trade, the Council offered to make a deal and pay Simone's organizing expenses if he turned over the men. The offer was refused. As Zanini saw it, "It was the legitimate thing to do at that particular time, for the union to go there — but Gus, oh, he goes up in the air! He says we ain't going with those sons-of-bitches."

With the organizing work successfully completed, it was once again time for Zanini to be removed from the scene. The men were in the union, and the contract was signed. His work was over. This became apparent as Simone isolated himself from Zanini. The relationship between the two became strained. There were a number of trifling differences that had weakened their friendship earlier. Zanini's abstinence from alcohol and tobacco was viewed by Simone with a mixture of amusement and suspicion. But the gap continued to widen as Simone spent less and less of his time in Zanini's company, now that the residential concrete formers had been organized.

The Lathers' boss was seen frequently at lunch with some of the subcontractors, and it was after one of these noon-hour gatherings in mid-November 1968 that Simone returned to the union office, his face purple with rage, uttering some incoherent vow as he walked past Zanini into the room where he kept his desk. Apparently he was angry at some contractor who had not gone along with the union. Zanini recalled: "He was drunk as hell. He comes in yelling, 'That bloody *Friulano*, he should be keeled!' Keeled — you know how he spoke? Then he calls me into the next room and wants to know where the guy lives. He was talking about Bianchini, you know. So I ask him, 'Why do you want to know that, Gus? What the hell did he do to you? He's with the commercial unions now. He's got a wife and two kids. You're not seriously thinking of that, are you? If you want to hit him, hit him in a different way. Hit his garage, hit his jobs. That's the way to do it.' So Gus says he'd think it over and he went and lay down. I could see that he was drunk."

On December 17, 1968 the head office of Leader Structures, a reputable forming company partly owned by Bianchini, was set ablaze. The fire destroyed the building. The Fire Marshal reported that a flammable substance had been spilled and ignited. The estimated damage was $75,000. On January 9, 1969 the jacks supporting a concrete floor on a Leader company job were lowered before the concrete had set. As a result, the floor sagged. Estimated damage on the project was $30,000. Two weeks later, after the damage had been repaired, the jacks were lowered again.

Four more fires hit Leader projects. One blaze broke out at lunchtime on an Ottawa building site. Another fire was set in Mississauga. Someone lowered an upper-storey apartment floor six inches; it had to be broken up with drills and the concrete repoured. Rumours began to circulate. Some accused one or two powerful residential forming companies of trying to take over commercial work from their competitor Bianchini. Others said it was the work of labour extortionists. And there were those who were convinced it was Zanini.

The private distress of Bianchini was described years later at a government inquiry. Zanini described a meeting in a restaurant near the office that had been destroyed by fire: "Gus and me go up to meet him. He was practically crying. He says, 'You know, Bruno, people phoned me up and said that you were doing all this stuff.' I says, 'Elio, I did not do these things. Why don't you get the names of who these people are?' He says, 'Well, they're just phone calls,' and that was as far as it went. And he related what is happening to him, that he's going out of business, and it was pathetic to see the man practically breaking down. Gus and I did not know what to say to the poor man."

In February there were more fires. This time heaters were manipulated to set a Leader building ablaze. Then projects contracted to a company owned by Kiriakos Vlahos were damaged. On one apartment project, an intense fire gutted the eleventh and twelfth storeys. Damage estimate: $175,000. Elsewhere, a cable broke on an elevator hoist. Three workmen fell eight storeys. A bucket of concrete overturned, narrowly missing workmen as they ran for their lives. On several occasions, tools were reported missing or stolen.

None of the sites where DiLorenzo crews worked were damaged, though the wealthy businessman discovered a death note attached to his garage door one day. It read: "You are at the head of all this upset in Metro. You think you have things all sewed up. Well, accidents happen to big wheels as well. Stop playing games or we'll play a game called Who Gets Nick's Head or *La Morte* Nick." The rear tire in his car blew out that morning as he drove along the highway. The slash mark of a knife was found on the tire.

It was clear that there was enough detective work for an army of police investigators and crime specialists, but despite the work of these authorities — by one count, five separate squads — not one bit of evidence surfaced. Invited regularly to appear at the Fire Marshal's office, Zanini maintained his innocence. "Look, I told the Fire Marshal," he explained, "I don't know how to lower cranes. It's not my business and I'm not a torch! See? These people knew how. They were pretty clever. It was the people in the industry that did it, the builders themselves."

Nearly everyone had some theory. On March 5, 1969, Toronto's chief of police, James Mackey, gave a summary of the whole affair while speaking to a group of evangelists at the Knox Presbyterian Church. In the midst of his lengthy address, he began to elaborate on his belief that an extortion racket was responsible for the wave of arson and sabotage in the construction industry. He said a small union headed by known criminals was to blame for the $750,000 in damage done to the two forming companies excluded from its contracts. Regrettably the chief had no evidence, nor could he name those directly responsible. Still, the idea that U.S.-style labour extortionists were at work in this well-policed and peaceful metropolis shocked Toronto residents. The newspapers gave generous coverage to Mackey's speculation.

Those intimate with the industry believed the chief had one man in mind: Bruno Zanini. The inference angered and depressed the controversial labour organizer, who immediately called reporter Frank Drea for advice. Drea's grasp of the industry made him a sympathetic listener. At his suggestion, Zanini agreed to an interview by the press to clear up any misunderstanding that could result from the chief's remarks. The lathing union, he told reporters, was not responsible. He argued that these misfortunes were the work of certain contractors trying to undermine unions. Some weeks later, he issued a second statement, calling for an inquiry to find the answers that had eluded police so far: "We want a royal commission to look into the financing of the building industry and the exploitation of construction workers."

Meanwhile, in April 1969, a bid to take over the controversial forming union was made by an official from the Labourers' international union in Washington. In a secret session with the

Labourers' chief, Peter Fosco, Gus Simone began negotiations for a Labourers' takeover of the forming workers' local — in the absence of Irvine. The exclusion of his crony was significant. Pressure was probably applied to make Simone swing everything to the Labourers. The move would clearly be contrary to Irvine's interests. Zanini was aware of the Labourers' interest but Washington officials preferred to negotiate with Simone.

The Labourers had been preparing for this takeover for several months. First, the international union had stripped its Toronto local of the right to bargain for labourers in the Forming Council. The jurisdiction was switched to Gerry Gallagher's local. The result was that the loss of the Labourers weakened the Forming Council's position. The Council would have been even more upset had they realized this was the first move by the Labourers in a campaign to take over all the workers in concrete forming. With all the forming organized into Gallagher's union local as a single trade, the Labourers would be in a position of unequalled strength on the Toronto construction scene.

Simone was being pressed. Outrageous as it seemed, he had successfully organized a trade completely unrelated to his own lathing union. Pressure to give up the men came from many directions in addition to the Labourers. Certainly the Forming Council was interested. So too was Irvine of the Plasterers, who was already working on the members of the unions' jurisdictional board in Washington for the local to go his way. Meanwhile Simone was at the centre. His own international president also came under pressure from the Labourers to turn over the men. The fight came down to Irvine versus the Labourers. Giles of the Operating Engineers would eventually throw his support behind the Labourers.

For the backroom deal to be concluded, Zanini himself had to be party to the negotiations. As before, it was only Zanini who could effect the transfer by persuading the men that it was desirable. When the Labourers had broken away in 1962, Zanini was instructed to lead the men. Nothing, of course, had changed. It was Zanini again who was now to inform the workers that the Labourers were the union to sign with.

Shortly before the formers were to pay initiation dues to finalize their membership in Simone's union, Simone and Zanini agreed to fly to Washington, accompanied by a lawyer for the Labourers' international union. The trip was necessary if the Labourers hoped to sign the men into their union instead. Their membership cards were already in Simone's desk. But Zanini was aware this time that he might well be dropped again, so he warned Simone not to sell the union or him down the river. Payments had to be made to him and to Irvine for their work and aid in financing the campaign. After an uncomfortable night on cots in the union's private gambling quarters in a Washington hotel, the two Toronto men met with Labourers officials the next morning. Apparently Simone and Zanini had both been promised jobs if the Labourers took over. The international union also made an offer to cover organizing expenses incurred by Simone. They proposed to settle everything for $15,000, but Zanini requested more money. Some $22,000 had already been spent without proper authorization by Simone's Lathers' union. As well there was money Irvine advanced for the campaign. Unfortunately Zanini had no receipts for Irvine, so the Labourers said no.

Everything broke down after this, as Zanini grew increasingly worried about the whole situation. They were selling the men into another union, but he himself didn't want to be sold out. There were no guarantees, only the word of these officials, who he began to suspect had no intention of hiring him at all. Nor would they repay Irvine. He'd been dropped once before by the Labourers; they could do it again.

The tension and his inability to negotiate the terms he wanted left him tired and depressed. He called Irvine, who had also flown to Washington. Unaware of what was happening with the Labourers, he was pleading before the International Building Trades' jurisdictional board for his right to organize the forming trade into his plastering union. Zanini unburdened himself to an irate Irvine, who called an immediate halt to the sell-out, threatening Simone a few days later. The plastering boss apparently warned him that if there were any further dealings with the Labourers, Simone might as well find himself a box. Shaking with rage, Irvine pointed to a funeral parlour across the street at this point in the conversation.

The threats were ignored by Simone. At the request of his Washington boss, he flew to Chicago to meet the Labourers, who had hastily convened a meeting between a number of officials, including several concrete forming subcontractors from Toronto. This time, Zanini had not been invited to attend. The group of lawyers and labour officials made an attempt to complete the deal. In attendance were Nick DiLorenzo and his public relations officer, George Orla. They were seeking a $2-million loan from the Labourers' union in return for their approval of the transfer.

This strange collection of employers and union officials, convening privately in a foreign city to settle matters that concerned a Toronto residential construction trade, offered a rare glimpse of the practices and powers wielded by the international building trade unions. The exclusion from the meeting of Zanini showed a marked inability to understand or appreciate the resourcefulness of the Toronto labour leader. He was a wild card.

14
THE INDEPENDENT UNION

Zanini decided he would not be duped one more time. It was time for him to try his old idea of an independent Canadian union in this new concrete forming trade. Fearing his efforts would collapse around him once the Labourers got the men he had just organized, Zanini obtained the support of Irvine and began to drum up more, bitterly accusing the international unions of trying to buy and sell men like cattle. He spoke to business agents, contractors and finally the men, disclosing the details of what was happening with their union. By the time Simone came back from Chicago, Zanini's independent campaign was underway.

One week later, before a gathering of more than 2,000 residential concrete formers, a nervous and pale Simone told the men that he had just been informed by Washington officials that he could no longer lay claim to this trade. Now that Zanini's resistance had soured the backroom deal, the last hope for the Labourers seemed to be to free up the union and allow the men to choose where to go. There seemed to be only two alternatives:

the Forming Council and the Labourers. What, then, was their pleasure? Before anything more was said, Zanini took over the microphone and began to whip up resentment against the international unions, explaining how the Labourers had worked out a shady deal to take over the union.

Suddenly there was a shout from the audience. "Why not make it Canadian?" Chairs shifted, men rose and clapped, put fingers to their lips and whistled their approval. When the vote was taken, only twelve men opposed it.

At the side of the stage stood the familiar figure of Charles Irvine. His open support for a Canadian independent union was certainly bizarre behaviour for an international union man with ties to the labour hierarchy in Washington. But he was willing to shake up the whole set-up, bitter over the backroom dealing by the Labourers. Irvine knew that if the union went independent, it would still be able to join his own international later. Irvine believed that the unit should not be destroyed now that the men were organized. So if for a time it was Canadian, he had no quarrel, as he told the workers that day: "They [the international unions] will fire me tomorrow but you go to it. Just buy yourselves a Canadian flag and stick together. You're Canadians now and nobody can tell you what to do."

Irvine was confident the men were now out of the reach of the Labourers. The deal had fallen through completely. What worried officials in Washington, however, was losing a key trade to a Canadian union. This meant membership dues would remain in Canada — a loss that no international union wished to tolerate.

Elated, Zanini immediately set to work on a constitution, signing up members and setting terms for a new contract that called for higher wages than Simone's old agreement. He threw out the proposed five-year term as well, settling for three years instead. He promised the workers that the contract would be effective as soon as the employers signed.

Even though Zanini had signed their employees, however, the forming subcontractors refused to recognize the new Canadian Concrete Forming Union. One of the strongest holdouts was DiLorenzo, who had thrown his cards in with the Labourers in the hope of getting a $2-million loan. The way DiLorenzo operated, Zanini's union with its higher wages could bankrupt his companies, wiping out any measure of profit. To break the company's resistance, Zanini threw up picket lines on all DiLorenzo projects.

His operation verging on collapse, DiLorenzo signed on July 16. The rest of the contractors followed. It was an enormous victory for the Canadian union, which unlike its predecessor had fought a bitter battle to raise men's wages and gain recognition. There was nothing sweet about the deal Zanini handed the forming contractors. He raised wages, the new rates to be in effect within two weeks. The contract would run for three years, not five. There were to be increased benefits and better vacation pay.

The intrigues that followed in the next few months to undermine Zanini's control of this trade began with the Labourers' union aligning itself with the Forming Council and the Building Trades Council. The former rival simply threw up the white flag and settled into a cozy relationship with its old enemies. The Building Trades Council soon announced its intention to call an illegal strike to organize all the trades in the residential field and force apartment builders to use only men affiliated with the commercial unions.

Days before the walkout began, the business manager of the Building Trades Council met privately with the apartment developers at the Sutton Place hotel. The whole event was somewhat unusual, as Alex Main was meeting with the companies he planned to shut down. The walkout would be illegal because there were no contracts. The developers stood to lose substantial sums of money. Emerging from these talks, business manager Alex Main commented only that the discussions had been fruitful.

The Building Trades then launched their strike. The massive 1969 walkout was financed largely by Washington and the international unions, and was aimed at breaking the remnants of the Brandon Group, Irvine's Plasterers and Cement Finishers; Simone's Lathers; and two other residential unions, the Independent Canadian Bricklayers led by John Meiorin and Zanini's new Canadian Concrete Forming Union. The idea was to organize the entire residential construction sector, establish uniform wage rates and force apartment builders to use only those subcontractors who hired union members belonging to the Building Trades Council in all trades. It was viewed by some as an ambitious effort to bring union solidarity back to the city and abolish residential locals — including Canadian ones — forever.

Irvine refused to honour the pickets set up by strikers. So did Zanini. Simone held out for a while with his residential lathing union before he switched sides, like the Labourers, and joined the strikers. Irvine never forgave Simone for this desertion. It was the end of whatever friendship or business alliance they might have had.

Once the strike took hold, the intensity of the internationals' desire to break the newly formed Canadian union became the topic of general conversation in Toronto. People began to take sides, aroused by the sentiments of independent Canadian unions separate from American influence. Professors, economists, labour experts and others were quoted daily in the press about the merits of Canadian unions.

When the strike failed to break the rebel union, tactics changed. Zanini said he was constantly followed; his phone was tampered with; women approached him. Then one of his business agents, Big John D'Alimonte, was threatened and bribed to leave the union. Zanini's old cohort, who had stayed on to help organize the Canadian union, woke up one morning to find his car destroyed completely. Someone had set fire to it during the night. Next, Gus Simone arrived at D'Alimonte's house the night before elections were to be held by the Canadian union. For nearly twelve hours, D'Alimonte was threatened and bribed to leave the union. The following day he told the workers he was quitting. The union, he said, was no good. And with that, he walked out the door. But this crack in Zanini's organization was healed quickly; in the workers' minds, D'Alimonte was a traitor. And so the union hung on, until the internationals and Alex Main called an end to it in September. The contract they signed with members of the Apartment Developers Association in the end appeared to give more benefits to the developers than the workers. The Building Trades Council won concessions from the builders in eight trades. But the agreement, significantly, excluded the concrete forming union and the Independent Bricklayers' Union. Gerry Gallagher's Labourers' local, which had failed in its bid for the concrete formers earlier, was now recognized by the builders voluntarily as the bargaining agent for labourers employed directly by builders. This choice indicated the popularity of Gallagher and his local with apartment developers.

By far the most significant concession by the unions in the agreement was the "owner–builder" clause. Any company building on land it owned could use cheaper residential unions whether the building was classified as commercial or residential. This had enormous implications for those residential developers who had the financial strength to undertake their own office building projects. Their labour costs would be far below the costs of their competitors in commercial development.

Only a handful of companies were capable of taking advantage of the owner–builder provision. As more and more commercial projects went to these firms building with cheaper residential labour, concern was felt among the commercial locals, who saw steadily declining employment opportunities for their men. As the apartment builders moved into commercial work, so did a number of subcontracting companies.

THE INDEPENDENT UNION

Although Simone had lost out in the forming campaign, his drywall union was doing extremely well. The only real thorn in the side of residential unions was Zanini's independent forming union, as it persisted in its demand for improved wages and benefits for the workers. Zanini's union survived; however, there were renewed efforts that would eventually have the desired effect of destroying the union completely. Zanini's power was weakened when the Ontario Labour Relations Board twice refused to certify Zanini's union to bargain for its members.

Charles Irvine then stepped in to rescue Zanini with promises of financial help from both his Plasterers' international and the Carpenters' international union. But the proposal was killed, apparently when one of the Carpenters' officials was informed by Toronto sources that Zanini was believed to be part of the Mafia. By March 1970, Zanini's union was barely managing to survive. To save the organization of his men, Zanini got together with the other independent residential construction union, the bricklayers, led by John Meiorin, who hoped to organize all construction workers into Canadian unions. It was largely through Meiorin's efforts that the forming union was finally legally certified some months later to bargain for formers employed by several companies.

As autumn neared, Zanini was preparing to finalize a contract for the employees of one of the largest public concrete forming companies, Acu-Forming Limited. Zanini had already been through several rounds of negotiations with the company, asking for wage increases and benefits. Zanini no longer had to rely on voluntary recognition. Nor did he have to call an illegal strike. The union was legally certified to bargain for these employees. At last, Zanini was able to negotiate at a table, drinking coffee, instead of running around with a baseball bat.

Just days before the final negotiating session, late one October night in 1970, a tense man of small stature stood up during a session of the Ontario legislature to make a speech that startled his political colleagues. Once a controversial coroner, then an MPP for the New Democratic Party, Morton Shulman claimed the Mafia was operating a phony union in the construction industry. He went on to describe at great length how Bruno Zanini was the front man in the union, and behind him was Charles Irvine. With some passion, he spoke of how the workers had been cheated of proper representation in international unions; instead, they were aligned with a Canadian union that was a front for the syndicate. To prove this, he had the word of one "honest" union agent, Gus Simone, who at one time had been threatened with a death note. There had been, he added, attempts at blackmail and arson. And sweetheart deals with crooked employers.

Shulman's outburst was not unusual. He was merely obeying an instinct that for years had put him in a number of precarious situations. Raising a furore as chief coroner had lost him that job. He took shots at the psychiatric hospitals. There were crusades about battered babies and abortion deaths, and investigations into strange machines that purported to cure cancer. Then he turned his talent to the stock market, where he shocked the upper crust by speculating in the bond market. He was a socialist, he said, of some wealth. He liked Renoir, so he bought the artist's work. He liked Krieghoff so much that he amassed one of the largest private collections of this painter.

Some said Shulman was an inspiration to the little people; others claimed he was a burr in the side of society. Sometimes he made errors for which he later apologized. One time he said the Attorney General had been seen at a barbecue given by a man convicted of price fixing, when the minister had not been within a hundred miles of the place. But he had his own peculiar rationale for firing at issues like clay pigeons: "The fact is . . . I can't get at the facts, so I'd rather look stupid occasionally if I also hit pay dirt occasionally. I'm prepared to get clobbered once a week if I get somewhere once a month. I'm prepared to take a calculated risk, though I know a lot of members [politicians] wouldn't agree. Yes, sure I lose credibility, but I don't intend spending my life as a politician. I don't want to be elected until I'm 99, so credibility to me is irrelevant."

Shulman's disclosure that October night was hampered by the lack of documented evidence. Most of his information came from a police report he had never seen. Pressed to produce some supporting evidence, Shulman later revealed that his information had been based partially on a seventy-page affidavit sworn by private investigator and one-time union-buster Norman Menezes. Then too there was the sworn statement of John D'Alimonte, a man who confessed he could neither read nor write.

Nevertheless, few people disputed Shulman's allegations that the Canadian union was a front for the mob. After all, Shulman was a self-proclaimed authority on the Mafia. Some weeks before this disclosure he had travelled to Sicily for a week to investigate Mafia links to activities in Ontario. At one point, he said, he was threatened and in great fear for his life.

It was an effective speech that won Shulman front-page headlines in the morning newspaper the next day — days before Zanini was to meet with Acu-Forming to sign the contract he had negotiated for some months. It was considered a good agreement, with improved wages and conditions for these forming workers, who in the past three years had been passed around like a dollar bill.

"Boom! They stabbed us — with Morton Shulman," said Zanini. "Just before we were to sign the contract — bang! Zanini's Mafia! It was a nightmare. They destroyed the Canadian union right there with them allegations. I couldn't do nothing about it. I couldn't sue him because he wouldn't repeat it outside the legislature. Why did he bring it out all now? Why didn't he say it a year ago when all this bit about sweetheart unions took place? Why?"

15
THE SALE

Discredited and with his union being described as a front for the mob, Zanini fell into a brief depression. Still, no one could pry the union from his grasp as he prepared to make one last attempt to win a contract for these men with his old labour crony Charles Irvine.

The most damaging blow so far had been Morton Shulman's unkind references to his character, his criminal past and, of course, to the Canadian union. He began to notice that people were becoming indifferent to him. Business agents, old friends and even some of the workers looked at him questioningly whenever they met him. The more he protested, the redder their faces grew, laughing too loud as they made their excuses and hurried on.

"People wanted to get away from me!" said Zanini later, the lines of his face folding in astonishment. "I certainly didn't belong to any criminal organization or I would have sold the men a long time ago. I would have something to show for it."

He described this period as a low point in his life. The contract for his men went unsigned while company officials politely made their apologies. In mid-November 1970, he entered hospital for an operation on his right ear. During surgery, his heart failed, and for a while he was clinically dead. He was left practically deaf in one ear. When he had recovered, more discouraging news awaited him. His union was running short of finances; bills for office rent and the telephone were going unpaid; the men were dissatisfied, restless, unable to comprehend what was happening to them. Zanini needed more money to call meetings, perhaps even a strike, but despite his passionate pleas to John Meiorin and the Bricklayers' union, the financing was cut short. The union had already spent $60,000.

But as luck would have it, Charles Irvine reappeared one day in the spring of 1971, his face glowing. It was a shame, he noted, to let the unit of men disintegrate after so much effort, and so he had taken the initiative: he had left the Forming Council and gotten a charter for these workers from his own Plasterers' international union boss in Washington. He needed a labour organizer and said there was a job for Zanini.

Zanini gave no immediate reply. The tiresome thought of campaigning again for yet another union disheartened him, as he would explain later: "You know, I was thinking and I went over my past. Where was I going? Was I making the right decision going with the Plasterers? Could I trust Charlie? What was going to happen to the men? I knew I was in the middle of some goddamn fight here. But then, I thought this was the last time, I'll give it a fair shake with Charlie and his international."

Irvine had wisely kept alive his friendship with Zanini. His support of the Canadian union may have been superficial but he garnered Zanini's loyalty in the process. And as both Irvine and the Labourers knew, Zanini was the only man the immigrant workers would follow. The Labourers used Zanini to split off from the Brandon Group before they dropped him. Irvine too had used Zanini to whip up his own residential unions, but he had never left Zanini out in the cold. So now, Zanini's old labour crony finally had a charter from the Plasterers to organize concrete forming. Why Washington decided to let Irvine have a crack at it is unexplained. The new residential charter came at a time when the Forming Council was making great progress in residential construction. Almost 60 percent of the formers were already signed up.

Irvine's decision to bring the men into the Plasterers earned him a number of enemies. The Forming Council took immediate reprisals and booted his three Plasterers' locals out of the Building Trades Council. Council official Alex Main gave this comment to the press: "Irvine sees his domain going down the drain and figures that if he can organize the Italian workers who do most of the forming work in this field he will regain control. He doesn't really love Italians any more than he loves anybody else. He is looking for power."

Supporting his charge, the labour boss mentioned the fact that Irvine had once stipulated in a contract that no more than 50 percent Italians could be hired by a firm. Irvine fired back with allegations that the Forming Council and the contractors were making a sweetheart deal. He accused the council of negotiating a five-year contract with employers already, even though only half of the formers had been organized.

The expectations of the Forming Council fell flat with Irvine's sudden bid for the same workers. What was even more worrisome was the re-emergence of Zanini under Irvine's wing. The alliance had proved unbeatable some years earlier. The significance of Irvine's entry into the race was that another union local had been created, if only to prevent the organization of forming as a single trade in the city under the auspices of the Forming Council, which had the right to organize these men nonetheless.

In the weeks that followed, the rivalry between the two groups intensified as the drive for the men escalated. Hundreds of curious workers turned out to hear what Irvine and Zanini had to offer. It was a grab bag of promises: higher wages, more benefits and a shorter agreement that would not extend beyond three years. Looking somewhat older and thinner, Irvine still managed to belt out his impassioned pleas: "You built a lot of buildings in this city, you built a lot of fortunes in this city. Now for God's sake, from this day on build something for yourself and your wife, your kids and those that come behind you. Leave them something." He paraded his virtues. Never, he told the workers, had he sold the men down the river. Always he concerned himself with the terms of contracts, the wages, the benefits; saying he dealt with the men, refusing to cook up private sweetheart agreements with employers.

The oratory moved nearly everyone who came and listened. At one meeting, the men rushed to the stage to sign up as new members halfway through Zanini's translation of one of Irvine's speeches. Clearly the immense popular appeal of these two beleaguered union leaders had not been lost over the years. The resurrected Irvine and Zanini team had quickly become a threat to the Forming Council, who faced half-empty halls at their rallies.

Then in April, Irvine was paid an unexpected visit by Paul Volpe. Familiar with Volpe's role in the past, the plastering boss inquired testily how he rated the honour of such a visit. As he told the press the next day: "Volpe threw down a union card and said he was in a new field — getting people together. I called him names and told him to come back when he felt tough enough. He phoned back in an hour and said he wanted me at a meeting the next night in a Yonge Street club. I called there the next day and told them to leave him a message — I was at the doctor's and couldn't be there."

Frank Drea, a reporter with inside knowledge, summarized the incident in a special report that appeared in the *Toronto Telegram*: "The mob had dispatched its hoodlum enforcers to try and carve out a labour racket empire from Metro-area inter-union chaos. The spoils concern just who will represent 2,000 immigrant construction workers who pour concrete on high-rise apartment projects."

The business card Volpe gave Irvine belonged to Gus Simone. It was a humiliating moment for the plastering boss. Now the persuasive labour consultant was aligned with Irvine's bitter enemy, Gus Simone. Or so Irvine believed. The incident may well have been a ruse to stir Irvine's anger against the lathing boss and thereby sow fear into Simone. For shortly after Irvine complained publicly about Volpe's visit, Simone hired one of Volpe's old acquaintances, Joey Bagnato, as a constant companion.

Perhaps Volpe saw a chance to heal the rift between Irvine and Simone. However, Irvine's public refusal to deal with Volpe did not improve his chances with the forming union. Six weeks later, with several hundred forming workers signed into a local of his Plasterers' union, he still was unable to gain voluntary recognition from employers. No one wanted to sign a contract with Irvine. To builders, it was like sticking their head in a noose. Too many companies had been felled by Irvine's tactics — illegal walkouts, alleged price-fixing combines — and the control he had once exercised with such expertise. Irvine was too costly.

So the talks continued to lag. The contract remained unsigned. Four, six, eight weeks went by with no result. Zanini pleaded with Irvine to strike, pull the men off job sites to get the contract signed. It had worked before. But for some reason, Irvine refused. Zanini soon came to suspect there had been a change in Irvine's thinking. He was convinced Irvine had been threatened.

The delay carried on into the hot summer of 1971. Then without warning, in a move that stunned nearly everyone in the industry, Irvine's former rivals, the Labourers, dissolved their ties with the Forming Council in July and began to campaign for the formers on their own. They had no more jurisdiction than Charles Irvine to represent these men as a single trade. "Can you imagine that?" said Zanini once, his eyes closing to two narrow slits. "They were trying to organize the men we signed up — our people," he exclaimed. "Going on job sites trying to get new members!"

At the same time, the Labourers started to negotiate with the contractors, undercutting the Forming Council's agreement on wages, and agreeing to drop welfare benefits. Said Zanini: "There's no doubt in my mind there were certain builders working with them. The other builders organized by the Forming Council had to go along too, because it was cheaper rates with the Labourers. They were pressured to sign, in a way, just to remain competitive."

Of the five trades that laid claim to forming, the Labourers were the lowest-paid. The interesting part of this move by the Labourers, at a time when the Forming Council was bargaining with employers, was that it met with success because of the concessions the union was willing to give forming contractors. The deal was too good for the employers to refuse.

The only remaining obstacle for the Labourers was to knock out the plastering local under Irvine, which had organized a number of formers. This was achieved through a backroom deal in New York between labour bosses for the Plasterers and the Labourers. The first Zanini heard of it was on August 5, when he arrived uninvited at a Toronto convention held for American and Canadian plastering officials at the Royal York hotel. On the fifth or sixth floor, he found the suite of the Washington president, whom he began to interrogate, demanding to know why there was no more money for the union to call a strike, or even a meeting. It was then he learned that a deal had been struck between the labour boys in New York. Everything, he was told, had to go to the Labourers.

There was a rumour that the Plasterers received some $500,000 for their cooperation. Six weeks later, Irvine's charter from the Plasterers was cancelled, and Zanini was left once again without a job and without a contract for the men he had organized. Weary and bewildered after five years of courtship by five different unions, the workers began to sign with the Labourers. The local then made clear its intention to move directly into the commercial field in concrete forming, using as justification the owner–builder clause granted the apartment builders and their associations back in 1969.

Meanwhile, a number of major forming companies under contract to the Forming Council changed corporate names and signed with the Labourers to remain competitive. And so the Labourers in the end were to organize the commercial concrete formers at cheaper rates. The union that had succeeded was the same union recognized by the builders some years earlier. Wages for forming workers dropped all across the board. The Forming Council had lost. So had Zanini.

16

THE SHOOTING

Dropped from the labour scene once again, Zanini fell unhappily into the ranks of the unemployed. Reduced to a meagre and spare existence, he began to make regular visits to his friends on the pretence of finding work; whenever it seemed appropriate he would ask for a loan. As one contractor said: "He didn't want a lot of money, just enough for bread, but at the time I was broker than him. I took out my wallet and I only had $30 in it, and he said to keep it. No one, of course, would ever hire him back into the labour movement and this Zanini knew. He had been dumped. This time he had been retired unceremoniously. In time, he became obsessed with the idea of trying to regain a measure of respect and prove that his Canadian union had been legitimate.

Late one day in February 1972, his old labour crony John D'Alimonte called. The former crane operator, who had betrayed the original Canadian union in 1969 to join the Labourers, was now, like Zanini, unemployed. The two got together, Zanini agreeing to drive D'Alimonte to Buffalo where he had to attend to the will of a recently deceased relative. At some point along the winding highway to the U.S. border, D'Alimonte bared his soul to Zanini, reworking the past, explaining how he had been threatened and bribed to desert the Canadian union and how he came to regard the Labourers, as he told them the day he quit the union: "You're a bunch of crooks. You are for the bosses. You are not for the men."

It was the first time Zanini had heard this and the news perked up his waning spirits. Now with this key bit of testimony, Zanini began to plan his return to the labour scene via a resurrection of the Canadian union. D'Alimonte also told him he had been asked to sign a piece of paper in some lawyer's office indicating the early Canadian union was phony. He was not sure what the paper said since he was unable to read. The union, he was willing now to testify, had been set up properly.

Of equal importance was D'Alimonte's charge that the Labourers cared little for the men they represented. This confirmed a number of incidents reported to Zanini by disgruntled formers, who claimed the union was cutting hours from their pay slips. He had also been told by some of the smaller forming contractors that the union was favouring certain companies. It was rumoured that one company owed the union several thousands of dollars in dues payments, a sum that had not yet been collected although everyone else was made to pay up. No one was sure any of this was actually happening as it appeared, but presumably, if it was, it amounted to an indirect attempt to force some companies abiding by the contract to operate at costs far in excess of those who weren't paying dues. Some contractors complained they might eventually be forced into bankruptcy.

Still it was the workers Zanini wanted to hear from, as he collected statements and scraps of evidence, wage slips to prove how benefits and hours had been cut. "Hell, there was one job where thirty men were getting beat for hours every week," Zanini once explained. "The foremen were cheating the men. The workers were keeping quiet because they were afraid. The only ones I know that ever played it straight were Acu-Forming, Del Zotto and Leader Forming."

Absorbed now with this new venture, Zanini's constant worry about his future faded. He bolted into action, trying to collect statements from workers who felt they were being cheated, the evidence that was needed to press for a royal commission of inquiry and the return, he hoped, of his Canadian union. But impatient as ever, he decided to deliver the story of exploitation to the newspapers. There were some hasty meetings in a damp cellar between a reporter and workers who refused to divulge their names. The news story did not appear as soon as Zanini had expected, and the strain of delay forced him to make a decision to proceed on his own by mid-August 1972. He felt there should be a rally of workers, with D'Alimonte explaining the entire saga of how he left the Canadian union. Zanini set the date for September 4, 1972.

A week before the meeting, as he sat outside a cafe, drinking coffee, a fat man with dark glasses came to his table. Dark suit, dark glasses was Zanini's recollection. "'Just watch yourself,' he says to me."

"Well goddammit!" said Zanini, his voice rising, almost breaking, "I was blacklisted. I couldn't get a job. And I wasn't a crook and I wasn't Mafia. And the goddamn Canadian union was honest, and it was the only union to be certified. Why should I let some thug like that fat guy talk me out of something that I worked all my life for?"

A few days later in the afternoon of August 23, 1972, Zanini took the elevator in his apartment building to the basement garage. Walking toward his parking spot, he passed two men working quietly under the hood of a car. He opened his mouth as if to say something, then changed his mind and continued in the same direction. When he arrived a few minutes later at his parking space, he unlocked the door, climbed in, turned the key with a sharp snap of the wrist and listened. Silence. He turned the key again and only then, when he raised his eyes, did he glimpse two men making their way between the cars toward him. Mechanics, he thought, coming to help me. With this in mind, he opened the car door and stood waiting. Suddenly one of the men raised a powerful flashlight and shone it into his face. Blinking, Zanini could now only barely see their faces. He heard one man shout, "Hold it, don't move!"

Then: the sound of a shot. And it was all over.

Zanini's leg buckled and he fell to the floor. Turning his head, he could see the men in the distance. They got into a white station wagon with a purple or red stripe in the centre, right across the body, and drove away.

Several minutes later, the phone rang in his apartment twenty-one storeys above. "Where's Bruno?" the caller asked.

"He's out."

"He's downstairs."

"What do you mean?"

"Are you his son?"

"Yes."

"Your daddy's downstairs. He's been shot."

According to a physician, one bullet had been fired into Zanini's leg at fairly close range. The incident was widely reported in the press, though no one could agree on the motive for the shooting. Frank Drea, who by this time had quit newspapers to become a politician, mused that the attack had been a warning to Zanini to end his demand for a government investigation of the industry. Morton Shulman said it was all part of a battle to control certain construction workers. A public relations consultant theorized in the Toronto Italian newspaper *Il Giornale* that Zanini had shot himself accidentally.

Meanwhile, the police questioned Zanini at his bedside in an unmarked room at the Humber Hospital, where he remained for two days under medical surveillance. "It's obvious they aimed down here," he said once, pointing to his left leg. "It's obvious they didn't try to kill me . . . unless the guy's a poor shot. So the police are asking me, 'What motive could it be, Mr. Zanini?' I says, 'Simple. There's certain subcontractors and builders who do not want me to expose the things that are going on in the construction industry, so why not cripple me up. They feared the way I was going with Frank Drea, eventually the Attorney General would know about it too. They were afraid I'd get the union back, too. See? There's people, unions, directly and indirectly involved with the bosses. Positive. But it just can't be proved.' It's obvious to me there were a couple of mobs in on the play. Maybe three but which ones, I don't know."

A week later, shortly after midnight, the premises of a lathing firm were hit by a blast of dynamite. Another company was slightly damaged by the explosion of two sticks of dynamite. All this activity aroused demands for another government inquiry into the industry, the third in a decade, following reports by Carl Goldenberg in 1962 and Ivan C. Rand in 1968. Goldenberg's recommendations had only partially been implemented; Rand's, following his inquiry into labour disputes, not at all.

Zanini was enthusiastic at the prospect of an inquiry, fully expecting to be exonerated and cleared of a number of accusations. There was some hope that he could shake the charges of Mafia involvement and vindicate himself as the one organizer who had built these unions for immigrants, almost single-handed — a hope his critics called illusory.

17
THE MAFIA IS WITH US

John Parmenter Robarts, former premier of Ontario, arrived for his farewell dinner in March 1971, in black tie, tailored evening suit and black velvet slippers. Stitched in gold on each slipper was a crown and his initials, JPR. For some time on that spring night, he stood greeting various business leaders and old political friends such as Darcy McKeough and Stanley Randall. Then the 135 invited guests sat down to a tastefully appointed dinner at the Board of Trade of Metropolitan Toronto's country club, just north of the city. Dishes of seafood on the shell and fillet of beef were served, followed by small plates of cheese and Emperor grapes.

At the end of the evening, Robarts was presented with a stereo-equipped colour TV. Accepting it, he gave a short speech. He told the gathering he was unsure of his future but it was likely that he would return to his law practice, a practice he had begun twenty years earlier. This ceremony concluded the smooth transfer of power by Ontario's ruling Conservative party from Robarts to the incoming premier, William Davis.

Part of Davis's inheritance was a proposal for new regional governments that would directly affect land and its development throughout the province. One of the senior advisers of the new premier was corporate land-use lawyer Eddie Goodman. His blunt, raspy talk and devotion to the party had earned him a measure of respect over the years as he canvassed for funds and helped shape party policy.

Another task passed on to Davis was the proposed reorganization of the cabinet into super-ministries. Next to Davis in power was Darcy McKeough, who now bore the title of minister of the provincial treasury, as well as minister of economic and intergovernmental affairs. It was McKeough, son-in-law of a prominent lawyer and party bagman, who was to decide how government money should be spent and how urban growth should proceed in the rapidly growing centres of southern Ontario.

Of course areas designated for potential development were of interest to land speculators. Information about provincial intentions was available to cabinet members, and to the embarrassment of the new premier, a number of his ministers began to speculate in real estate during the crucial first months of his rule.

The transportation and communications minister, Gordon Carton, had acted as a lawyer in numerous purchases of land near the proposed site for a new airport, prior to his appointment to the cabinet. He denied he had any financial interest in properties purchased by his clients. Attorney General Dalton Bales purchased ninety-nine acres of farmland east of Toronto in a partnership with two other investors at a time when cabinet ministers were discussing privately plans to limit growth west of Metro Toronto while promoting easterly expansion. Provincial solicitor general John Yaremko speculated as a private investment in an area being considered for development on the Niagara Escarpment. Then there was the satellite city project, Century City; it was never built, losing the developer a substantial sum of money, despite private assurances from the government during the initial planning stage. McKeough himself came under fire for his quick approval of a subdivision proposal in which he had a personal interest.

In the summer of 1972, the Davis government corrected the situation, making public a code of ethics that forbade a minister to deal in land. Officials were also ordered to disclose to the premier the extent of their current land holdings. These conflict of interest guidelines were designed to remove any doubt in the public mind that the practice had been ended. They did not, however, embrace other areas of conflict; for instance, an incident when Eddie Goodman acted for a land development company that was exempted by a cabinet decision from paying $660,000 in provincial land speculation tax on the sale of 280 acres.

Other men of less stature and influence tried repeatedly and sometimes successfully to win political favours. There was one real estate broker, Ross Shouldice, who raised funds on a voluntary basis for the party. His flood of letters to cabinet ministers requesting favours in return for political funding prompted one official to say, "He must have had writer's cramp."

Shouldice learned in 1971 of a piece of land that was on or near the route of a highway extension proposed by the Ministry of Transportation, whose major task was deciding routes of arteries and roads throughout the province. If the government were to purchase this property, he offered, the Tory party would receive a $30,000 donation, and the broker, a six percent commission.

The president of the company holding the land was Alan Feldman. Several government ministers remained vague as to whether or not they had heard of this offer. Eventually he was asked to discontinue his fundraising activities.

When the ministry finally purchased the 100-acre property through other brokers, it paid close to $1.5 million. The peculiar thing was that two maps existed for this section of highway. Only one of them showed the route crossing the property Feldman wanted to sell, and it was this map the ministry finally accepted, blaming the existence of the other map on an error by a draftsman.

Easing over these disruptions in his office, Davis maintained a presence of reserve and calm, preserving the political stability so gratifying to investors. Strong and able urban and regional planning at both local and provincial levels had set the stage for dynamic yet orderly growth.

So when the construction industry was rocked once again by a few bomb blasts and unaccountable vandalism in the summer of 1972, the government was less than enthusiastic about responding to renewed demands for a provincial inquiry. Some said the industry should be examined at all levels, from unions to investors. In fact, Zanini had been among the first to demand an inquiry to look into the financing of the industry. He believed, as did others, that the exploitive system of subcontracting and open tenders in the housing industry was the ultimate cause of all violence in that sector.

Pressure intensified until the government finally relented and announced its intention to set up a royal commission to examine specifically the violence — not the industry as a whole. The one-man inquiry was limited in scope to studying the activities of certain unions during the past five years. The premier chose Judge Harry Waisberg, a soft-spoken, fair-minded county court judge who had served on previous royal commissions. Among Waisberg's own political acquaintances was Eddie Goodman, who had hired the judge's son to work in his law practice. Waisberg appointed as counsel to his inquiry Albert Shepherd, the London lawyer who had worked on the arduous and lengthy Atlantic Acceptance inquiry some years earlier.

There was now an air of optimism that, at last, the whole convoluted tale of the construction industry would be put before the public. There was much to disclose: the horse-trading of workers in the concrete forming trade, bought and sold by U.S.-based unions; the undercutting of wages and workers' benefits by unions trying to sweeten deals and induce employers to hire from them; and the role of some builders, both developers and subcontractors, in trying to suppress labour organizers.

A key decision relating to how the inquiry would proceed was made early in the investigation, when Waisberg and Shepherd learned that Gus Simone was willing to testify at length on what he knew about the construction business. Simone, the ex-lather who got into the union business in the mid-1960s while Zanini was serving his term for possession of burglary tools, had acquired intimate knowledge of how some unions operated. His experience was, however, limited to the residential unions and it was here he had met with his greatest success. There had been the original lathing union, then the drywall workers and finally his attempt in concrete forming. Simone had played a part too as a union agent, willing to regulate a bid-depository set up among drywall contractors anxious to end the cutthroat business and allot jobs to each other. He was inclined to accept gifts whenever they were offered. So it was true that Simone had an understanding of business as well as unions. He was, of course, involved in several misdemeanours, and part of the deal he made with the royal commission was that his testimony would be given under the protection of the *Canada Evidence Act* so that anything he said could not be used later in court proceedings against him.

The unsolved violence in the industry was the focus of the inquiry. There were the incidents of arson and sabotage, the estimated $750,000 of damage sustained in 1969 by two forming contractors, the bombing of two lathing companies in 1972 and the shooting of Bruno Zanini, as well as numerous reports of threats and intimidation.

Despite the request of a local group of concerned tenants and citizens for the inquiry to include the activities of three Toronto developers — Cadillac, Greenwin and Meridian — none of the principals of these companies participated. Only one major residential development firm in Toronto had its owners subpoenaed to answer questions directly before the inquiry. They were Angelo and Elvio Del Zotto, two of three brothers who ran a family-owned apartment development business and some other enterprises. Unlike most builders, the Del Zottos maintained their own work crews and did much of their construction themselves. They did their own concrete forming and drywall by taking a percentage interest in the subcontracting firms performing the work, rather than following the general practice, which was to sublet the entire project. When the Del Zottos' drywall subcontractor, Cesidio Romanelli, intimated his desire to expand into projects undertaken by other developers in 1971, he set up a new company to do this independent of Del Zotto interests. It was after this initiative that Romanelli lost a number of non-Del Zotto jobs owing largely to a bid ring and payoffs to company agents by major firms in which Romanelli would not participate.

According to Simone, Romanelli had met during this period with Angelo Del Zotto at the Mona Lisa tavern to discuss his need to hire a bodyguard. In his recollection of the incident, Simone told the inquiry that Del Zotto gave Romanelli the name of a man to contact. Complying with the judge's subpoena, the Del Zotto brothers gave testimony, and they refused the protection of the *Canada Evidence Act*. They denied the meeting, as did Romanelli. The only concrete evidence that was produced to support Simone's account of the meeting was the name of Del Zotto's secretary scribbled into Simone's notebook, allegedly by

Del Zotto himself. The builder said he didn't know whether or not it was his handwriting when shown the name.

In a chapter of his final report subtitled "Organized Crime," the judge discussed one aspect of the role of the Del Zottos in the construction industry. He found that "following that contact, a sinister array of characters was introduced to this industry." Romanelli did hire a man with a criminal background, sometime after the alleged meeting, who was known to Paul Volpe. It was Volpe who persuaded Romanelli to switch from lawyer Elvio Del Zotto to another lawyer, John Rosen, whom Volpe used frequently. The new lawyer incorporated two new companies: Redvale Investments Limited and C. Romanelli Drywall Limited. Volpe's name appeared in the incorporation papers for Redvale Investments Limited. Rosen held 25 percent of the shares of Romanelli's company in trust.

The "sinister characters" the judge later made reference to were Volpe and the two men hired by Romanelli while trying to expand his operation. Romanelli said that the Del Zottos knew nothing of his hiring of these two men nor of his friendship with Volpe. Not only did Romanelli change lawyers, after encountering Volpe he also had a change of heart with respect to the combine of drywall subcontractors, which he had at first resisted. In fact, Romanelli began to collect from other drywall subcontractors regular payments that were intended for Simone, whose alleged role was to regulate the combine through his union. Simone said he never saw the money.

Another matter investigated by the inquiry was the shooting of Bruno Zanini. Evidence was introduced that a bouncer named Frank Veltri, sometimes known as "The Angel," had been hired to cripple Zanini for a fee of $1,500. Police investigators had recorded a phone conversation between Veltri and his girlfriend in which he discussed the shooting:

Veltri: I phoned the Monarch yesterday to talk to him and . . . somebody knows already. I'm gonna get nailed on one. And plus I might have to be called up on that inquiry.

M.J.: But listen, I did a bit of research into that guy . . . you was supposed to have, you know what . . .

F.V.: Yeah . . . he was labour . . .

M.J.: Yeah . . . but he's a fink anyway now . . .

F.V.: He's a . . . stool pigeon.

M.J.: He belongs to the Mafia.

F.V.: Yeah. No, he don't . . . no, he's a stool pigeon. He's copping out on all the Mafia.

M.J.: Well, he's no good anyway.

F.V.: I know. You know what one copper said to me in the station?

M.J.: Should have finished him off.

F.V.: He says . . . how come you missed, why don't you do a good job to him?

M.J.: That's what I mean . . . he was no good.

F.V.: Because they don't like him anyways, you know . . . said, lookit, if that . . . was me, I would've done a good job to him. [laughter] That's right.

M.J.: Were you supposed to get 15 for that?

F.V.: Yeah.

M.J.: Did you?

F.V.: No ... [laughter]

M.J.: [laughter] Oh ... I wouldn't like you to get mad at me.

F.V.: [laughter]

M.J.: ... Cripes ... I wouldn't need to have my cartilage taken off ... you'd shoot them off.

As Veltri saw it, Zanini was not part of the mob. In fact, he reasoned that there was some worry among criminal elements that Zanini would tell more than he should. At the same time, Veltri denied any involvement in the shooting to police. At the inquiry, when confronted with the tape, he told the judge that he was lying to the woman, "trying to impress her." There had been no conviction because the gun was never found.

Neither has the motive for the shooting ever been confirmed. Veltri in his phone conversation suggested that it was because Zanini had threatened to tell the whole story about mob involvement in construction labour unions. Another theory was that it was to intimidate Zanini at the point where he seemed ready yet again to disrupt other people's carefully laid plans for the large and powerful residential concrete forming union local. Others involved in the union business knew that Zanini could disrupt schemes that they had almost succeeded in bringing to fruition. Indeed the shooting had that effect; it put Zanini out of circulation, and ended for the last time his efforts at interfering with the transaction between the international unions, as a result of which the residential concrete forming local was transferred to the Labourers' international.

Whether Zanini had also understood the shooting as a warning against telling all he knew, however, was not clear. He had, after all, been one of many calling for an inquiry.

Zanini was a familiar face at the hearings, attending each session, making notes as he listened to the statements made before the judge. Several weeks before he was to give his own version, two men approached him at the close of a morning session. They claimed they were business agents, scouting for an organizer to set up a new union for barbers. Zanini suspected there was something more to the invitation. Curious, he agreed to meet them for lunch. He met them a second time. Still there was talk of unions and nothing else. Then, on the third occasion, as Zanini later told the story, "They told me to meet them at the King Edward hotel for lunch. So I walk into the lobby and there was one of the guys, Max — that's not his real name — and with him, there's some new guy, flat-looking face, supposed to be a big shot from the United States.

"Well, I figured we're going for lunch. I'm starved. 'No,' says Max, 'let's go outside.' We go outside and there's a big Lincoln parked there. So Max gets in the back. This big Tony, about 55, gets in the front and drives me around the block. What the hell is going on here? I'm thinking. So I start to use a bit of their lingo, more or less cooperating because it was obvious these guys weren't union guys. So I'm hearing Max tell Tony that I was the guy that got shot in the leg. Christ! I says, 'Let's go to some restaurant and talk. We'll have a coffee, you know?' But no, they tell me. I figure this guy was on the run because he didn't want to stop anywhere or go anywhere.

"We get to talking about the inquiry and I says to myself, I better watch out. These guys are definitely out to see what the hell I know and what I'm going to do. See? I hadn't testified yet. Then out of the blue sky, the big guy says, 'Listen, you better watch yourself. Next time, you could get one between here.' 'For what?' I says. The guy didn't say nothing. That's all. Never saw him again. That was his message and that was the end of it."

When Zanini's turn to testify came, he failed to mention this unsettling incident. His hesitations and frequent omissions made for an uneven and unsatisfactory testimony, in the opinion of Judge Waisberg. Zanini was incapable of answering questions directly and seemed confused at times. He also appeared to be telling less than he knew.

The inquiry itself turned out to be less than satisfactory as a compelling study of the industry. Many key matters were left unstudied: for instance the Operating Engineers, the union running the cranes used in hoisting material on all high-rise projects, received little mention although it had played an important role by supporting Simone's organizing activities with the concrete forming workers, and later the Labourers' bid for the same men. The inquiry examined only five years of the industry, in spite of the fact that many of the disruptions were the result of earlier disputes.

Nearly a year and a half after completing his hearings Judge Waisberg produced his findings in a two-volume report. In it he acknowledged that organized crime had played a role in the construction business, but the report's discussion of this matter was limited to only a portion of that role, concentrating on the Del Zottos, Romanelli, and Paul Volpe and his associates. Waisberg agreed that Zanini had not shot himself, concluding that the shooting had been tied to his activities in the industry. In his assessment of Zanini's role, the judge had this to say: "It is obvious throughout that Zanini's one concern was to provide himself with funds from union organizations. While witnesses have indicated that Zanini, at one time, had considerable influence with the men due to his oratorical ability, it seemed to me that he did not have any concept of the duties and obligations of a business agent nor of the principles involved in labour–management relations. In his role as a union business agent, there were many instances of improper conduct."

Waisberg's portrait of Simone was less critical, balancing the union agent's concern for the workers along with what the judge termed irregular practices of accepting gifts from employers of the men in his union. In his recommendations, the judge called for licensing of contractors, improved inspection of union books, quicker certification and a province-wide welfare plan. In the end, Waisberg offered no conclusive findings with reference to the violence that rocked the industry in 1969. But he was praised by editorial writers from the press for his revelation that, as one newspaper put it, "the Mafia is with us," even though little hard information was provided on the role of criminal elements in the industry.

PART VI
Semi-Retired

18
LABOUR EMPIRES

More than twenty years after the suicide of the young Italian mother, Gerarda Trillo, and the first stirrings of immigrant workers' outrage in the Toronto housing industry, some union officials were still shaking their heads solemnly. The residential trade was a jungle then, recalled one spokesman. Union bosses would peer out their office windows, looking across the city skyline, and wonder how they were ever to organize these thousands of Italians. There were only a handful of men, fighting considerable odds, who were finally able to improve the conditions for these workers. Whatever these men may have done to disrupt the industry, they also helped to organize it: that was the unsolicited comment from one international union man who had battled both Irvine and Zanini in union-related squabbles through the years.

But as Zanini once said of himself, he was "just a little fish in a big pond." By 1974, he was a man in his 50s, his hair still red although he bore the look of a hollow man, burned out. He still carried his briefcase of opera scores and at times talked excitedly about the Waisberg report that had come out that year. The judge shared the opinion of the police that Zanini had not shot himself. From this Zanini felt a measure of vindication.

He was, however, unable to find steady work, living with his two sons in a two-bedroom apartment. At times he would visit Charles Irvine's plastering union office. The labour boss had grown frail-looking. Someone said his spirit was broken. He had been accused of a number of misdemeanours throughout the inquiry. Stories had been told in public about how Irvine had used one of his plastering locals to regulate a price-fixing combine for the contractors in 1961. Although no documentary evidence was produced to link Irvine with this activity, a former business agent had testified that he had been used to enforce the combine. Irvine dismissed his former colleague as a drunk with too much taste for the Hot Stove Lounge and the Ports of Call.

Then there had been the suggestion that Irvine had tried to gain control of the residential concrete forming workers to force developers back to using plaster instead of drywall in their apartments. There were reports that Irvine had tried to falsify dues receipts when his membership was dwindling to convince Washington that the union was prosperous. But there was no money to send to Washington. Accountants examining the union's financial records found numerous places where Irvine, as trustee of whatever money was in the union funds, had apparently made considerable transfers of cash to his own personal account. His bookkeeping system was called "Kafkaesque." Expenditures were written on scraps of paper marked laconically "cash re negotiations" or "cash re pickets." And there was the 1971 fire in the union offices, which partially destroyed the records. When Irvine saw the results of the fire he began to laugh, recalled a former business agent. "Irvine was happy about the fire but I don't know the reason why." For some years after, Irvine kept a phone, the plastic deformed and melted by the blaze, on top of a desk in his office.

But Irvine was a defeated man. Two of his three plastering locals were destroyed through lack of membership and dissension. Members quit to join the Bricklayers' union. Others simply left the industry. Irvine himself was soon to disappear into semi-retirement. For a short while, he worked with his son in a record shop near his home in the northeast part of the city.

Only one of Irvine's locals survived by 1974. The business agent for these cement finishers at the time was Frank Amis, a man who had been kicked out of the local years earlier. When Amis was reinstated in the early 1970s, after appealing to Washington, he appointed himself financial and recording secretary. Within fourteen months, he and his wife had paid themselves about $70,000 in salary. Amis's share of $54,300 was three times the amount the local had paid his predecessor as business manager, according to an accountant who inspected the books for the Waisberg commission.

And so came the ungracious decline of a celebrated and respected trade. Because plastering and lathing are part of the same construction method, on the heels of the decline of the plasterers came the end of the Lathers' union. But lathing union business agent Gus Simone was less concerned about the disappearance of a craft that was no longer popular because he had secured a new position for himself in the drywall business. The man from Pescara had grown stouter and more prosperous, realizing a number of New World dreams. He had a $100,000 home outside of Toronto in Bolton, a sprawling ranch-house affair built in 1972, with a backyard swimming pool. Architectural plans and materials had been supplied by a number of drywall contractors. Many of the contractors merged their drywall and lathing companies into a new association called the Interior Systems Contractors Association of Ontario. Apart from pieceworkers, Simone was the sole supplier of their labour crews. The commercial lathers' trade was dissolved in a different manner.

The local had been destroyed by the loss of work to Simone's cheaper residential lathing union. Members of the commercial local drifted into the Carpenters' union.

In 1976, Gus Simone was charged and convicted of income tax evasion for failing to report to government officials $33,200 in cash payoffs from lathing and drywall companies. These kickbacks, which had come to light during the Waisberg inquiry, had been described by Simone as gifts.

Simone's autonomy in residential drywall was not to last. Three years later in 1979, Washington bosses shuffled that local into the commercial local of the Carpenters while retaining Simone as a business agent. The move was ratified by its members. It was the end of yet another residential construction union local.

The only other union in residential construction with a significant membership today is the Independent Canadian Bricklayers' Union headed by John Meiorin. Efforts to dissolve this union by the Building Trades Council have been only partially successful. The commercial unions won an agreement from the apartment developers in 1978 that restricted Meiorin's workers to residential construction.

Earlier hard-line tactics by the Council had brought another victory when they struck the owner–builder clause from the 1974 contract with apartment developers. This clause had been a loophole under which builders had used residential labour for commercial work if they owned the land under development. How many developers actually benefitted from this arrangement during the five years it existed in the union agreement is difficult to determine. After 1974, builders were forced to pay higher rates for labour on their commercial projects, a change indicating a hardened attitude on the part of the international unions, who had already witnessed the destruction of one commercial local, the Lathers.

On the other hand, Gallagher's Labourers' union local continued to secure their stronghold, emerging as one of the most powerful unions in the city, the winner of the battles with other unions for the allegiance and dues of the concrete formers. After winning the formers in 1971, the Labourers had bargained with individual contractors for the first few years. Then in 1974, the union signed a contract with the association of concrete forming subcontractors. At this time, the Labourers won wage and fringe benefits and introduced a comprehensive welfare plan (which had been previously absent) as well as a new pension fund. With the membership of the concrete formers, the Labourers' union had boosted its membership considerably; nevertheless, by 1974 officials were already planning to expand their operations in the apartment field by organizing maintenance and service employees as well as superintendents.

At the centre of this expansion was labour boss John Stefanini, an early protégé of the Brandon Group, who took over the local after the death of Gerry Gallagher in 1978. He went on to mould it into one of the most powerful trades in the union business. By the late 1970s his membership was estimated at around 8,000 men. The union covered a wide range of labourers employed not only in construction but also in mining and industrial plants, and dental technicians, oil burner mechanics and security guards.

After 1974 the Building Trades Council continued its efforts to achieve labour unity in the city. The major new threat to their craft union structure was the trend toward industrial unions. It was another twist that in the end would provide employers with labour at cheap rates. The Labourers' boss, John Stefanini, was moving in this direction. Stefanini's local had organized fourteen house-building companies as early as 1974, classifying all the workers as members of an industrial unit rather than a craft unit. The men who put basements in single-family residences were to be paid 50 cents an hour less than those employed on high-rise construction. The crafts involved in forming had dissolved in a similar manner.

Unchanged today is the fact that many Toronto construction workers are still immigrants; some have entered the country illegally simply to find work and send money back home to their families. The majority of these labourers are no longer Italians but Portuguese, hard-working, fearful men, often illiterate and unable to speak English. Many of these men are working without union benefits and, as before, no one dares to complain.

19
END OF AN ERA

Before the old Harbord Collegiate was torn down in 1976 there was a wonderful party for the school's alumni. Nearly everyone who had become successful came: lawyers, politicians, men with silk ties knotted under drooping chins. As Phil Givens once said, they had all aimed high and most of them had made it, this long rocky journey out of an earlier era of poverty, depression and prejudice.

The former Toronto mayor had tried to realize his own political ambitions in federal and provincial politics; he settled in 1977 for an appointment as chairman of the city's police commission. His friend and colleague Eddie Goodman had doubled the size of his father's law practice, acting for a number of high-powered developers whose own businesses had also flourished during the 1960s. Goodman had also excelled politically as a backroom adviser and policymaker.

Then there was the success story of Leonard Blatt and his old diamond-polishing partner, Phil Roth, who with Max Merkur made their company, Meridian, a developer of high-rise apartments in the same rank as Greenwin and Cadillac. But there were management problems and the partnership ended. Roth himself geared down after he suffered heart failure.

These men and Herb Stricker, another Harbord graduate who was the developers' spokesman as well as a developer himself, did not have the high-rise apartment field all to themselves. There was, for instance, the company run by the three Del Zotto brothers. Their interest in building was an inheritance from an immigrant father who spent his life working as a bricklayer. Over the years, their company had expanded from house building to apartments, construction companies, building materials, property management, hotels, restaurants, bakery interests, home furnishings and farming.

But the real newsmaker in Toronto land development had come out of Montreal. The son of a shoemaker, developer A.E. Diamond continued to score impressively in the development business, first residentially and then commercially. The culmination of his career came in 1974 when a merger was proposed between his Cadillac, Canadian Equity and Development Company, another real estate concern, and the Bronfman family trust's real estate subsidiary, Fairview, the same company that had bought so many of Principal Investments' holdings fifteen years earlier. The accumulation of properties in the portfolio of Cadillac Fairview gave the new company revenues of about $1 million every working day for the following year, through its ownership of 29-million square feet of rentable space across Canada and the U.S. Financial experts agreed that the merger, which combined Cadillac's depth of management and Fairview's access to money, would turn Cadillac Fairview into the pre-eminent corporate real estate giant in Canada.

For a time, Diamond ran the new, merged company's affairs before he retired voluntarily to an honorary position, turning the management over to Jack Daniels. His former partner, Joseph Berman, had long since retired with so much money that he pledged to make $1-million payments annually to the United Jewish Appeal for the next ten years. Overseeing Cadillac Fairview was Leo Kolber, a lawyer and trustee for the Bronfman family interests.

By the mid-1970s, becoming disenchanted with excessive regulations and government planning, and fearing political turmoil in Quebec, Cadillac Fairview had begun to look for new fields to conquer. It was also coming close to exhausting the possibilities for major development projects in Canadian cities. It found new opportunities south of the border and soon closed the doors on its single-family construction arm in Canada. The company's main thrust into the U.S. market is now in shopping centres and malls, office buildings and suburban land development. As one developer remarked, the U.S. in the mid-1970s had conditions similar to those in Canada in the 1950s. Properties could still be acquired at relatively cheap prices, and there appeared to be no prospect of political upheaval or excessive regulation such as began to plague the Canadian industry after two decades of spectacular growth. Rent control, land speculation taxes and restrictions on urban growth were all clamps on the industry's progress in Canada. But the U.S. market was wide open after a 1975 recession that knocked many American builders out of business. Attracted by the lack of competition and the low land prices, Canadian builders made their move.

Cadillac Fairview opened a shopping centre in 1978 at Hickory, North Carolina, and built the $70-million Galleria centre in Westchester, New York. In Atlanta, Georgia, there was the 667,000 square foot Shannon Mall. Cadillac Fairview made other shopping centre deals in Mississippi and Connecticut. There was an office tower in Denver and plans for an industrial park near Los Angeles, as well as numerous residential projects slated for Nevada, California and Florida.

The large size and financial capacity of these builders was a big advantage in producing large-scale projects and carrying the costs; by contrast the many small, independent American house builders, whose yearly construction averaged 10 homes each, often could not acquire the financial backing to expand. Usually the banks they relied on for financing were limited to operating in one city or state. This was of course not the situation in Canada, where developers dealt with only a handful of chartered banks whose operations spread across Canada and into the U.S.

The pattern for builders like Cadillac Fairview was to form joint ventures with small U.S. builders, using the local companies for the actual construction work. In 1978, for instance, Cadillac Fairview purchased through a wholly-owned U.S. subsidiary the share capital of General Homes Consolidated Cos. Inc. of Houston, Texas, for $24 million. General Homes was a private building and land development company with operations extending into Mississippi and Alabama.

However, the influx of Canadian residential builders to the U.S. was met with growing concern, particularly on the part of small builders. There was some fear the cost of development land would escalate. "Canadian companies will be destroyed if they think they can go in and just raise the price 10 percent," said one U.S. real estate analyst. Many Americans felt that there was not a shortage of land that would warrant substantial increases in the price of real estate.

Although the Canadian housing business differed somewhat from that in the U.S., Americans were confused as to why Canadian suburban land costs were so high. One spokesman for the U.S. National Home Builders Association made this comment: "Land in Canada is so expensive it is incredible. I just can't believe it. Here you are one of the largest countries in the world with a small population and such an enormous amount of land with Hong Kong prices."

The connection to Bronfman money and the transition from a handful of entrepreneurs to professional corporate management had led to Cadillac Fairview's aggressive move into the U.S. real estate market. The other big Toronto developers had occasional American projects; condominiums in Florida, often catering to Canadians going south for holidays or retirement, were one favourite kind of scheme. By the end of the 1970s, however, the developers themselves were easing into retirement. It was the end of an era.

The boom years of the 1960s and early 1970s, when high-rise apartments sprang up all across the city, were over. Growth had slowed down, and new approaches to urban planning and housing design were superseding the simpler days. City residents had fought the high-rise builders to a virtual standstill in the older residential neighbourhoods of the city. When high-rise apartments were built, it was either on central-city land previously scheduled for offices or in the farther reaches of the suburbs.

Replacing the simple high-rise were new kinds of buildings advocated by the new kinds of city politicians who had succeeded the enthusiastic pro-developer boosterism of people like Phil Givens. The new projects emphasized row-houses opening onto the street. They often preserved old buildings on the site, and limited new construction to fill in around the old buildings. Apartments were less massive, designed to minimize the anonymity of the high-rise.

The city itself moved into the housing development business, a move that would have been scorned by Mayor Givens in the early 1960s, and at the end of the 1970s, the biggest single housing development project in the city was not a high-rise village along the lines of St. James Town but rather a city-sponsored non-profit project called St. Lawrence, just east of the downtown. There were many ironies in the growth of St. Lawrence. The project was initiated while David Crombie was mayor; he was considered by many to be middle-of-the-road, if not a reformer opposed to the developers and their schemes. But it was when John Sewell was Toronto's mayor that the first housing in St. Lawrence was occupied. It was Sewell who had most strongly opposed Phil Roth and Meridian when they wanted to expand the St. James Town project southward. Now Sewell was the president of the city housing development company, and the general contractor putting up the project for the city was, irony of ironies, a subsidiary of Meridian.

20
NO REGRETS

With his friend Luciano dead from heart failure for some years, Lansky took extra measures to care for his own weak heart and the three ulcers that continued to flare up now and then. In February 1970, he flew south to Acapulco for what he termed a badly needed rest. Surrounded by friends from as far away as Canada, he sat amid the palms on the grounds of the Acapulco Hilton, a hotel of some splendour where the concrete pool winds around the grounds like a river. But the mid-winter vacation was disrupted by local police authorities, who interrogated him and searched his room on the pretence that he had been involved in a robbery of valuable paintings from a Mexican museum. While they took apart his suitcases, Lansky tried to make it clear he was not in the business of art theft. After taking some photographs, they left.

During the rest of his stay, Lansky was seen with Vic Cotroni, owner of a Montreal meatpacking plant, and Cotroni's partner, Paolo Violi (who died some years later from a bullet wound at a poolroom bar). It was difficult not to imagine that sooner or later the conversation among these men turned to gambling. Some believe plans were made that February for future expansion of casino halls for Miami, Atlantic City and, of course, Quebec.

Tanned and looking fit, Lansky returned to Miami, where he was now living, and was immediately detained by airport officials. Some days later he was charged (but later acquitted) with possessing barbiturates without a prescription. Complaining of lack of privacy, he closed his Miami apartment and flew to Israel in 1971, avoiding the indictment of a federal grand jury in Nevada for conspiring to defraud the U.S. government of income tax on $36 million in profit from crime and syndicate operations in Las Vegas.

Lansky had other problems. The U.S. attorney for the Southern District of New York, Robert M. Morgenthau, had been investigating mob income tax evasion. He had uncovered the well-guarded flow of funds skimmed from gambling casinos into Swiss banks. Morgenthau had become convinced that this money was being returned to the U.S. in the form of investments used to finance the purchase of land and construction of hotels and apartments. Of particular interest to Morgenthau was the Miami National Bank, now controlled by Sam Cohen, a one-time partner of Lansky in a Las Vegas casino operation. He believed Cohen routed some of the gambling profits through his bank to accounts in Tibor Rosenbaum's International Credit Bank of Switzerland. One of Cohen's business associates was Lou Poller, who apparently invested money for Teamsters union boss Jimmy Hoffa.

By 1971, Hoffa had been charged and convicted of misuse of Teamsters pension funds. A secret ledger of Teamsters loans, made public in late 1971, disclosed that the union pension fund had ploughed hundreds of millions of dollars into loans that were not merely unwise but often fraudulent. In the words of one Wall Street journalist: "Through such loans . . . the fund has passed millions of dollars to companies identified with

Mafia members and their cronies. It has also lent millions of dollars to employers of teamsters; and according to . . . rank-and-file teamsters, the union has sometimes deserted members' interests in favour of the employer–borrowers." Hoffa had, for instance, given Moe Dalitz, an old Detroit crony, some $19 million for the construction of a California resort called La Costa. An additional $27 million was forwarded for expansion of the same club.

Through Lou Poller's adept financial management, some of this money was sent to Rosenbaum's Swiss bank and then returned as clean money. The Swiss banker himself was something of a financial genius, diversifying his own wealth through real estate acquisition in Liberia, Brazil, Nigeria and Italy. However, according to one Israeli intelligence report, Rosenbaum's troubles began when he bought a $12-million estate from the Italian royal family, a 1,200-acre tract of land that he had hoped to develop into an apartment and hotel complex. Despite considerable pressure, the land was rezoned by the Italian government and made into a national park.

To shore up his collapsing property deals, Rosenbaum apparently used some of the funds collected by a charitable organization, the Israel Corporation, which had collected money from Jews around the world for the state of Israel. An Israeli government official was found to have transferred $100 million in cash, collected by philanthropists and fundraisers throughout the world to build Israel's economy, to Rosenbaum's bank just before it collapsed. Only $8 million was recovered for the charity. Lansky was saved embarrassing losses by withdrawing his money some time before the crash.

Swiss investigators began to inquire into the unauthorized movement of funds and the money lost by the Israel Corporation. At the Israeli official's one-day trial, he pleaded guilty and was sentenced to fifteen years' imprisonment. Rosenbaum himself was rapped by Swiss authorities for "dishonest management." He moved his bank to a new address.

As a result of his investigations and discoveries, Morgenthau began to press for new legislation to control the outward flow of funds from the U.S. to Switzerland, in the hope of ending the traffic of illegally obtained money used to finance enterprises controlled by the syndicate. Legislation was drafted but the bill never became law. In 1972, Morgenthau was fired by the Nixon Administration, leaving him without any official involvement in investigating national and international crime.

Canadian police authorities sometimes said they thought some syndicate money was being laundered and then turning up in land-buying and development schemes in this country. Where the money originated, they weren't sure. Some authorities thought that a ready supply of mob cash chasing after real estate in southern Ontario in the early 1970s was a major factor contributing to rocketing prices, before the provincial government's imposition of a land speculation tax in 1973.

One investor in Canadian land in the early 1970s was a familiar figure, John Pullman. Though he retired to Switzerland in the early 1960s, Pullman continued to visit friends and relatives in Toronto. He left his Canadian investments in the care of some relatives and a former law partner of Sam Gotfrid, Joe Burnett.

Ben Yuffy, a Windsor lawyer and a Pullman in-law, and his brother Henry Yuffy, a chartered accountant, both acted on occasion for Pullman companies. One company, Pullman Holdings Ltd., was involved in mortgage investments. Another, Chillon Investments, owned real estate property that was later sold.

In 1977 John Pullman was in a Toronto courtroom, faced with charges of stock fraud in connection with the promotion of a company that went bankrupt. Testifying on his own behalf, the white-haired ex-banker described himself as a "successful" stock speculator who had made "maybe two or three" million dollars over the past fifty years trading securities. He also said he had a number of other business interests, including a U.S. bakery chain that went bankrupt and valuable real estate holdings in Toronto. Pullman was acquitted.

For some years now Pullman's activities as an investor have been studiously followed by both Canadian and American tax investigators. According to a recent report in *The Wall Street Journal*, "Senate investigators and other federal agents are convinced that he has a wealth of information about organized crime's banking practices. The Senate permanent subcommittee on investigations is especially interested in Pullman's activities." The same article quoted Pullman as saying he has never handled any deposits for others.

Less fortunate than Pullman at the hands of justice was a former Toronto lawyer, Sam Ciglen, who was charged and convicted for his role in a stock fraud along with his brother-in-law Sidney Rosen, a Canadian agent for the Corporate Bank in Nassau. Ciglen, now in his 70s, had represented Archie Bennett in the mid-1960s, acting for a company once named as a borrower of Pullman money. Although Bennett is now dead, Ciglen's ties to the family are still close. Another Bennett brother, A. J. Bennett, was appointed trustee along with family in-laws for a $400,000 trust set up for Ciglen's four daughters.

Ciglen's law practice had begun in 1929 and continued until 1970, when he was prosecuted by the Department of National Revenue concerning income arising out of oil and mining promotions since the 1950s. He was imprisoned in Kingston penitentiary from March to December 1970 and disbarred that year. During the mid-1960s he was apparently involved indirectly with Racan Photo-Copy, a money-losing company that was siphoning money out of Atlantic Acceptance. His most recent conviction, in 1979, arose out of a $1.8-million stock fraud.

Another Toronto resident who ran into legal trouble was Paul Volpe. He was convicted in 1980 of keeping a common gaming house; he pleaded guilty and paid a fine of $8,000.

But the Volpe brothers were still wearing short pants at the time Sam Bronfman was setting up his bootlegging routes to the U.S. After some forty years of business, his Montreal-based distillery firm, Seagram's, filed a report to the U.S. Securities and Exchange Commission disclosing that the company had made $1 million in questionable payments involving political contributions and certain trade practices. But this was no longer a concern to Sam Bronfman, who had died in July 1971.

Meyer Lansky, whose activities as a bootlegger in New York were closely tied to the supply of booze from Sam Bronfman's Canadian operations, was less successful than his colleague John Pullman at finding a retirement haven. The homeland he raised money for in his casinos refused him citizenship in 1972. Five days before his tourist visa ran out, he left Israel voluntarily. His flight from the country was the beginning of a wearisome journey. Barred from entry into Switzerland, he arrived in Buenos Aires, only to be flown four hours later to Paraguay, where authorities forced him back onto the plane. Refused permission to deplane in La Paz, Lima and Panama, Lansky ended the ordeal by returning to the U.S. A crowd of journalists and three officers of the Federal Bureau of Investigation awaited his arrival at the Miami airport.

In February 1973, Lansky went on trial, faced with charges of criminal contempt for failing to obey a court subpoena concerning his evasion of taxes. In the following years he was interrogated by several committees seeking answers to, among other mysteries, the death of John Rosselli, a man allegedly involved in a plot with the Central Intelligence Agency to assassinate Castro. There were questions too about the disappearance of Teamsters union boss Jimmy Hoffa, whose body has never been recovered. Meanwhile, Lansky was fighting other charges, of conspiring to conceal ownership in the Flamingo hotel and evading taxes on $36 million in earnings.

The end draws near for Meyer Lansky; now well into his 70s, he has few regrets. As he once explained: "I wouldn't have lived my life any other way. It was in my blood, my character. Environment certainly had something to do with it, but basically my own personality determined my fate. But I don't mean the personality that the books and magazines give me. People have accused me of all sorts of crimes, but the accusation I still mind the most is that I killed Bugsey Siegel, who was my dear friend always. I kept in touch with his family after he was killed and I saw his granddaughter in the summer of 1971 when she visited Israel. I told her how her grandfather and I had grown up together and I talked about how it used to be for Jews in this country. When we started out, most of Florida and many resorts in other parts of the country were out of bounds to Jews. Before the Second World War, Jews were forbidden to step inside some hotels and casinos and apartment houses. Our casinos were pleasant places and open to everybody, Jews, Christians, Arabs, anybody could come and gamble.

"And as to bootlegging, I'm not ashamed of that either. A lot of respectable people bought respectability with the money they made."

The enormous success of the Bronfman family, with an empire that includes Cadillac Fairview, Seagram's, oil and gas interests, a 5.5% holding in the Club Mediterranee and investments in a whole range of publishing and media companies, is a source of bitterness to Lansky. He asks: "So why am I considered the criminal today because I was also part of the bootlegging business? Why is Lansky a 'gangster' and not the Bronfman and Rosenstiel families: I was involved with all of them in the 1920s, although they do not like to talk about it today and change the subject when my name is mentioned."

Epilogue

Lou Chesler died of natural causes in his home on Golden Beach, Florida on November 23, 1983. A native from Belleville, Ontario, he attended the University of Toronto until he quit to work as a stock salesman. He showed a talent for picking the right stocks and then grew rich underwriting dozens of mining projects. In later years, he headed up a Canadian-controlled production and distribution corporation, Seven Arts, which was capitalized on Toronto's stock exchange.

As well, he was a major housing developer in Florida, where he owned a real estate company, General Development Corp. He was described as a front or associate of underworld figures Vito Genovese and Meyer Lansky. Through his company, Chesler and his associate Wallace Groves introduced gambling to the Bahamas, buying up half the island and setting up The Grand Bahama Development Corp. in early 1960s to build a hotel-cum-casino. He was forced out of the Bahamas in a power struggle in 1964. He and his wife Molly gave a generous donation to Mount Sinai Hospital that was redirected to nuclear medicine.

Charles Irvine died in 1981 at the age of 74, five years after retiring from the labour movement.

Meyer Lansky died from cancer on January 16, 1983 at Mt. Sinai Hospital in Miami Beach. He was admitted December 31st, suffering from dehydration. Born Maier Suchowljansky, a Russian-born Jewish immigrant, he came to the United States and New York's Lower East Side in 1911 after his family experienced pogroms in Grodno, Belarus. He left a widow and three children. He was accused of many crimes, ranging from assault to contempt of court and tax evasion. But aside from a few minor run-ins with the law as a teenager, he went to jail only once. That was for two months in 1953, on a gambling conviction in Saratoga Springs, N.Y.

John Pullman was arrested in 1975 as he checked in at the Sutton Place Hotel in Toronto. The charge was defrauding Aquablast Resources Ltd. of $1.6 million in money or securities through a debenture issue. He was acquitted. During the 70s the Department of National Revenue launched a major probe into Pullman's considerable moneylending operations in various legitimate concerns such as construction companies, nursing homes, and firms in the food business. The investigation lasted until 1983 when the case wrapped up. Pullman won and two years later he died. Born Wolhyn Pullmer in Russia, he came to Canada in 1908, moved to the U.S., became a bootlegger and was convicted in 1931 of a Prohibition offence. Returning to Canada in 1948, he invested money in real estate and mining ventures before moving to Geneva, Switzerland during his final years.

Toronto organized-crime figure **Paul Volpe** was found in the trunk of his wife's car at Toronto's Pearson International Airport on Monday, November 14, 1983. His throat was slashed. Apparently, he left his home about 9 a.m. the day before, promising his wife he'd be back around noon after meeting someone at the airport. He never returned. Police were notified and found his car with blood on the rear fender. Inside was the body of Paul Volpe, fully-clothed. At the time of his death, he was awaiting trial in Peel Region on a charge of conspiracy to commit fraud in connection with the purchase of a building on Queen Street East in downtown Toronto that is currently leased to CityTV.

EPILOGUE

Bruno Zanini died of heart failure on Saturday August 29, 2009 at the age of 87. He left a son, John, and five grandchildren. His obituary described him as a prominent union leader in the 50s and 60s who applied his fiery personality and formidable energy to ending worker exploitation in the construction trades. He signed up more than one thousand bricklayers in 1955 and was later involved in creating an association of five Italian construction locals. After his union career ended, he worked with his son in real estate and construction. He was passionate about opera and sang in several restaurants.

The **Del Zotto brothers**, who are still in construction, received the 2013 Regional Builders Award of the Year.

Acknowledgments

This story was a challenge for me, and the often difficult experience of writing it was shared by my family and dear friends. The patience and encouragement of my husband when I was at the typewriter helped me greatly in this work. I am also thankful to those reporters, journalists and authors who gave a full account of the times, as well as the assistance of the librarians.

— C. W.

Appendix A

PRINCIPAL INVESTMENTS LIMITED
REAL ESTATE OWNED OR HELD ON BEHALF OF COMPANY
AT DECEMBER 31, 1949

PROPERTY	LAND	BUILDINGS
21 Adelaide St. W.	$ 13,035.80	$ 16,413.53
33–43 Adelaide St. W.	—	40,070.00
2448 Bloor W.	4,367.11	10,717.71
2310 Bloor W.	6,557.02	22,030.75
333 Bloor E.	21,031.09	84,366.21
Brantford	20,205.64	10,014.28
599 Bayview	15,468.85	23,426.83
2278 Bloor W.	14,643.55	21,665.33
2330 Bloor W.	15,570.36	26,526.74
636 Bay St.	43,235.02	158,959.10
3014 Bloor W.	37,532.00	147,840.07
3022 Bloor W.	14,700.00	—
3020 Bloor W.	30,000.00	40,974.89
8 Royal York Rd.	7,500.00	18,288.24
18–28 Bloor W.	275,288.25	79,310.70
2314 Bloor W.	10,281.73	16,743.27
879–81 Bloor W.	20,060.50	3,556.00
Chatham —144 King St.	37,829.33	111,440.96
75 Crescent Rd.	9,026.26	38,131.32
234 Courtleigh Blvd.	5,375.00	21,064.35
Chatham — 98 Stanley St.	2,586.63	9,948.22
1275 Castlefield Ave.	1.00	232,863.61
2874 Dundas St. W.	23,011.37	27,913.13
583–5 Danforth	37,897.08	92,121.22
2057 Danforth	13,892.06	75,413.66

771 Danforth	$ 26,431.94	$ 62,198.28
2903 Dundas W.	8,420.41	25,870.90
1426 Danforth	980.00	37,420.00
Dundas, Ont.	3,665.10	7,334.90
2050 Dundas St. W.	6,754.39	57,140.95
1879 Eglinton Ave. W.	2,465.27	70,644.89
1909 Eglinton Ave. W.	30,000.00	96,540.63
420 Eglinton Ave. W.	21,123.54	29,876.46
Eglinton & Bayview	36,430.42	—
247 Fleet St.	92,961.78	275,864.81
10–16 Front St.	105,475.00	107,900.00
Galt — 9 South Water St.	6,892.00	41,162.24
Gwillembury Cottage	500.00	6,808.11
111 Howland Ave.	2,554.95	17,300.36
Hamilton — 303 Ottawa St. N.	49,000.00	91,000.00
Hamilton — 217 Ottawa St. N.	29,525.00	65,260.97
King & Cowan	18,149.98	70,035.57
Kingston — 176 Princess St.	—	4,165.00
Kingston — 160 Princess St.	42,766.47	22,233.53
988 Kingston Rd.	3,556.00	17,544.00
Kingston — Princess & Queen	28,845.60	48,700.35
175 Lakeshore Rd.	624.91	1,249.82
London — 91 Dundas St.	9,723.08	40,723.08
786 Lakeshore Rd.	24,713.85	51,610.30
Mavety St.	6,322.79	21,638.36
Midland	10,430.19	6,095.00
Mattawa (dep.)	500.00	—
33 Norwood Rd.	650.00	1,450.00
Niagara Falls — 430 Bridge St.	1,350.00	3,150.00
Niagara Falls — 507 Queen St.	20,779.60	30,730.00
Niagara Falls — 481 Queen St.	21,773.90	31,997.31
Owen Sound — 968 2nd Ave.	21,724.34	115,423.44
Ottawa —109 Sparks St.	25,332.46	143,292.27
Ottawa —78 Rideau St.	144,204.67	279,562.53
Ottawa —Plaza Bldg.	44,900.00	321,269.28

APPENDIX A

Ottawa — 104 Rideau St.	$ 39,138.00	$ 36,910.00
Ottawa —178 Queen St.	44,072.51	105,927.49
Orillia — Mississauga St.	80,000.00	169,566.84
Orillia — Residence	2,300.00	7,700.00
Port Arthur — 227 Arthur St.	4,220.00	7,600.00
Parry Sound — Metropolitan	5,681.34	25,910.22
469 Parliament St.	20,424.31	12,863.86
Penetang Bowling Alley	4,048.53	17,074.67
Parry Sound— James St.	3,340.00	17,527.89
Penetang — Vimy Inn	4,510.00	6,591.20
Penetang — Pen Theatre	—	75,351.54
489 Parliament St.	7,692.00	12,308.00
Peterborough	5,000.00	—
2054 Queen E.	8,344.95	12,012.60
1508 Queen E.	8,448.05	12,508.40
12 Queen E.	16,745.17	32,835.58
187 Roncesvalles	4,590.40	8,308.22
437 Rogers Rd.	4,950.75	27,520.00
67 Richmond St. W.	94,639.45	629,759.03
112 Richmond St. W.	28,250.00	83,170.35
Stratford — 28 Wellington	17,596.03	24,000.00
250 Simcoe St.	6,561.60	—
966 St. Clair W.	21,735.38	36,112.00
St. Catharines — King & James	13,218.55	104,080.86
St. Catharines — 232 St. Paul St.	37,254.71	53,620.87
950 St. Clair	17,300.00	72,000.00
Sarnia — Christina St.	10,000.00	26,245.35
1223 St. Clair W.	21,600.00	90,234.15
St. Catharines — 102 King St.	8,528.35	30,903.00
Sault Ste. Marie	29,478.42	38,364.97
Sarnia — 112 Christina St.	195,252.65	—
Temperance St. lot	36,000.00	—
434 University Ave.	20,111.79	229,203.19
516 University Ave.	171,230.16	255,168.55
Windsor — 1484 Ottawa St.	17,067.43	33,333.33

Windsor — 439–57 Ouellette	$ 98,885.23	$ 385,028.91
Windsor — 459–63 Ouellette	48,292.79	119,703.62
Windsor — 1262 Ottawa St.	16,881.42	20,740.89
Woodstock, Ont. (leasehold)	—	31,567.19
763 Woodbine	12,719.40	28,000.00
Waterloo — 31 King St.	5,811.21	17,001.19
3178 Yonge St.	3,322.86	3,730.00
3198 Yonge St.	3,322.86	3,730.00
3200 Yonge	3,115.86	3,445.00
323 Yonge St.	19,746.15	59,184.77
271 Yonge St.	18,217.13	20,971.18
106 Yonge St.	44,742.70	101,950.81
3212 Yonge St.	3,244.85	15,739.65
1375 Yonge St.	22,970.79	120,840.83
177 Yonge St.	107,311.83	75,711.92
3434 Yonge St.	15,634.31	90,729.69
141 Yonge St.	105,000.00	105,000.00
2300 Yonge St.	21,781.98	52,179.20
3202 Yonge St.	6,192.00	15,008.00
36 Yonge St.	15,900.00	44,175.00
464 Yonge St.	33,554.08	19,805.09
470 Yonge St.	36,735.00	35,484.00
330 Yonge St.	13,139.25	4,000.00
958 Yonge St.	18,750.00	18,750.00
111 Yonge St.	—	69,841.38
1329 Yonge St.	60,000.00	99,551.14
1119 Yonge St.	25,520.00	2,513.53
5237 Yonge St.	16,903.45	59,138.96
369–71 Yonge St.	54,303.62	24,953.90
302–04 Yonge St.	—	109,498.69
168–80 York St.	1,000.00	—
	$3,370,952.59	7,585,700.16

Appendix B

PULLMAN LOAN TRANSACTIONS, 1972

Following is an extract from court records filed by the Department of National Revenue in 1977 in connection with income tax that the Department claimed John Pullman owed for 1971 and 1972.

In the taxation year 1972 the Plaintiff earned the amount of $934,691.04 from a moneylending business carried on by him in Canada, which amount was earned in respect of the following loan transactions:

LOAN TRANSACTIONS	DATE	AMOUNT
1. Jose Vedra Development Corporation	Jan. 14, 1972	$ 10,000.00
2. Ruthbern Holdings Limited	Jan. 20, 1972	75,000.00
3. M. Suson Enterprises Inc.	Feb. 8, 1972	21,300.00
4. Hoben-Huron View Apartments	Mar. 7, 1972	7,500.00
5. Barlovento Inc.	Mar. 28, 1972	75,000.00
6. Banco Obrero De Puerto Rico	Mar. 28, 1972	23,000.00
7. Juando Ville Development Corporation	Mar. 28, 1972	98,200.00
8. Petoskey Hall Properties Inc. RE: Sosnick Convalescant Home	Apr. 24, 1972	25,000.00
9. Les Galleries Drummond Inc.	May 2, 1972	143,424.94
10. Edmundo De Jesus Atalaya Gardens Inc.	May 5, 1972	15,000.00
11. Jose Vedra Developments Corporation	Jun. 23, 1972	26,000.00
12. Ruthbern Holdings Limited	Jul. 5, 1972	60,277.32
13. Prince Edward Square	Oct. 24, 1972	49.98
14. Prince Edward Square	Nov. 21, 1972	302.67
15. Prince Edward Square	Dec. 13, 1973	1,808.10
16. Prince Edward Square	Oct. 24, 1972	273.36
17. Prince Edward Square	Nov. 21, 1972	1,366.50
18. Prince Edward Square	Dec. 13, 1972	1,347.90

19. Three M Construction	Jan. 20, 1972	$ 1,041.66
20. Three M Construction	Feb. 15, 1972	1,041.66
21. Three M Construction	Mar. 24, 1972	1,041.66
22. Three M Construction	Apr. 10, 1972	1,041.66
23. Three M Construction	May 8, 1972	1,041.66
24. Three M Construction	Jan. 20, 1972	932.29
25. Three M Construction	Feb. 15, 1972	932.29
26. Three M Construction	Mar. 24, 1972	932.29
27. Three M Construction	Apr. 10, 1972	932.29
28. Three M Construction	May 6, 1972	932.29
29. Three M Construction	Jan. 20, 1972	1,292.06
30. Three M Construction	Feb. 7, 1972	1,398.92
31. Three M Construction	Mar. 10, 1972	1,516.99
32. Three M Construction	Apr. 10, 1972	1,678.68
33. Three M Construction	May 5, 1972	1,823.98
34. Three M Construction	Jun. 16, 1972	1,929.19
35. Three M Construction	Jul. 28, 1972	2,049.01
36. Three M Construction	Aug. 23, 1972	2,193.85
37. Three M Construction	Sep. 15, 1972	2,384.32
38. Three M Construction	Oct. 23, 1972	2,485.02
39. Three M Construction	Nov. 22, 1972	2,552.34
40. Triple B Investments	Jan. 10, 1972	340.00
41. Triple B Investments	Feb. 7, 1972	340.00
42. Triple B Investments	Mar. 3, 1972	340.00
43. York Management & Consultants Ltd.	Jan. 6, 1972	500.00
44. York Management & Consultants Ltd.	Feb. 7, 1972	500.00
45. York Management & Consultants Ltd.	Mar. 1, 1972	500.00
46. York Management & Consultants Ltd.	Apr. 4, 1972	500.00
47. York Management & Consultants Ltd.	May 4, 1972	500.00
48. York Management & Consultants Ltd.	Jan. 6, 1972	2,830.00
49. York Management & Consultants Ltd.	Jan. 6, 1972	500.00
50. York Management & Consultants Ltd.	Feb. 7, 1972	500.00
51. York Management & Consultants Ltd.	Mar. 1, 1972	500.00
52. York Management & Consultants Ltd.	Apr. 4, 1972	500.00
53. York Management & Consultants Ltd.	May 4, 1972	500.00

APPENDIX B

54. York Management & Consultants Ltd.	Jan. 6, 1972	$ 1,380.00
55. York Management & Consultants Ltd.	Feb. 7, 1972	1,380.00
56. York Management & Consultants Ltd.	Mar. 1, 1972	1,380.00
57. York Management & Consultants Ltd.	Apr. 4, 1972	1,380.00
58. York Management & Consultants Ltd.	May 4, 1972	1,380.00
59. York Management & Consultants Ltd.	Jan. 6, 1972	220.00
60. York Management & Consultants Ltd.	Feb. 7, 1972	220.00
61. York Management & Consultants Ltd.	Mar. 1, 1972	220.00
62. York Management & Consultants Ltd.	Apr. 4, 1972	220.00
63. York Management & Consultants Ltd.	May 4, 1972	220.00
64. Cernuik Construction Limited	Jan. 14, 1972	350.00
65. Cernuik Construction Limited	Feb. 11, 1972	350.00
66. Cernuik Construction Limited	Mar. 13, 1972	350.00
67. Cernuik Construction Limited	Apr. 14, 1972	350.00
68. Cernuik Construction Limited	May 9, 1972	350.00
69. Cernuik Construction Limited	Jun. 15, 1972	350.00
70. Cernuik Construction Limited	Jul. 4, 1972	350.00
71. Cernuik Construction Limited	Aug. 16, 1972	350.00
72. Cernuik Construction Limited	Sep. 13, 1972	350.00
73. Cernuik Construction Limited	Oct. 16, 1972	350.00
74. Cernuik Construction Limited	Dec. 19, 1972	700.00
75. Edmundo De Jesus	Feb. 18, 1972	1,500.00
76. Edmundo De Jesus	Mar. 6, 1972	1,500.00 77.
77. Edmundo De Jesus	Apr. 10, 1972	1,500.00
78. Edmundo De Jesus	Apr. 26, 1972	1,500.00
79. Omega Investments Limited	Jan. 4, 1972	168.75
80. Omega Investments Limited	Feb. 1, 1972	168.75
81. Omega Investments Limited	Mar. 6, 1972	168.75
82. Omega Investments Limited	Apr. 4, 1972	90.00
83. Omega Investments Limited	Apr. 6, 1972	8.85
84. Omega Investments Limited	Jan. 4, 1972	393.75
85. Omega Investments Limited	Feb. 1, 1972	393.75
86. Omega Investments Limited	Mar. 6, 1972	393.75
87. Provincial Mushrooms	Jan. 14, 1972	712.34
88. Provincial Mushrooms	Apr. 4, 1972	164.35

89. Provincial Mushrooms	Apr. 7, 1972	$ 2,000.00
90. Provincial Mushrooms	May 9, 1972	1,000.00
91. Provincial Mushrooms	Jun. 15, 1972	1,000.00
92. Provincial Mushrooms	Jul. 6, 1972	466.62
93. Juando Villa & Development	Mar. 30, 1972	69.74
94. Juando Villa & Development	Apr. 30, 1972	77.63
95. Juando Villa & Development	May 30, 1972	78.43
96. Juando Villa & Development	Jun. 30, 1972	93.98
97. Juando Villa & Development	Jul. 30, 1972	128.56
98. Juando Villa & Development	Aug. 30, 1972	172.52
99. Juando Villa & Development	Sept. 30, 1972	228.13
100. Juando Villa & Development	Oct. 30, 1972	274.47
101. Juando Villa & Development	Nov. 30, 1972	354.98
102. Juando Villa & Development	Dec. 30, 1972	412.71
103. Ruthbern-Maron Alma	Jan. 3, 1972	1,029.16
104. Ruthbern-Maron Alma	Feb. 1, 1972	1,029.16
105. Ruthbern-Maron Alma	Mar. 6, 1972	1,029.16
106. Ruthbern-Maron Alma	Apr. 4, 1972	1,029.16
107. Ruthbern-Maron Alma	May 1, 1972	1,029.16
108. Ruthbern-Maron Alma	Jun. 5, 1972	1,029.16
109. Ruthbern-Maron Alma	Jul. 4, 1972	1,029.16
110. Ruthbern-Maron Alma	Jul. 19, 1972	507.45
111. Ruthbern-Maron Alma	Jan. 3, 1972	704.19
112. Ruthbern-Maron Alma	Feb. 1, 1972	704.19
113. Ruthbern-Maron Alma	Mar. 6, 1972	704.19
114. Ruthbern-Maron Alma	Apr. 4, 1972	704.19
115. Ruthbern-Maron Alma	May 3, 1972	704.16
116. Ruthbern-Maron Alma	Jun. 5, 1972	704.16
117. Ruthbern-Maron Alma	Jul. 6, 1972	704.16
118. Ruthbern-Maron Alma	Jul. 19, 1972	347.40
119. Triple B Investments	Mar. 17, 1972	856.00
120. Triple B Investments	May 2, 1972	1,041.66
121. Triple B Investments	Jun. 5, 1972	1,041.66
122. Triple B Investments	Jul. 4, 1972	1,041.66
123. Triple B Investments	Aug. 2, 1972	1,041.66

APPENDIX B

124. Triple B Investments	Sep. 6, 1972	$ 1,041.66
125. Triple B Investments	Oct. 3, 1972	1,041.66
126. Triple B Investments	Nov. 1, 1972	1,041.66
127. Triple B Investments	Dec. 4, 1972	1,041.66
128. York Management & Consultants Ltd.	Jun. 6, 1972	500.00
129. York Management & Consultants Ltd.	Jun. 7, 1972	230.13
130. York Management & Consultants Ltd.	Jun. 6, 1972	1,385.00
131. York Management & Consultants Ltd.	Jun. 16, 1972	637.47
132. York Management & Consultants Ltd.	Jun. 6, 1972	220.00
133. York Management & Consultants Ltd.	Jun. 16, 1972	101.26
134. York Management & Consultants Ltd.	Jun. 6, 1972	500.00
135. York Management & Consultants Ltd.	Jun. 16, 1972	230.13
136. Les Habitation Côte Nord	Sep. 6, 1972	965.21
137. Omega Investments Limited	Jul. 10, 1972	578.58
138. Omega Investments Limited	Aug. 16, 1972	2,989.33
139. Omega Investments Limited	Sep. 19, 1972	2,989.33
140. Omega Investments Limited	Oct. 25, 1972	2,892.90
141. Omega Investments Limited	Nov. 16, 1972	2,989.33
142. Omega Investments Limited	Dec. 4, 1972	2,892.90
143. Omega Investments Limited	Jul. 10, 1972	394.50
144. Omega Investments Limited	Aug. 16, 1972	2,038.25
145. Omega Investments Limited	Sep. 19, 1972	2,038.25
146. Omega Investments Limited	Oct. 25, 1972	1,972.50
147. Omega Investments Limited	Nov. 16, 1972	2,038.25
148. Omega Investments Limited	Dec. 4, 1972	1,972.50
149. Food Chain Properties Ltd.		6,062.11
150. Bremar Convalescent Homes	Jan. 4, 1972	633.75
151. Bremar Convalescent Homes	Feb. 7, 1972	633.75
152. Bremar Convalescent Homes	Mar. 6, 1972	633.75
153. Bremar Convalescent Homes	Apr. 4, 1972	633.75
154. Bremar Convalescent Homes	May 3, 1972	633.75
155. Bremar Convalescent Homes	Jun. 5, 1972	633.75
156. Bremar Convalescent Homes	Jul. 7, 1972	308.80
157. Idak Convalescent Centres Inc.	Feb. 7, 1972	1,083.33
158. Idak Convalescent Centres Inc.	Mar. 1, 1972	1,083.33

159. Idak Convalescent Centres Inc.	Apr. 7, 1972	$ 1,083.33
160. Idak ConvalescentCentres Inc.	May 17, 1972	1,083.33
161. Idak Convalescent Centres Inc.	Jun. 12, 1972	1,083.33
162. Idak Convalescent Centres Inc.	Jul. 17, 1972	890.25
163. Lennon Green Acres	Jan. 4, 1972	1,125.00
164. Lennon Green Acres	Feb. 2, 1972	1,125.00
165. Lennon Green Acres	Mar. 6, 1972	1,125.00
166. Lennon Green Acres	Apr. 4, 1972	1,125.00
167. Lennon Green Acres	May 4, 1972	518.94
168. Lennon Green Acres	May 2, 1972	248.08
169. Lennon Green Acres	Jun. 1, 1972	227.50
170. Lennon Green Acres	Jun. 15, 1972	57.84
171. Roberts Construction	Jan. 3, 1972	740.00
172. Roberts Construction	Feb. 1, 1972	740.00
173. Roberts Construction	Mar. 1, 1972	740.00
174. Roberts Construction	Apr. 4, 1972	740.00
175. Roberts Construction	May 4, 1972	740.00
176. Roberts Construction	Jun. 5, 1972	740.00
177. Roberts Construction	Jul. 6, 1972	740.00
178. Roberts Construction	Aug. 4, 1972	740.00
179. Roberts Construction	Sep. 6, 1972	740.00
180. Roberts Construction	Oct. 10, 1972	740.00
181. Roberts Construction	Oct. 25, 1972	486.40
182. Roberts Construction	Jan. 3, 1972	216.66
183. Roberts Construction	Feb. 1, 1972	216.66
184. Roberts Construction	Mar. 1, 1972	216.66
185. Roberts Construction	Apr. 4, 1972	216.66
186. Roberts Construction	May 3, 1972	216.66
187. Roberts Construction	Jun. 5, 1972	216.66
188. Roberts Construction	Jul. 7, 1972	85.44
189. Maron Properties — Sorel	Jan. 7, 1972	937.50
190. Maron Properties — Sorel	Feb. 7, 1972	937.50
191. Maron Properties — Sorel	Apr. 6, 1972	1,886.71
192. Maron Properties — Sorel	May 12, 1972	937.50
193. Maron Properties — Sorel	Jun. 6, 1972	937.50

APPENDIX B

194. Maron Properties — Sorel	Jul. 6, 1972	$ 437.50
195. Multi Grow Developments Limited	Jan. 26, 1972	500.00
196. Multi Grow Developments Limited	Feb. 15, 1972	500.00
197. Multi Grow Developments Limited	Apr. 6, 1972	1,000.00
198. Multi Grow Developments Limited	May 12, 1972	500.00
199. Multi Grow Developments Limited	Jun. 15, 1972	500.00
200. Multi Grow Developments Limited	Jul. 19, 1972	500.00
201. Multi Grow Developments Limited	Aug. 16, 1972	500.00
202. Multi Grow Developments Limited	Sep. 13, 1972	500.00
203. Multi Grow Developments Limited	Sep. 22, 1972	115.01
204. Multi Grow Developments Limited		2,595.93
205. Omega Investments Limited	Jan. 6, 1972	1,380.21
206. Omega Investments Limited	Feb. 1, 1972	1,380.21
207. Omega Investments Limited	Mar. 9, 1972	1,380.21
208. Omega Investments Limited	Apr. 4, 1972	1,380.21
209. Omega Investments Limited	Apr. 6, 1972	136.11
210. Omega Investments Limited	Jan. 4, 1972	1,192.50
211. Omega Investments Limited	Feb. 1, 1972	1,192.50
212. Omega Investments Limited	Mar. 9, 1972	1,192.50
213. Jose Vedra Development Corporation	Jan. 3, 1972	1,592.50
214. Jose Vedra Development Corporation	Feb. 2, 1972	1,592.50
215. Jose Vedra Development Corporation	Mar. 3, 1972	1,592.50
216. Jose Vedra Development Corporation	Apr. 4, 1972	1,592.50
217. Jose Vedra Development Corporation	May 8, 1972	1,592.50
218. Jose Vedra Development Corporation	Jun. 5, 1972	1,592.50
219. Jose Vedra Development Corporation	Jul. 28, 1972	942.30
220. Jose Vedra Development Corporation	Jan. 3, 1972	1,744.16
221. Jose Vedra Development Corporation	Feb. 2, 1972	2,858.39
222. Jose Vedra Development Corporation	Mar. 3, 1972	3,109.16
223. Jose Vedra Development Corporation	Apr. 4, 1972	3,109.16
224. Jose Vedra Development Corporation	May 8, 1972	3,109.16
225. Jose Vedra Development Corporation	Jun. 5, 1972	3,109.16
226. Jose Vedra Development Corporation	Jul. 28, 1972	1,668.90
227. Multi Plus Ltd.	May 9, 1972	536.22
228. Multi Plus Ltd.	Jun. 6, 1972	604.16

229. Multi Plus Ltd.	Jul. 4, 1972	$ 604.16
230. Multi Plus Ltd.	Aug. 16, 1972	604.16
231. Multi Plus Ltd.	Sep. 22, 1972	604.16
232. G.J. Simpson Construction	Jul. 10, 1972	597.69
233. G.J. Simpson Construction	Aug. 2, 1972	2,020.00
234. G.J. Simpson Construction	Sep. 1, 1972	2,020.00
235. G.J. Simpson Construction	Oct. 2, 1972	2,020.00
236. G.J. Simpson Construction	Nov. 1, 1972	2,020.00
237. G.J. Simpson Construction	Dec. 4, 1972	2,020.00
238. G.J. Simpson Construction	Jul. 10, 1972	326.16
239. G.J. Simpson Construction	Aug. 2, 1972	1,102.50
240. G.J. Simpson Construction	Sep. 5, 1972	1,102.50
241. G.J. Simpson Construction	Oct. 2, 1972	1,102.50
242. G.J. Simpson Construction	Nov. 1, 1972	1,102.50
243. G.J. Simpson Construction	Dec. 4, 1972	1,102.50
244. Hubert S. Garner	Feb. 7, 1972	1,373.33
245. Hubert S. Garner	Feb. 28, 1972	1,373.33
246. Hubert S. Garner	Apr. 4, 1972	1,373.33
247. Hubert S. Garner	Apr. 17, 1972	1,373.33
248. Hubert S. Garner	Jun. 6, 1972	1,373.33
249. Hubert S. Garner	Jun. 15, 1972	1,373.33
250. Hubert S. Garner	Jul. 28, 1972	1,373.33
251. Hubert S. Garner	Jul. 28, 1972	99.99
252. Hubert S. Garner	Sep. 11, 1972	655.54
253. Hubert S. Garner	Feb. 7, 1972	293.33
254. Hubert S. Garner	Feb. 28, 1972	293.33
255. Hubert S. Garner	Apr. 4, 1972	293.33
256. Hubert S. Garner	Apr. 17, 1972	293.33
257. Hubert S. Garner	Jun. 6, 1972	293.33
258. Hubert S. Garner	Jun. 15, 1972	293.33
259. Hubert S. Garner	Jul. 28, 1972	293.33
260. Hubert S. Garner	Sep. 11, 1972	515.05
261. Brighton Mall Inc.	Apr. 10, 1972	919.82
262. Brighton Mall Inc.	May 15, 1972	2,543.66
263. Brighton Mall Inc.	Jun. 14, 1972	2,543.66

APPENDIX B

264. Barloventa Inc.	May 5, 1972	$ 971.85
265. Barloventa Inc.	Jun. 20, 1972	750.00
266. Barloventa Inc.	Jul. 10, 1972	345.10
267. Commercial Builders	Jan. 3, 1972	350.00
268. Commercial Builders	Feb. 1, 1972	350.00
269. Commercial Builders	Mar. 3, 1972	350.00
270. Commercial Builders	Apr. 4, 1972	350.00
271. Commercial Builders	May 2, 1972	350.00
272. Commercial Builders	Jun. 1, 1972	350.00
273. Commercial Builders	Jun. 20, 1972	218.63
274. Grouse Nest Resorts	May 23, 1972	892.50
275. Grouse Nest Resorts	Jun. 15, 1972	991.66
276. Humber Wood Products	Aug. 4, 1972	4,474.88
277. Humber Wood Products	Aug. 16, 1972	11.80
278. Idak Convalescent Centres	Jan. 4, 1972	1,004.99
279. Idak Convalescent Centres	Feb. 15, 1972	1,389.44
280. Idak Convalescent Centres	Feb. 28, 1972	1,389.44
281. Idak Convalescent Centres	Apr. 17, 1972	1,389.44
282. Idak Convalescent Centres	May 17, 1972	1,389.44
283. Idak Convalescent Centres	Jun. 23, 1972	1,706.64
284. Idak Convalescent Centres	Jun. 12, 1972	1,389.44
285. Inducon Construction	Feb. 1, 1972	1,888.33
286. Inducon Construction	Mar. 6, 1972	1,241.60
287. Maron Properties Limited — Miramichi	Jan. 7, 1972	175.00
288. Maron Properties Limited — Miramichi	Feb. 7, 1972	175.00
289. Maron Properties Limited — Miramichi	Apr. 6, 1972	352.04
290. Maron Properties Limited — Miramichi	May 12, 1972	175.00
291. Maron Properties Limited — Miramichi	Jun. 6, 1972	175.00
292. Maron Properties Limited — Miramichi	Jul. 6, 1972	104.94
293. Maron Properties Limited — Miramichi	Jan. 7, 1972	375.00
294. Maron Properties Limited — Miramichi	Feb. 7, 1972	375.00
295. Maron Properties Limited — Miramichi	Apr. 6, 1972	754.68
296. Maron Properties Limited — Miramichi	May 12, 1972	375.00
297. Maron Properties Limited — Miramichi	Jun. 6, 1972	375.00
298. Maron Properties Limited — Miramichi	Jul. 6, 1972	225.00

299. G.J. Simpson Construction	Jun. 5, 1972	$ 1,541.89
300. G.J. Simpson Construction	Jul. 10, 1972	1,538.73
301. G.J. Simpson Construction	Aug. 2, 1972	1,535.54
302. G.J. Simpson Construction	Sep. 6, 1972	1,532.32
303. G.J. Simpson Construction	Oct. 3, 1972	1,529.06
304. G.J. Simpson Construction	Nov. 1, 1972	1,525.78
305 G.J. Simpson Construction	Dec. 4, 1972	1,522.45
306. G.J. Simpson Construction	Jun. 5, 1972	1,024.67
307. G.J. Simpson Construction	Jul. 10, 1972	1,022.57
308. G.J. Simpson Construction	Aug. 2, 1972	1,020.45
309. G.J. Simpson Construction	Sep. 6, 1972	1,018.31
310. G.J. Simpson Construction	Oct. 3, 1972	1,016.45
311. G.J. Simpson Construction	Nov. 1, 1972	1,013.97
312. G.J. Simpson Construction	Dec. 4, 1972	1,011.75
313. M. Suson Enterprises	Apr. 6, 1972	1,557.56
314. M. Suson Enterprises	Apr. 17, 1972	2,060.00
315. M. Suson Enterprises	May 16, 1972	2,060.00
316. M. Suson Enterprises	Jun. 15, 1972	2,060.00
317. M. Suson Enterprises	Aug. 8, 1972	2,060.00
318. M. Suson Enterprises	Aug. 30, 1972	2,060.00
319. M. Suson Enterprises	Oct. 1, 1972	2,060.00
320. M. Suson Enterprises	Oct. 23, 1972	2,060.00
321. M. Suson Enterprises	Nov. 24, 1972	2,060.00
322. M. Suson Enterprises	Dec. 21, 1972	2,060.00
323. M. Suson Enterprises	Feb. 28, 1972	517.77
324. M. Suson Enterprises	Apr. 6, 1972	1,750.00
325. M. Suson Enterprises	Apr. 17, 1972	1,750.00
326. M. Suson Enterprises	May 16, 1972	1,750.00
327. M. Suson Enterprises	Jun. 15, 1972	1,750.00
328. M. Suson Enterprises	Aug. 8, 1972	283.00
329. M. Suson Enterprises	Aug. 30, 1972	283.00
330. M. Suson Enterprises	Oct. 1, 1972	283.00
331. M. Suson Enterprises	Oct. 23, 1972	283.00
332. M. Suson Enterprises	Nov. 24, 1972	283.00
333. M. Suson Enterprises	Dec. 21, 1972	283.00

APPENDIX B

334. M. Suson Enterprises	Jan. 4, 1972	$ 2,545.83
335. M. Suson Enterprises	Feb. 2, 1972	2,545.83
336. M. Suson Enterprises	Mar. 6, 1972	2,545.83
337. M. Suson Enterprises	Apr. 4, 1972	2,545.83
338. M. Suson Enterprises	May 1, 1972	2,545.83
339. M. Suson Enterprises	Jun. 5, 1972	2,545.83
340. M. Suson Enterprises	Jul. 7, 1972	2,545.83
341. M. Suson Enterprises	Aug. 8, 1972	2,545.83
342. M. Suson Enterprises	Sep. 19, 1972	2,545.83
343. M. Suson Enterprises	Oct. 1, 1972	2,545.83
344. M. Suson Enterprises	Nov. 1, 1972	2,545.83
345. M. Suson Enterprises	Dec. 4, 1972	2,545.83
346. Foodchain London	Jan. 4, 1972	291.67
347. Foodchain London	Feb. 7, 1972	291.67
348. Foodchain London	Mar. 14, 1972	291.67
349. Foodchain London	Apr. 26, 1972	291.67
350. Foodchain London	May 11, 1972	291.66
351. Foodchain London	Jun. 6, 1972	291.66
352. Foodchain London	Jul. 1, 1972	291.66
353. Foodchain London	Aug. 8, 1972	291.66
354. Foodchain London	Oct. 2, 1972	291.66
355. Foodchain London	Oct. 10, 1972	291.66
356. Foodchain London	Nov. 16, 1972	291.66
357. Foodchain London	Dec. 11, 1972	291.66
Total		**$934,691.04**

Select Bibliography

Following is a list of the books, government reports, periodicals and newspapers that I found particularly useful in the research for this book.

BOOKS

Anderson, Annelise Graebner. *The Business of Organized Crime: A Cosa Nostra Family.* Stanford: Hoover Institution Press, 1979.

Aubin, Henry. *City for Sale.* Montreal: Editions l'Etincelle, 1977.

Charbonneau, Jean-Pierre. *The Canadian Connection.* Montreal: Optimum Publishing, 1976.

Eisenberg, Dennis; Dan, Uri; and Landau, Eli. *Meyer Lansky: Mogul of the Mob.* New York: Paddington Press, 1979.

Gage, Nicholas. *The Mafia Is Not an Equal Opportunity Employer.* New York: McGraw-Hill, 1971.

Gambino, Richard. *Blood of My Blood: The Dilemma of the Italian-Americans.* New York: Doubleday & Company, 1974.

Goldenberg, Carl, and Crispo, John, eds. *Construction Labour Relations.* Ottawa: Canadian Construction Association, 1968.

Gosch, Martin A., and Hammer, Richard. *The Last Testament of Lucky Luciano.* Boston: Little, Brown and Company, 1974.

Harney, Robert F., and Troper, Harold. *Immigrants: A Portrait of the Urban Experience, 1890-1930.* Toronto: Van Nostrand Reinhold, 1975.

Kaplan, Lawrence J., and Kessler, Dennis. *An Economic Analysis of Crime.* Springfield, Illinois: Charles C. Thomas, 1976.

Lorimer, James, and Phillips, Myfanwy. *A Citizens Guide to City Politics.* Toronto: James Lewis & Samuel, 1972.

Messick, Hank. *Lansky.* New York: Putnam, 1971.

Moldea, Dan E. *The Hoffa Wars.* New York: Paddington Press, 1978.

Mollenhoff, Clark R. *Strike Force: Organized Crime and the Government.* Englewood Cliffs, New Jersey: Prentice-Hall, 1972.

Moore, William Howard. *The Kefauver Committee and the Politics of Crime, 1950-1952.* Columbia, Missouri: University of Missouri Press, 1974.

Newman, Peter C. *Bronfman Dynasty.* Toronto: McClelland and Stewart, 1978.

Speisman, Stephen A. *Jews of Toronto: A History to 1937.* Toronto: McClelland & Stewart, 1979.

Tyler, Gus. *Organized Crime in America.* Ann Arbor, Michigan: University of Michigan Press, 1962.

REPORTS

Province of Ontario, Royal Commission on Certain Sectors of the Building Industry (the Waisberg Commission), December 1974.

Province of Ontario, Royal Commission on Labour-Management Relations in the Construction Industry (the Goldenberg Commission), March 1962.

Province of Ontario, Hansard, October 1970, December 1972.

PERIODICALS
Bimonthly Reports
Corriere Canadese
Canadian Builder
Financial Post
Canadian Grocer
Toronto Globe and Mail
Life
Il Giornale
Maclean's
New York Times
Monetary Times
Toronto Sun
Toronto Life
Toronto Star
Weekend Magazine
Toronto Telegram
The Wall Street Journal

Index

Ahearn, Daniel Francis, 33
Anti-Semitism, 10, 15–18, 21
Apartment Developers Association, 159, 196
Atlantic Acceptance Corporation, 134, 138, 142, 143, 148–51, 154, 216, 243

Bagnato, George, 173
Bagnato, Joey, 24, 174, 175, 204
Bank of World Commerce, 80, 145
Batista, Fulgencio, 37, 38, 76, 77, 138, 139
Belmont Construction Company, 54
Bennett, Archie, 17, 18, 82, 243
Berman, Joseph, 54, 235
Bianchini, Aurelio, 56, 161, 184–87
Blatt, Leonard, 21, 54, 233
Brandon Hall Union Group, 105, 116
Bricklayers, Masons and Plasterers International Union, 63
Bronfman, Charles, 93
Bronfman, Samuel, 18, 34, 38, 39, 41, 56, 245
Broward Amusement Company, 40

Cadillac Contracting (1959) Ltd., 56
Cadillac Contracting and Developments Ltd., 54, 56
Cadillac Fairview Corp. Ltd., 234–237
Canadian Bricklayers' Association, 73
Canadian Jewish Congress, 17, 18
Capone, Al, 35
Casino International (Haiti), 153
Castro, Fidel, 139
Cellini, Dino, 144
Cellini, Eddy, 152
Cemp Investments Ltd., 56, 83, 93
Chesler, Louis A., 41, 141, 143, 147, 148, 149, 151, 153, 247
Ciglen, Sam, 82, 149, 243
Colonial Inn (Miami), 41
Crombie, David, 237
Costello, Frank, 78, 88
Cotroni, Vic, 239
Coyne, James, 91, 93
D'Alimonte, John, 183, 195, 196, 199, 206, 208, 209
Davis, William, 213–216
Del Zotto, Angelo, 217, 218
Del Zotto, Elvio, 217, 218, 184

Del Zotto Enterprises Ltd., 209, 218, 222, 159, 173, 234, 249
Dennison, William, 97
Diamond, Allen Ephraim, 54, 55, 92, 234
DiLorenzo, Nicola (Nick), 56, 152–55, 178, 182–84, 187, 191, 194
Dorfman, Allen, 152
Dorfman, Paul, 86, 87
Drea, James Francis, 69, 100, 188, 204, 210, 211
Dupuch, Sir Étienne, 143, 144
Duvalier, Dr. Francois, 144

Eagle Star Insurance, 94
El Cortez Club (Las Vegas), 40

Fairview Corporation Ltd., 83
Federation of Jewish Philanthropies, 18
Ferdmann, Sylvain, 38
Fitzsimmons, Frank, 85
Forming Council, 179, 180, 182, 183, 185, 189, 193, 194, 201–206
Frost, Leslie, 110

Gallagher, Gerry, 99, 189, 196, 231
Giles, Frank, 182, 184
Givens, Philip (Givertz), 20, 21, 94–97, 233, 237
Goldenberg, H. Carl, 211
Goldhar, Max, 21
Goodman, Edwin (Eddie), 21, 54, 95, 213–215, 233
Greenwin Construction Limited, 54
Gotfrid, Sam, 81
Grand Bahama Development Company Ltd., 141, 142
Grand Bahama Port Authority, 141
Grau San Martin, Ramon, 76
Green, Al, 92
Grossman, Al, 54, 92
Groves, Wallace, 140–42

Harbord Collegiate (Toronto), 15, 19, 233
Hoffa, James R., 37, 69, 84–87, 111, 112, 124, 153, 240, 241, 244
Home Builders Association, 109, 236
Hotel Nacional (Havana), 38, 77
Hughes, Samuel, 150

INDEX

International Credit Bank of Switzerland (Geneva), 79, 145, 240
International Hod Carriers, Building and Common Labourers Union, 99
International Union of Operating Engineers, 183
Irvine, Charles, 70–73, 98, 101–14, 116, 118–21, 165–66, 167, 169, 171, 174, 180–82, 189–93, 195, 197, 198, 200, 201–206, 227, 229, 247
Italian immigrants, 7, 9, 11, 23, 24, 25, 28–29, 32 48, 56, 58, 59, 63

Jenoves, Bill, 68, 70, 71, 103
Jewish Times, 17

Kamin, Jack, 54
Kanner, Naftali, 174–75
Kefauver, Estes, 41
Kefauver Committee, 75
Kolber, Leo, 83, 235

Lambert, Jean, 148
Lansky, Meyer, 151–64, 239–41, 244–45, 246–48
League for the Defence of Jewish Rights, 17
Luciano, Salvatore (Lucky), 32–37, 39, 77, 88, 239
Lucayan Beach Hotel (Grand Bahama), 143–45, 146–48, 149, 150, 151, 152
Lundquist, Fred, 39

McKeough, Darcy, 158, 212–214
Mackey, James, 188
McClellan committee hearing, 88
Main, Alex, 194, 196, 202
Mary Carter Paint Company, 146, 152
Meiorin, John, 195, 197, 201, 230
Menezes, Norman, 162, 163, 199
Meridian Property Management Limited, 54
Miami National Bank, 87, 240
Modular Precast Concrete Structures Ltd., 164
Morgan, C. Powell, 147, 150
Morgenthau, Robert M., 240, 242
Mussolini, Benito, 27

Nevada Projects Corporation, 40

Operative Plasterers' and Cement Masons' International Association, 70

Phillips, Lazarus, 56, 93, 146
Pindling, Lynden 152

Poller, Lou, 87, 240, 241
Principal Investments Ltd., 51, 54, 82–83, 94, 149, 234
Prio Socarras, Carlos, 76, 139
Pullman, John, 79–83, 142, 145, 242–43, 244, 248

Rasminsky, Louis, 19, 93, 94
Real estate, 95, 120, 140, 153, 157, 159, 159, 163, 213, 234, 235, 237, 241, 243
Robarts, John, 213
Romanelli, Cesidio, 173, 217, 218
Rosenstiel, Lewis, 39
Rosenbaum, Tibor, 137, 146, 240, 241
Roth, Philip, 21, 54, 92, 233, 234, 238

Sadlo, George, 75, 145
Sewell, John, 238
Shepherd, Albert, 150, 215, 216
Shulman, Morton, 198–99, 100, 210
Shouldice, Ross, 178
Siegel, Bugsy, 40, 214
Simone, Agostino, 167–76, 189–92, 195, 197, 198, 204, 216–218, 226, 223, 229, 230
Sands, Sir Stafford, 140–142, 146, 151
Stacher, Doc, 75, 78, 80
Stefanini, John, 241
Stricker, Herb, 21, 234
Subcontracting system, 100
Summerville, Donald, 95

Trillo, Gerarda, 64, 66, 227
Trizec Corp. Ltd., 93
Toronto Building Trades Council, 66

Union National Bank of Newark (N.J.), 80
Ungerman, Irving, 22, 24
United Brotherhood of Carpenters and Joiners, 103

Veltri, Frank, 218–20
Vlahos, Kiriakos, 162, 163, 184, 185, 187
Violi, Paolo, 239
Volpe, Albert, 120
Volpe, Paul, 119, 120, 121, 122,173, 174, 175, 203, 204, 218, 222, 243–44, 248

Waisberg, Harry, 215, 216, 222, 223
Wood, Wire and Metal Lathers' International Union, 168

Zanini, Bruno
   childhood, 23, 24, 25
   black market, 29

    independent organizer, 66–68
    international bricklayers' local, 67–69
Zanini and Irvine, 98;
Zanini and Volpe, 118–122
    arrest 1963, 123
    release, 179
    forming union with Simone, 179–181
    "enforcer", 183–84
    Royal Commission request, 188, 209, 215
    Chicago sellout, 191, 192
    Independent forming union, 197
    Plasterers and forming, 196
    shooting, 209–211
    inquiry, 215
Zanini, Amilcare, 64
Zanini, Giobatte, 22, 23, 28
Zeckendorf, William, 92, 93
Zwillman, Abner "Longie", 34